The Cottage Woman

Discovering that reality is more than human consciousness—a true story

by AUGUSTA

 FriesenPress

One Printers Way
Altona, MB R0G 0B0
Canada

www.friesenpress.com

Copyright © 2021 by Augusta
First Edition — 2021

All rights reserved.

No part of this publication may be reproduced in any form, or by any means, electronic or mechanical, including photocopying, recording, or any information browsing, storage, or retrieval system, without permission in writing from FriesenPress.

The drawing of the stove was done by the author as was the oil painting of the cottage woman.

ISBN
978-1-5255-9371-0 (Hardcover)
978-1-5255-9370-3 (Paperback)
978-1-5255-9372-7 (eBook)

1. BODY, MIND & SPIRIT, REINCARNATION

Distributed to the trade by The Ingram Book Company

A Strange Visitor

> *"There are more things in heaven and earth, Horatio, than are dreamt of in your philosophy."*
>
> *~ Shakespeare*

Dedication

I dedicate The Cottage Woman to my grandchildren and their generation who will see beyond and dare to take their own life adventures into the unknown in whatever form it might be offered.

This book also bows to those who journeyed forth into uncharted territory decades ago, listened, and continue to do so to this day.

Beyond what your eyes see.
That which cannot be seen is called invisible.
That which cannot be heard is called inaudible.
That which cannot be held is called intangible.
These three cannot be defined . . .
You can see it,
Hear it,
And feel it
Then the unseen,
Unheard, and untouched are present as one.

~ Lao Tzu

Table of Contents

Testimonials from the Readers	xiii
Introduction	xvii
The First Fall and Winter	xxiii
A Strange Visitor	1
First Encounter ~ Finding the Missing Piece	3
Getting Acquainted ~ You Won't Mind This Trip	13
Several Weeks Before the Cottage Woman Arrived ~ A Loon Calls	23
First Time Alone with the Cottage Woman ~ The Door Is Open	27
The Invisible Is Listening	41
I Am Real, Ask Your Questions ~ It All Feels Nebulous	43
The Invisible Has a Reality of Its Own ~ A Steep Learning Curve	55
The Spirit Needs Us to Ask ~ You Need to Be Still to Hear	57
We Are All One and The Same ~ Break-Through	67
A New Year's Visit ~ Life Is A Schoolroom For Our Human Lessons	71
A Winter Reflection a Week Later ~ A Journal Entry	83
Discovering That Reality Is More Than Human Consciousness	85
You Don't Need to See Oxygen to Know It's There	97
Personal Pain Work Leads to the Most Honoured Human State	109
The First Spring & Summer	127
Mrs. Jordan Dies and Easter	131
What I Am Learning From Working With the Cottage Woman	135
Exposed To A Reality Other Than the Human Side	139
Being Observed as I Write ~ A Pleasure for the Other Side	153
Light Comes Through but Is Not of You	155

Images Become a Third Eye ~ An Important Tool for Seeing beyond the Surface	175
A Healer Must Maintain Life-Giving Boundaries for Herself	185
The Second Fall & Winter	**189**
The Seas Are High ~ And the Sailboat Moves in Harmony	191
Death Is but an Opportunity to Stumble into a Larger Reality	193
Nature Has Feelings	203
Yah, a Great Bold A ~ A New Name	211
The Other Side Is Separate, but Much the Same as Yours	215
The Many-ing and One-ing of God ~ The Cottage Woman Seems to be One of the Many-ing	221
A Gauge of Intuition ~ An Opening to a Main Area of Work	225
Christmas Preparations ~ Arriving for Christmas	235
The Second New Year ~ A Time of Refinement	243
Stumbling into a Nineteenth-Century Garden Party	255
A Time of Intense Learning ~ Much Work to Freeing Oneself	259
The Second Spring & Summer	**269**
A Drop-In Visit ~ And an Effective Way to Pray	271
Baked Beans, Brown Bread, and Presence	277
A Critical Time, a Breakdown ~ Dysfunction Repeats Itself	281
Attending to a Breakdown ~ It's Scary	287
What Constitutes a Family Is How One Perceives It?	295
Loving the Raw Life of It All	303
A World Rapidly Changing ~ I Stayed Too Long	309
Allow Pain to Be with Whom It Belongs ~ Much Freedom	313
Late Summer Transition ~ And Too Much Company	321
The Third Fall & Winter	**323**
Life Changes Require of Me a New Relatedness ~ A New Wine	325
A few days later ~ possibly a giant step	329
An Opportunity to Grow, Exploring a New Frontier	333

Jan Revisits ~ A Loving Heart	343
A Reunion, the Cottage Woman Must Be Invited	345
A Mini Visit and a Little Party ~ Two Glasses of Wine	351
Court ~ Acting as a Satellite When Praying	355
Guides Are Presented to Different People in Different Ways	359
Blessed Are Those Who Know They Have Helpers	369
A Christmas Visit ~ Much Illumination, Must Let the Heart Sing	379
Your Work ~ Compassion for Others, the Foundation of Life	393
Much Like Old Friends ~ A Clear Conduit	401
Epilogue ~ An End with a New Beginning	405
Acknowledgements and Gratitude	411
About the Author	415

TESTIMONIALS FROM THE READERS

"The Cottage Woman is a compelling introduction to an expanding spirituality and an effective vehicle for this ancient spirit woman's important nuggets of wisdom. This (book) is the mark of a great idea. I have never read anything quite like it and I'd venture that your future readers haven't either. What you bring to the table is an original presentation that makes her lessons—and their life-changing power—come alive. As a result, the words jump off the page, and they have the potential to touch the lives of your readers. You also have the ability to perfectly capture a feeling, a moment, or an idea in a single paragraph. Thanks again . . . It is a great read, and I am confident . . . that your readers won't be able to put The Cottage Woman down!" — **FP**

"The author takes you on a journey beyond the 'everyday' world. She weaves her personal

journal entries, the actual recordings, and reflections of what transpired as two unknowing souls met with a third wise one. They, the author and the cottage woman, pull you into an adventure that is both unnerving, at times bewildering, and leaves one wanting to know more. The insight, wisdom, and larger perspective that are offered are invaluable. Advice on everyday life will surprise the reader. I found the book intriguing, educational, and touched with humour. It draws you in as the author herself learns about the mystery and wisdom that is found in this ancient woman and so-called 'invisible' world. By the end of the book, I was stretched, awakened, and left wanting more. I can't wait for the next book." — **LM**

"Most of my adult life has been one of searching for spiritual truths. I have taken part in conferences, meditations, and healing practices in which I delighted, and I also have read more books on the subject than I can remember. However, The Cottage Woman is truly an extraordinary read. The content is astonishing. The lessons she imparted are profound. I found the book a life changer and I loved it. The Cottage Woman would make a great movie." — **JA**

*"The Cottage Woman is an amazing read. It is an engaging and meaningful guide to exploring the possibility that there is another reality other than the one we live in daily. The reader is provided with guidance for anyone interested in personal and spiritual growth. It was most interesting to read about Augusta's journey as she discovers a larger reality first-hand. The Cottage Woman was hard to put down. It is a manual for life. I can't wait till I get the book in my hands and start underlining. — **JC***

*"This book certainly cemented for me the knowledge that there are guides and they are available to each of us. The author captures the personality of the cottage woman. This book also shines the light on the power of prayer and that death is 'not a word we use.' The word 'transition' was more acceptable to her. I also see it as a very personal journey and applaud the author for the guts it took to put such a story out there. The storyline kept building and I was very sorry when the book ended." — **JT***

INTRODUCTION

Come to the edge.
We might fall,
. . .
COME TO THE EDGE!
And they came
and (she) pushed
and they flew.

~ Christopher Logue

This book is an invitation to come to the edge of what we believe to be true. We, a small group of friends, said it was too fearful; we might fall. Then the cottage woman pushed with the beat of the universe, and we flew. This book is about one of the most important and most unusual adventures in my long life. It is also about a growing friendship that changed me and others. It has taken me three decades just to have the courage to write it and make it public.

The cottage woman entered our life unexpectedly and shockingly. She was a bit unusual (and possibly more than a bit.) This is a human story, an adventure story, and a true story. It is an invitation by the universe to live life largely and more splendidly. When we do, beautiful power awaits us so long as we dare go beyond the bounds of what we believe is true and absolute. There is a bigger story under us and beyond us.

The cottage woman's first words to us when we met her were, "Love, I teach love." And she was a woman of her word, thus changing us and changing our world. She told me, "You must have confidence in yourself and walk with assurance and love. You must be very aware of being loving. Walk in it. You do not do these things by yourself." (And during these years, it was shocking to realize how much help the universe gives us—and for the most part, we are unaware of it.)

This wise, ancient woman invited us to see further, to climb the mountain higher. Like a telescope that sees into the heavens, just when we thought we had seen it all, the lens updated; she replaced the old with the new, and we were asked to go further. The telescope she gave us looked inside, as well as out beyond ourselves. It took us decades to catch up with what she meant, and we are still on our way.

This book's truth is a witness to the reality that there is another side, the seemingly invisible side where the reality of things exists and where the function of all exists. The book shows how the other side relates to us, how it sheds light, and how it transforms us, just as it changed and expanded those who met her. The cottage woman stretched us beyond our banalities, our three-dimensional knowing, to discover that physical reality is not the total reality (as any quantum physicist and ancient sage today will tell us). The reader will discover not only that there is another side, but how loving and caring the other side is and how close and tangible it is to us.

Context

The cottage woman came into our lives thirty-five years ago, in a small village in Nova Scotia. She gave us information that was beyond our understanding at the time. In the 1980s, words like "guides," "out-of-body experience," "near-death experience," and "entity" were simply not in our vocabulary. Angels were too religious to be real. It was also before the iPhones, the internet, and You Tube; quantum physics was in its infancy for the layperson. We had never heard of any of it.

Our reality was solid matter, whereas now quantum physics states that matter is ninety-nine percent dancing particles. Countless people have had experiences of dying, entering a tunnel of light, and seeing what some call angels. Doctors, scientists, and honest people are witnessing the authenticity of these experiences.

Different universities have studied mediums, monks, and shamans the world over. Researchers study consciousness and how meditation affects brain waves, neurons, and the physical body. We are evolving human beings. Einstein was right: life, in its solidness, is an illusion, albeit a convincing one.

The Cottage Woman is not a "how-to" book, even though its namesake thought that life was a schoolroom and that we came here to do our human lessons. As she informed us,

"Doing one's life-lessons is a much-honoured state." I was counselling at the time, doing personal development programs at the provincial training centre, working in hospice and several other organizations. Thus, many of her visits dealt with human emotions, spiritual growth, and a larger vision of what it means to be human.

There were many opportunities for humility in this woman's presence. This ancient woman responded to questions about fear, pain, relationships, life-after-death, comas, suicide, abuse, past lives, and streams of consciousness, to name a few. And we were to discover that her wisdom was generic—it was not only reserved for the particular person asking the question. Her answers could easily apply to any human situation. In my discussions with the cottage woman, there were also countless occasions where I was referring to a situation or conversation with someone and she knew what was said without my saying a word. On these occasions, she answered generally, with greater depth of understanding of the encounter than I had, even though I had personally been there.

As this old friend advised, "You cannot compromise truth and still have it remain truth." Thus, I spent several years listening to the old tapes of her visits, as they had faded through time. In writing this book, my main concern was to capture as much of the original dialogue as possible. I also used books of notes, journal entries, and observations written at the time because these gave voice to who we were; our life was the chalice, the container that held our experience. However, names and places have been changed to protect the privacy of those involved and their families. It is also worth noting that in some of the recollections that follow, one visitor sometimes spoke for several others.

The Cottage Woman invites the reader to take an unusual and beautifully empowering adventure. New freedoms await. This ancient, spirit woman's words speak to this book: "You are given here an exposure to another reality, other than the human side." Thus, in these uncharted waters, the reader is invited to go beyond the edge into an expanding reality, beyond one's conventional beliefs and experience.

The First Fall and Winter

Discovering that, not only the visible is real.

A STRANGE VISITOR

Once Upon a Time

Once upon a time, I met with a wise woman in a little cottage on the North Atlantic coast. We talked every couple of weeks, on average, for five years. In winter, applewood often burned in the wood stove as snow drifted through the cracks around the windows of the cottage. She seemed partially invisible at times, and she reminded me of the women staretz of Russia in the 19th century.

And like them, living at the edge of the village, people came to her for healing and wisdom. The woman's advice was practical yet, at times, it seemed beyond the reach of everyday awareness, much like a monk who had lived in a cave above the snow line for many years.

When this stranger entered our lives, my own life was full, and our house was a gathering place for family and friends. I was not only giving development programs at The Center, but privately working with people who were in emotional crisis and doing personal-growth work.

At the time, I would regularly meet with several friends who lived on the same country road as me. We aimed to learn how best to live with deeper meaning and creatively engage our everyday challenges. We were the most ordinary group of mothers and housewives, and we met in an old cottage not far from my house because our kitchens were generally occupied with family and lacked privacy for personal sharing.

Life was full of challenges. The people who knocked at our door needed a very large heartbeat and a greater wisdom than mine. They included Philip, a young family man who had a brain tumour; Tom, a minister who needed help with his ministry; and Donna, who continually cut herself and wanted to die. There was also a young woman lost in a coma who needed contact at a deeper level, parents whose son had gone missing, and Ellen, who thought the world was against her. These were the situations we were immersed in when this wise woman, whom we could never have thought up in our wildest imaginations, dropped into our lives.

In regard to faith, we were traditionally lukewarm Christians, if we were anything. One afternoon, in our total ignorance of what might exist beyond our five senses and our one-dimensional world, we were introduced to a strange visitor. That afternoon initiated the five-year friendship that changed each of our lives.

FIRST ENCOUNTER ~ FINDING THE MISSING PIECE

Prior to this encounter with the cottage woman, my two cousins, Jan and Kay, arrived from the west for a family visit. One afternoon, Pam, one of the group, also dropped in at the cottage for a visit. The early fall was beautiful with its coloured leaves and sun.

When I first met Pam, she had three small children, and one of them was in my son's class. Her house was on my morning jogging route, so I began to drop in once in a while. We had the same sense of humour, and her kitchen was always welcoming with its smells of homemade bread or baking cookies. I also found her wise beyond her years and education. After a year or two, my monthly drop-ins turned into weekly drop-ins, and we became good friends. I started asking her what she thought about certain challenging, and emotional situations people brought to me. Her responses were helpful. She began to meet some of the people with me when I was counselling.

She had met my two cousins several days ago and liked them, so I invited her for a visit to the cottage this afternoon. The four of us sat around talking, laughing, and catching up on each other's lives. When counselling in the cottage, I often taped the conversations so I could study them later. This afternoon, I had turned the recorder on for fun. However, Pam introduced a more serious vein into the conversation. Apparently, she felt there was "a missing part" to our counselling work.

I asked, perplexed, "What do you mean?"

She replied, puzzling, "I don't know, but maybe if I could relax and go deeper into myself, I might find out."

My cousin Jan had taken a course in hypnosis. For fun, she had tried hypnotizing the family the night before, but no one had succumbed. This caused much hilarity. Pam, who was quite conservative, shocked me somewhat when she suggested trying it. I thought: *This could be fun entertainment if it works.*

What followed is something none of us had ever read about or imagined. By the end of the afternoon, we were gobsmacked and very scared. And what a quiet, head-down, sober group we were, as we walked back down the little path to the house, later that afternoon.

Uncharted Waters ~ Alarmed

Jan begins to hypnotize Pam. I expect nothing to happen, except maybe a little entertainment. However, after a few minutes, she seems to be relaxing, certainly better than any of the family did the night before. Her eyes close, her breathing deepens. Jan keeps counting and suggesting she go deeper. Yet the more Jan relaxes her, the more agitated our friend becomes. Having had four children, I know what labour looks and sounds like; weirdly, I am being reminded of it. The intensity of Pam's response is alarming. Jan asks if she is okay. No answer. We wait. After more worrisome agitation, she ventures, "What is the missing piece, Pam?"

Struggling with her words she rasps, "I have to go deeper."

Then, after what seems like an age, my friend's body continues to contort and struggle, and now her hands shoot out in front of her. My cousin, keeping her voice steady, encourages her. More agitation. Then Pam sits straight up in the rocker and states (which feels like a plea), "My hands, I need to use my hands." *Oh, that is panic in her voice.*

Jan and I eye each other warily. My cousin asks, "Why do you have to use your hands, Pam?"

"I have to," she stresses.

"Are your hands to be used for healing?" I interject. *Maybe physical healing will be the area we will move into with our counselling work.*

"But they are not my hands," Pam insists.

"What*?" My breath catches. Keep calm.* "Then whose hands are they?

"They are not my hands. I have to know how to pick them up. I am in the way."

"Do you know how to move out of the way?" Jan queries.

"I think I do. I am not quite at home with it."

"Are you referring to hands that heal?"

"I am, but I don't have enough strength yet to do it."

"How do you get the strength?"

"By going deeper."

"So, the hands you are going to use in the people-work are somebody else's hands?" Jan shrugs her shoulders and furrows her eyebrow, giving me a puzzled look. *What is she talking about?*

Again, my stomach grabs my backbone as I watch rigid, boney, oddly positioned hands laying on Pam's lap.

"I can't pick my hands up. I can't control them."

Jan jumps in, her voice slightly shrill, "That's alright, Pam."

Catching my cousin's eye, I see my own fear in hers.

"No, it isn't," I croak. *I can hardly breathe.*

Shaking her head, Jan whispers to me, "I've never had this happen before. Pam is now reacting independently of my suggestions. I have no idea what is going on."

I whisper back, rather stoically for the panic I am feeling, "Then you might say, dear cousin, we are in uncharted water."

"We certainly are." *More eye-rolling between the three of us.* And not knowing where to guide the conversation, Jan returns to what now feels more like a problem than fun.

"Well, Pam, do you know how to put yourself aside so you can use your hands for healing?"

"I think I do, but there is still the missing piece I don't have yet."

"Is there anywhere inside you that knows where the missing piece is?" I interject.

She whispers, "I have to go deeper."

Love, I Teach Love ~ We Don't Need Names

Again, we wait. More silence. Watching her, I feel uneasy. Pam's neck and face seem to be slightly distorted. Her hands also appear somewhat different.

After more agitation and several attempts to speak she says, as if stating a common fact, "It is like there are many parts of me, like I am many people. I am not the person." *Oh God, what have we gotten ourselves into?* "I am many people." *Oh, the weird is just becoming weirder!*

"What do you mean?" Jan asks, sitting on the edge of her chair.

Pam (or is it Pam?) shifts in the rocker. Then in a raspy voice, she states, "I teach."

The energy in the room feels electrically charged. This is not Pam's voice! This croaky voice is much older than a thirty-six-year-old's—plus, it has an accent! And while Pam is psychic, she is not old, and she would never consider herself a teacher; she dropped out of school early.

Jan soldiers on, "What do you teach?" Then, this stranger sits back in the rocking chair and again states, "Love, I teach love."

"When did you teach?" Jan asks cautiously, with a raised eyebrow.

"Many, many times. You see, I am me now."

"Who? You mean Pam?" *This is incredible.*

"No," she responds empathically.

Jan proceeds rather bravely. "Do you have a name?"

"I have many names. We don't need names. We don't relate on that level."

"Who is 'we'?" I interject, totally perplexed.

She ignores the question and continues, "I can come to you from that level, yet I have to wait. It will come. The Person knows it's there."

Does she mean Pam? And what's a "level" and where is "there"?

I am about to ask these questions when the rocker stops. Pam squirms and is agitated again. We wait nervously. Suddenly, her eyes pop open. Looking around and somewhat stunned, she thankfully asks, "What happened?"

My cousin and I look at each other. We have no idea, so I suggest we all go down to the house and play the tape. Besides, we have had enough for one afternoon. And little did we know, the strangest part was yet to come.

• • •

What's That Beat?

Entering the house, we go into the living room. No one is home, thank goodness. We are desperate to make some sense out of what just happened in the cottage. Turning the tape on, we initially hear Jan's soothing voice followed by Pam's ensuing struggle. Then panic can be heard creeping into our voices as we realize the situation is getting beyond our control.

Yet this time, as the raspy voice talks, we hear a thumping noise. It is barely perceptible at first, then it grows louder until it seems to be bouncing off the walls of the living room. Glancing at my friends, fear, shock, and total disbelief look back. Pam is chalk white. There was no sound, absolutely none like that in the cottage. As it mounts to a deafening crescendo, we are frozen with near heart-stopping fear. No logic comes to my rescue.

The back door opens. A voice shouts, "Anyone home?"

Oh no, no. It's my neighbour, Fran. No one can hear this. I dash from the living room, my heart pounding, and I try to stop her in the kitchen. It's pointless, as she hollers to be heard, "What's that Beat?"

"What Beat? I don't hear any Beat," I croak. *My breath is interfering with my ability to speak. I cannot be hearing this. It's just not possible. The room in the cottage was silent except for our ordinary voices, and that strangled, oddly accented voice of Pam's.* I repeat to her, "There is no Beat. There's no Beat." And yet here it is, filling the house.

We continue to the living room; Fran's face is full of questions. Then, gathering my courage and without any explanation, I play the tape again. Like before, everything sounds normal, just the four of us talking and laughing. However, as we listened to my cousin relaxing Pam, the struggling noises begin. Again, what sounds like an odd, accented voice emerges—it was definitely not Pam speaking.

This time, halfway into the conversation, the thumping begins when the voice announces, "Love, I teach love." I can hardly hear it at first. And again, increasing in crescendo, the thumping sound starts to roll like thunder through the house. I look up the stairs thinking: *It's even thumping off the bedroom walls.* I shiver. *This is not right. It just can't be. What have we gotten ourselves into?*

• • •

Reflections the Next Morning ~ The Deal

The next morning, my nerves are still sizzling like the breakfast bacon in the frying pan. Indeed, what have we gotten ourselves into? How did the throbbing, thumping Beat get recorded when it was unerringly silent during the visit in the cottage, except for our voices? And who exactly was talking to us? Pam cannot remember anything. She also looked and sounded weirdly different. Her mouth changed and her neck muscles took on an odd shape. Yet, as scared as we were, that strange transformation was mesmerizing.

As I ponder the situation, the bathroom toilet flushes. Footsteps scurry down the stairs. I hope my cousins have slept better than I. One look at them both, and I know they have not. Kay tells me she has dreamed of a scary monster. Our imaginations are taking their toll! Looking toward me, she instructs, "I don't think you should do this again, but if you do, I'm going to imagine a cross protecting you." Desperate measures for an atheist, yet her comments add their own chill.

I feel suspended in non-reality. The eggs and bacon are tasteless. The phone rings. I jump. It is Fran. She states, "You have no business fooling around with Pam's mind. After all, she has a husband and three children." Being a fundamentalist, she also mentions the devil. I hang up. I don't believe in any devil, but I am badly rattled.

Minutes later, the phone rings again. This time, it is Pam. In a panic, she asks, "What happened yesterday? Am I going crazy? Are you sure you didn't hear a Beat, noise, thumping or anything odd when you taped that conversation? Why can't I remember what we talked about?"

I have no answers, no soothing words, no comforting logic. Letting my breath out slowly, I wonder to myself, "*Where is my dependable solidity?*"

The remains of my breakfast go into the compost as I escape out the back door to pace the cement foundation that has surrounded our house for years. Today, I need its realness and solidity under my feet. As I walk, thoughts attack me like shotgun pellets. *Could that strange encounter be evil?*

Pam seemed to be possessed by someone yesterday. And what ratchets up that weirdness is hearing that thundering Beat on the tape that gobsmacked us beyond logic.

As I pace the veranda, I remember asking the stranger, "Who are you?" Then whoever it was sat back in the rocking chair, paused, and whispered, "Love, I teach love."

Reflecting on what the voice said and continuing to walk around the veranda in the crisp morning air, I consider: Maybe "it" is of God. Lots of weird stuff happened in the New Testament—water turned into wine, and an angel got Paul out of prison. Yet, before I leave this solid, cement foundation, I must make a decision: Will we or won't we continue to help Pam "go deeper?"

The Deal ~ Only Your Spirit-Love

After pondering awhile with my hands thrust into my apron pockets, I begin to feel the strength from the ever-present North Atlantic lapping the edge of our lawn. I make a deal with God.

"You know how scared we are, yet if this weirdness teaches love, if it will help us in our own personal growth and work, I will take this strange encounter as an opportunity and a gift. But we need protection. I only want your spirit-love if I am to continue."

Then, as if God has bad ears, I repeat my deal out loud more than once until the September sun warms me through my blouse.

GETTING ACQUAINTED ~ YOU WON'T MIND THIS TRIP

My cousins only have a week and a half before they leave. I don't want another weird visit alone. Will we or won't we relax Pam again? Maybe this stranger was just from Pam's unconscious, or is it another aspect of her personality? Yet she is as scared as we are, and I am sure she knows nothing more about this than we do.

I have known Pam for fifteen years. She is county-homespun and straight-honest. Plus, she seemed to be out cold yesterday. Then there is that illogical Beat. Now, having made a deal on the cement, I need to find out more—if this teaches love, we need it not only for ourselves, but for larger wisdom in our counselling work.

Who Is "We" ~ And Where Is "There"?

A few days later, having no idea if the same event will happen again, the four of us (Pam, Jan, Kay, and myself) gather our courage and meet in the cottage. I pray for protection and repeat the deal I made on the cement; I only want to meet with Spirit and nothing else. (And at the same time, I am desperately hoping there is nothing else!)

Besides, who are we talking to? Who is "we" and where is the "there" that this voice refers to? Yet, most importantly, where is Pam, and what have we gotten her and ourselves into? She has a family and three young children. Recently, a movie came out about people having multiple personalities. God, I hope we haven't awakened a monster!

After Pam settles back in the rocking chair, Jan begins relaxing her. Her eyes close, her mouth puckers, her facial muscles begin to contort, and her hands take on the same crooked shape as the day before. We watch, fearful, fascinated, and somewhat breathless. We wait as my cousin keeps talking in the quiet of the cottage. Again, the grunting and the laborious sounds begin to accompany my friend's squirming. After a little while her lips begin to move, but the raspy words come out sounding weak and a bit garbled.

Pam—or whoever—suddenly thrusts out her hand to me. "Feel it." She insists. My breath catches; I don't want to. Then, getting a grip on myself, I bring my hands within inches of hers. A current instantly jolts my fingertips, setting me back by the shock of it.

"It is energy." She calmly assures me. *I am not reassured.*

"Does it hurt you?" I ask. *My fingers don't hurt but are tingling.*

"Oh no, I am used to it. Power is centred in the hands. It has to be used in love. It's power surging. I have to be careful. I will be motivated by love, nothing else. It is a time of learning." *For us, I assume.*

Then I ask, "But who are you, really?"

"Roots." The raspy voice is terse.

"Of what?"

"The universe. This Body is a conduit, but not all are." She continues, "This Body (Pam) has work to do. Must get closer. You must not touch it, must not ask questions until ready. Centring prayer needs to be used. The power of healing needs prayer to be centred and concentrated. The Body cannot do it alone. And this Body has reservations and needs reassurance. The Entity has given permission for me to come in, but it is not ready."

Odd, she is referring to Pam as "the Body" or "the Entity." What an interesting distinction. I am dead sure Pam is not ready for this, but she apparently gave her permission anyway.

The old woman present in my friend turns her head towards me. Although her eyes—or rather Pam's—are shut, I feel she is seeing me clearly.

Pointing her crooked finger at me, she instructs, "You are the director. You have questions: Research and find your questions. Plan for the next session. Stay open in your mind. Concentrating with your mind adds strength to the Person."

Her closed eyes feel like they are piercing me. Then she adds, "You are new to this, yet you have the keenest intuition. But you will have to listen, as you tend to put the brakes on." *You are so right on both accounts.*

"So, Pam and Paige have work to do with you?" Jan reiterates.

"Yah, indeed." *Oh, interesting, Pam and I have work to do with her. And she actually sounds friendly!*

"Is our counselling work going to be, okay?" I ask.

The cottage woman shoots back, "You won't mind this trip. You will learn. The human part will be a wild ride." *No wilder than the one I'm on at the moment.*

As if reading my mind, the old woman tilts her head and points her slightly curled hand toward me. "I am real. I am real." O*bviously, she is reading my still uncomprehending and doubting mind.*

Is she real? How could she be real? Yet here I am, looking right at Pam, but knowing this is not Pam I am addressing, nor is it her voice I am hearing. Plus, none of us can deny that thumping Beat in the living room. I almost wish I could.

Was She Real? ~ How Could She Be?

I have to ask the next question: "Is this a trick?"

Not wasting a breath, she quickly retorts, "Indeed not, indeed not." *She is right. There is nothing about this person that resembles Pam. She feels like an old woman, yet at the same time it is unbelievable that a real person is coming through another real person.*

However, if we don't believe that, what do we do with the Beat we heard on the tape, which still gives me goosebumps? Besides, I have known Pam for years. This person thinks differently, talks differently, and even looks different. Plus, Pam would never, ever claim to be the love of the universe, nor would I or anyone I know!

Pam shifts in the rocker, agitated again. I look at my cousins. Jan and Kay both shrug their shoulders. We wait.

Do You Have a Name?

After a few minutes and more agitation, I explain that even though she has said that "they" don't need names at her level, it still would be easier for me to talk and relate to her if I can call her something.

She stops rocking, seems to ponder, then states rather garbled, "My name is Metude." She repeats it several times as initially I can't make it out. I ask her to spell it, as I have never heard it before.

Then, she continues her instructions on what to do during the visits. "We will guide you through each step. One must concentrate and listen. Do not touch the Body. You must have questions ready, and you must reassure the Person."

What Was That Beat?

Now, knowing her name and feeling slightly more comfortable with her, I ask the burning question: "What was that Beat thundering off the walls in the living room the first day we met you?"

She leans forward in the rocker, her index finger beginning to move slowly, up and down just above her knee. Then, with the slightest smile, she states, "Ah, that Beat takes great energy. It is the love of the universe. You needed it." *Ha, we certainly did, or we wouldn't be sitting here without it.*

"Oh Metude, on reflection, it was like a heart beating! Yet, we were so scared."

She nods and looking kindly, responds, "Indeed, no need to be, 'tis good."

Then, the cottage woman says in a weak voice, "The body is closing me out. I must leave." Again, we observe, more fascinated and a little less fearful as neck and mouth muscles change. This is an unsettling process to watch. Pam stretches and is back to herself. Again, she remembers nothing. *I am relieved, though. Metude seems like a real person, as unbelievable as that is!*

• • •

The Beat never happened again. Even so, now instead of fear, it fills me with awe. And the old woman is right—we needed it desperately. Later, as my cousins repeatedly say, if it wasn't for the Beat, we would never have continued with the visits—and thus, we would have lost the opportunity of a lifetime.

Besides, prior to the cottage woman, the only things I believed real were basically what I could see, hear, touch, and feel. I knew there was spirit. I loved it. Yet, the invisible still felt nebulous and very cloud-like. However, talking to this person without a body, hearing the thundering Beat when there was no sound originally in the room was proof that the invisible was not as formless or empty as I had previously thought.

After that last visit with the cousins, walking the few steps from the cottage to the house and hearing this mysterious person confirming the Beat, I felt like skipping—or better still, *flying*—over the grass. The sun was gloriously warm for a chilly, fall afternoon. I started laughing at how scared we were about the Beat when it was simply love! The love of the universe! And I knew that she wasn't lying.

• • •

A Secret Place to Visit ~ Tell No One

We needed to keep this stranger a secret, as our country road was not ready for a multi-dimensional experience like talking with this strange visitor. Thus, we also needed a secret place to meet with her where we would not be disturbed. Once this strange presence came through, I could not have anyone just dropping in. The old woman's low, accented voice and the rearrangement of her muscles on Pam's face were simply too weird.

The cottage was perfect, as no one ever went up there during the day but me. Its isolation was ideal for our visits. Our motto became: "Tell no one." My family was well-liked on our country road, but I sensed that "witch-burning" (figuratively speaking, of course) could easily be kindled. After all, we were talking to someone who did not have her own skin-and-bone body. Plus, we wouldn't have believed it ourselves. Now she was there, right before our eyes and even then, we were struggling. If it had not been for the undeniable evidence of the mysterious Beat on the tape and my deal with God on the cement, I expect we would not have exposed Pam and ourselves to such an abnormal, scary encounter the second or third time.

Another vital consideration was that I did not want this unexplained phenomenon affecting my relationship with my husband, Roger. I did not want it to be a secret or cause a distance or rift between us. We had tea every night around nine o'clock and talked about the day's events. Now, I began telling him more about this old woman coming through Pam. He had heard the Beat on the tape. In fact, we repeatedly listened to it. I also wanted him to keep his reality expanding with mine so we could continue to grow in "abnormality" together.

One day, when we were stacking the winter-wood in the garage for our kitchen stove and talking about the recent events, he concluded that there were just some things that "cannot be explained or denied." Extremely relieved that he felt that way, I quickly agreed. The door was open for me to talk about the cottage woman.

• • •

The Cottage ~ Alias an Old Barn

When buying our home in Seaforth years ago, we moved an old "barn" from down the road onto our new property. Our oldest child, Doug, wanted a pony, and we had to have a place to keep the hay. Our three younger children Haley, Callie, and Dev also had many a ride up and down our country road. When we sold the pony several years later, we changed the name of the old, dilapidated grey-shingled building to "the cottage." It was about thirty feet from the house and consisted of one long room with a large window facing the house with the ocean about twenty feet beyond.

Spruce trees leaned against the windows on the backside of the cottage. The space between the clapboards initially let in the rain and snow. Eventually, Roger covered the cracks with tar paper, added new shingles, and he and the children put on a new roof.

My painting studio was in one half of the room, and we met with the cottage woman and our guests in the other half. In the middle of the room, against the back wall, was an antiquated early-eighteenth-century wood stove. Our strange guest and her visitors huddled around its heat in fall and winter. Thus, her nickname came naturally: the cottage woman.

• • •

Being in Presence ~ And Book Friends

For years before meeting the cottage woman, I kept a weekly journal about my encounter with life—its insights, learnings, and joys. During those years, as our children were growing up, I was beginning to recognize a love larger than myself, a deeper spiritual awareness, and also a Presence that was tangibly felt in my husband, children, and community.

Roger, my husband and father of my children was also a caring presence. I met him in my first year of university. He was in engineering, and I was in the social sciences. We shared special interests like music and art, and we had similar values. Yet, most importantly, he had an integrity and a flexibility of thought about him that I loved.

In addition, as a young mother, slowing down to be in a larger presence than myself was difficult with the minute-by-minute demands of four children, aged five and under. Taking them to the grocery store, two in the basket and two getting a lift by hopping on its rungs, not only taxed a muscle or two; it also, at times, disturbed my ease of spirit.

One day, I came across a quote that marked all future trips to the store. It read, "Those in a hurry are without hope of splendour." (Unfortunately, I did not record the author's name at the time.)

Also, my book friends were often mystics: Meister Eckhart, Thomas Kelly, John Woolman, Soren Kierkegaard, Pierre Teilhard de Chardin, Simone Weil, Frank Laubach, and the liberation theologian Gustave Gutierrez. Their experiences with the presence of God—their awareness, discovery, and relationship to the divine spirit within their own beings—inspired me. A rich spirituality was developing within me.

At the time, I was also discovering Teilhard de Chardin's observation that we are spiritual beings *immersed* in human experience rather than human beings *having* a spiritual experience. Upon reflection, maybe this is what the cottage woman was referring to when she said, "Love, I teach love." And that her source or root was "the love of the universe." Maybe she would help me discover more about the love I was experiencing and reading about from these mystic writers. They recognized a Presence larger than themselves and experienced a deeper spiritual awareness of God.

SEVERAL WEEKS BEFORE THE COTTAGE WOMAN ARRIVED ~ A LOON CALLS

Sept 7/85 I am here on the deck, a loon calls from across the water. The moon is rising up behind Potato Island and God, as Laubach writes, is "tenderly wounding my soul with such loveliness." I wonder, what is your word for me? What does your Spirit want from me? And, like Laubach, I wait for an answer; unlike him, I hear nothing. Practising the constant awareness and that lovely feeling of God is hard to maintain. I don't think I can learn to see and feel the Presence in each activity. I get glimpses, like that old man today so bent over at the grocery store, but I had to slow down in order to see him with spirit-eyes. Maybe walking slower will help.

Ah, the moon is full now with its sad, hollow eyes. It occurs to me that if I can ever establish myself in constant Presence, there will be no me! I am feeling a bit unsure that the "little i" wants that. But that's the call. It is not for everyone, but it is for me. I know this in my bones. I don't think I can do it, but I'll try.

Two weeks later, after the cottage woman arrived

Sept 20/85 A lovely evening, I am here on the deck, writing by the light coming through the living room window and waiting for the full moon to come up. Ah, there is a pink slip of light rippling the trees across the water to Strawberry and Potato Island. Roger and I canoed down the river after supper. It was beautiful.

Jan and Kay have left for the west. I need a break from all the intensity of the past few weeks. I won't meet with the old woman again until I am more rested and more back to normal.

There is also a fall crispness in the air; I smell it as I write. The brownish leaves are beginning to dry and curl. A sign of summer's ending and fall's beginning. I wonder if this isn't the most intense year of my life. The past weeks have been stressful and busy for Jan, Kay, Pam, and me. Meeting the old woman in the cottage was not contemplative or emotionally restful for us. I need silence,

*aloneness, and inner calm for myself. I
am exhausted. Looking in the mirror this
morning, my eyes looked punched. Roger
suggested I take a month off. Not possible,
yet I will make more space. I must.
Are there not different melodies in our lives?
Husband, children, friends, prayer, painting,
human development work, each of these play
a different melody—all of which requires a
balance that is definitely necessary.
However, despite the oddity of the situation,
this cottage woman could offer significant
wisdom in our life, but she comes in such
a different way that she needs to be kept
a secret.
I have had three days of normalcy, and I
feel more human tonight. Thank God, it's
time to do ordinary things. It's a housework
day, and how few and far between those
days have been! After the last weeks, this
seemingly predictable mundaneness feels like
a friend. Just before waking, I asked myself,
"What do I do or how do I work with
people?" (I am not a professional therapist or
counsellor, yet when I listen and talk with
people, they seem to find a wisdom that is
helpful and emotionally healing.) Then an
inner voice seemed to reply, "You walk along
with people and share their burden. It may
or may not be resolved, but you are there."*

Augusta

That's about it.
This type of emotional work with others'
problems takes an energy that comes
from deep within. The family nurturing,
painting, and karate are a balancer. Roger
fixed up the painting studio in the cottage
yesterday. Finally, I have space away from
the phone. I need a few days painting,
a little weeding of the garden, or better
still—a week not talking to anyone.
Roger's birthday was yesterday. He is fifty. It
doesn't seem so old anymore. We had family
and friends over. Dev, our youngest son,
also had his seventeenth birthday. My, that
sounds old for our youngest child.

FIRST TIME ALONE WITH THE COTTAGE WOMAN ~ THE DOOR IS OPEN

Pam and I decided this morning that we would try for a visit. It is November-cold, so I went up to the cottage early to set the fire in the old wood stove. Before starting, we prayed for protection and direction, stating clearly that we only wanted to visit with this old woman. We didn't know what to expect; after all, we never knew that the cottage woman existed, who knows what other possibilities are out there?

This would be my first time visiting with her alone (except for Pam, who was not present, anyway.) I was nervous. Could I help the old woman come in by myself? In any event, I had to try. The people we saw in counselling and our little group of friends needed more wisdom than I could give them on my own. Plus, I was also beginning to feel that she had come for a greater purpose as she was already stretching me beyond my limited perception of reality.

The visit was excellent, yet disappointing. The tape-recorder only worked sporadically. I later learned that

Pam—or maybe the old woman—could turn it off energetically. Thus, when I turned the recorder on afterwards, we discovered that it had only taped about half the visit. Luckily, I had made notes, so filled Pam in on the rest of the visit after the fact.

Nervous to begin, I count like my cousin did with a soothing voice, encouraging Pam to relax. After a short time, I am watching muscles rearrange themselves, which hopefully is announcing the presence of this strange, new acquaintance. Pam must now have a little more confidence in the cottage woman's entry, as she isn't physically struggling as much as she was before.

I wait until she looks settled, then after some apprehensive thoughts, I ask, "Are you Metude?" *Two people in one body: How utterly weird is that?*

After a slight pause, she replies in a throated, accented voice, speaking in a business-like manner, "Yah, indeed. Proceed." *I feel the relief in my stomach.*

Later, I tell Pam, "Oh, I can't believe it! Our old woman did come in, and she is delightful! I am so excited! She is not scary at all. She kept her head tilted to one side and wagged her finger just above her knee when she wanted to emphasize a point. Her mouth and chin muscles arranged themselves almost in a pucker, as they did before. She does feel way older than we are. (Pam was in her thirties, and I was forty-six.)

I continue, "Really, a visit with her is rather like a visit with my dear older friend Mrs. Jordan. And get this—she told me she enjoys the rocking chair and gave it a little rock!"

"What a dear old soul."

"Yes, but she's not that old. She's got the vitality and vigor of a person in their fifties, even though her wisdom seems ancient. I do feel her inner strength. Yet when I ask her something, she does not answer right away."

"Why?"

"I'd say she listens expectantly, then gives me an answer that relates exactly to the situation. Yet, I don't know if she sees it or how she picks up the information. And Pam, this is also interesting—she says she is not only *Metude* because she is not one person. She continually refers to 'we.' I don't know. It is like there are different aspects of her or something. We'll have to ask her again to explain because I really don't understand her thinking."

Only Positive Thoughts Are Real ~ And with Them, We Make the World

"Then Pam, I asked about my good friend Ellen. She is a lovely person, but she is extremely unhappy with her life. It has left her bitter, angry, and feeling worthless. (Often, she projected these feelings onto others and onto me.) I also told the old woman that Ellen sees things negatively, and we have tried to ignore that. But listen to this, she said straight out, 'Ellen is like a horse with blinders on.' I was taken aback by her bluntness, but as soon as she said it, I thought, *this old woman is right*.

"She continued, 'What she believes other people are doing to her is exactly what she is doing to others.' So, I asked how we could help her. She replied rather tersely that when Ellen is being negative about people, we need to call attention to it, rather than just ignore it. She kept repeating 'must be brought up,' but I told her this friend is very refined and is easily hurt. Metude quite agreed and added, 'Must be done gently, carefully. Only positive thoughts are real.' She repeated that several times."

Pam and I had never considered a thought solid enough to be real. No one else we knew did either. Several decades ago, before the iPhone, the Google search engine, computers, Skype, and the new science, no one on our country road considered a thought *real!* Thoughts were just *thoughts*, like clouds floating by. We believed in what could be seen and touched. (Buddha and quantum physics had not made it yet to Seaforth.) And for the next five years, the cottage woman reminded us that thoughts are real in almost every visit.

> *We are what we think.*
> *All that we are arises with our thoughts.*
> *With our thoughts, we make the world.*
>
> *~ Buddha*

"Also, listen to this," I continue. "Metude stated emphatically that you and I are not to have negative thoughts either. That sort of shocked me because I think we are really positive people."

Pam frowns, "This old woman does not mince her words." *Quite true, it seems.*

Who Can Visit ~ A Readiness Is Needed

"Pam, I am eager for the rest of our group to meet this old woman who is beginning to feel like a miracle arriving in our midst. She could be a great help to each of us. And, if she is real as she keeps telling me, life certainly is a lot larger and full of more mystery than I or they have previously thought. I think our group would be interested.

"So, I asked her if I could tell Ellen about these visits because she is more spiritual. And guess what, the old woman's answer was emphatic, 'No, the person is not ready.' Now that's disappointing because I thought it would help Ellen's concern about the subject of death that she brought up the other day. Seems to me that this old woman is living proof that there is an incorporeal side to humans, even if Metude is in your body, Pam. Yet, what a mind stretch that is! Most people aren't ready to understand. Therefore, we will have to be careful, as we just can't invite whoever we want to meet her. And that's too bad." *Pam is nodding vigorously.*

"In addition, who would ever believe that we are visiting with someone that does not have her own skin-and-bone body? No one we know, even I am struggling when she is sitting right before my eyes. However, what I can't deny is that she is a totally different person than you. This person literally does seem to be from the other side.

"I also asked if Fran, who believes as you know, that there is a devil, could visit. I was sure the answer would be 'no.' However, the old woman reflected a minute then said, 'Very difficult right now. Thinks narrowly. Needs to hear what is going on here to expand her reality. Needs to listen with her heart rather than her ears. She will hear.'"

Pam muses, "It's getting rather complicated. I hadn't thought of these differences. So, we will always have to ask rather than guess who can visit."

"Right my friend. I hadn't thought of it either, but I will need to prepare Fran before she comes."

Pam is nodding again, and I am guessing she cannot imagine how I ever got permission to invite our fundamentalist friend for a visit. *It's beyond me too.*

You Need Not Borrow Fears ~ About the Other Side

Then, I remember something else that Pam had mentioned the other day, "Oh yes, did something trouble you at church on Sunday? The old woman mentioned it."

Pam looks puzzled, then laughs and replies, "Oh, I bet it was when the minister was saying he doesn't believe in ghosts."

"Well, she said that you were intimidated."

"I was!"

"She suggested you work against that. Besides, you have heard voices when no one was in the room. The old woman says you must have confidence, yet continue to question all such issues. Then she added, 'You need not borrow fears.'"

"Hmm, that will be hard." *Pam is right, as she is full of fear about this stuff.*

"I know, but she said you need to work at it. And what is really neat, Pam, is that the cottage woman is probably here in this room listening to us right now and seeing how well

I am doing in giving you this feedback. Plus, I am not even scared. How neat is that?" *We laugh, nervously.*

"And isn't it weird to think of someone being here, knowing what we are saying and knowing the different situations in detail without me telling her anything, even when you were not present in the situations yourself. How amazing is that!

"Plus, what's really exciting is I could feel her enthusiasm about our counselling work. When I mentioned it to her, the old woman leaned forward in the rocker, pointed her finger at me and said, 'There is much work to do.' And imagine, we have her wisdom available to us!

"So, I asked her how often she will come back to visit us. She replied, 'If the need arises, I'll come back.'" *Oh, then you are here forever, I said. We will always need your largeness of spirit.*

"The old woman also keeps telling me to reassure you that she is real. And Pam, at every encounter, she seems so totally a separate person from you that she must have had a different history. So, I asked about her life. And with a surprising lilt and slight nod, she answered, 'Yah, indeed. What would you like to know?' She seemed somewhat amused. I was tempted to say everything, but restrained myself.

"So, I asked her, 'Are you a spirit guide?' For me, at times, there seems to be a wise voice or feeling in my head that directs me which I call a guide. We have talked about this. However, in response, the old woman bent her head, frowned, and said her visits are different than what we call 'guides,' which must mean there really are guides!

"Then, she tried to explain again. 'Metude is an aspect of Me, like what you call a personality. There are different planes.'

"I sensed the 'Me' is more knowing even than her, maybe a larger divine resource. She said some other stuff Pam, but I can't get it.

"I then asked why she comes to us now and she replied, 'The door is open, and permission is given from the person.' That must have happened when you decided to find the missing piece within yourself when we first met the old woman. She also said she's been waiting a long time to come to us. Apparently, she was with us often but has not been allowed to speak.

"I responded to her, laughing, 'Well, you are going to be allowed now.'"

I glance at Pam and wonder if she will disagree, as she is still so iffy about what is happening. She raises an eyebrow but says nothing, so I add, enthusiastically. "Pam, she is so delightful. I wish you could meet her."

"Me too," *she sighs, but I am not at all sure she actually wants to meet her at all.*

Past Lifetimes ~ Are Continuous Life Experiences

"Now Pam, this is where the visit got stranger. When I asked the old woman where she was from, she seemed to not understand the question, so I added, 'in one of your past lifetimes.' She began to rock, looking as if she was considering something. The slightest smile began to form at the corners of her puckered mouth. I think she was checking to see if we were ready to hear her answer. Then she began to speak, and I struggled to understand her accent."

So, I click on the tape recorder again for Pam to catch the cottage woman's words firsthand. "We don't consider them past lifetimes but merely continuous life experiences. Which aspect do you want?"

I ask about her accent since it is so noticeable.

"Ah, Sweden, many, many years ago."

"Really? What did you do?" Again, she didn't seem to understand what I was asking.

"Your occupation," I add.

"I worked in a shop with clocks and was a clockmaker. I knew the Person at that time. She was a schoolteacher."

Pam's eyes widen. "I knew her? I was a schoolteacher in Sweden?"

"That's what the old woman says. Something like you both manifested at the same time, whatever that means. *At least, I think that is the word she used.* I have to say it sounds far-fetched, but I do trust her. She is not going to lie."

The expression "continuous life experiences" somehow made sense when I heard it—I understood that there is one life or aliveness from which we emerge here on earth to have a life experience. If that is the case, there must be many people alive, although invisible on the other side like Metude. It quite boggles the mind. She must have died out of that physical life, and now she is also having this experience, as limited as it must be for her. I believe this wise, spirit woman because I am looking at her! I also feel her essence.

Plus, until five minutes ago, Pam merely thought of herself as a housewife and mother with very little education. Now, even though she might not have a readiness to accept that the cottage woman is real, she is considering the possibility that she might have been a teacher.

Jolting me from my thoughts, Pam laughs and asks, "Did you ask about anyone else in our group?"

"Well, with the size of our families and community I have lots of choices, but I don't know if it is appropriate to ask about everyone, out of a respect for their privacy. So, I tried to keep the questions focused on a problem.

"But Pam, she is so nice. I am starting to feel affection for her even though she doesn't show me any emotion. I wanted to tell her, but I don't know if one says that to someone like her. Yet, I braved it.

"With the slightest smile, the old woman nodded, 'That is good. It is important.' She repeated the word 'good' twice."

She Is Here to Learn Too ~ But Seems to Know Everything

"When she was leaving, I thanked her for coming to us so we could learn. She replied, 'I am here to learn, too.' Now isn't that something? She seems to know everything, so what can she ever learn from us? Maybe, not to give too much information or answer our questions in a 'yes' or 'no' fashion, as that might stunt our growth. And, as it is, I can only understand so much anyway.

"Oh Pam, and she also assured me that she'll be back. This is a whole new world opening to us."

My younger friend replies, "Well, I feel terrific, full of energy." *That is different, she rarely feels terrific nor has extra energy.*

"I am telling you; this old woman is a gold mine. She really is. She will help us see below the surface."

I query Pam again to see if she remembers any of this visit. As it is hard to believe she does not recall at least a snippet of what was said in the last hour or so. Shaking her head, she states, "No, sometimes I have a slight memory, but only after you mention something. If you were to ask me, I couldn't tell you what was said."

Then Pam gives me a razor-sharp look. "Do you think this Metude is a subconscious part of me?" *What a great question.*

"I have given this some thought myself. No, she is so different than you. Of course, I considered that, but I honestly think you are two separate and very different people. It is just not you I am experiencing. I have known you for years, and we have had hundreds of tea-talks. I know you! This might help: In a dream when the person doesn't look like themselves, but you know who it is because you feel the essence of their personality, I would know yours in a second. Besides, when the old woman comes in, you change physically and you are even shaped differently. It's like this cottage woman has to rearrange your muscles to fit into your body.

"No, my friend, I experience her as a different person who knows a lot more than we do. I think we just have to trust her and follow our instincts. Maybe that's what the old woman means when she repeatedly tells me to listen. And she did tell us she is the love of the universe. It does sound a bit grandiose, but somehow, I can feel it in her.

"However, this listening thing she keeps reminding me to do is very nebulous. Unfortunately, when I try to listen inside myself, I can't hear anything but silence and the lap of waves, as if I am outdoors. Besides, what do I listen for? Am I supposed to be hearing a voice? It's pretty hard to get direction that way." Pam shrugs her shoulders. *She doesn't know either.*

Checking my watch, I know it was time to end the visit. My friend always wants to be home when her children get off the school bus.

• • •

A Culture Allergic to the Psychic Gifts and Getting the Hives

Pam was gifted. She could hear voices and was visually clairvoyant. Yet back then, our culture was so allergic to psychic phenomena that it would break out in hives knowing we were talking to someone without a human body. And Pam's family reflected the prevailing wind.

I, on the other hand, did not consider myself particularly psychic; but as the cottage woman said in the first visit, I have okay instincts. Early in my life, I began to vaguely identify a thought or feeling that sometimes seemed to come from a place larger than myself. I began to like the guidance (intuition, insight), as things seemed to work out better if I followed it. Eventually, I named this feeling a "spirit guide," as it felt caring, wise, and I couldn't see it! Besides, it guided! God was a bit big for me to handle. So, I started to call it a seemingly crazy name I had never heard before. Thus, over the years and in desperate situations, I called on this wisdom and it responded.

THE INVISIBLE IS LISTENING

Nov 14/85 Jack Frost has begun to paint his beautiful artwork on these bedroom windows. The patterns are exquisite. My throat and ear are sore. Need to start the cod liver oil. Thank goodness I feel rested, productive, energetic, and balanced again. Life seems to have fallen into some kind of blissful, bit-size order, and it is a far cry from a month ago, when I was struggling to adjust to the cottage woman.
Plus, this old woman is finding a place in my psyche and in my affections.
I woke this morning from a dream, and I felt love. Pam and I had our heads together. She stroked my hair, telling me it was beautiful. And I replied, "Well, it's just hair, ordinary hair." I am surprised at the comment because my hair isn't really beautiful, and Pam never gets personal. Later I looked hair up in the symbol book and got a pleasant surprise: hair on the head symbolizes spiritual forces and signifies spiritual

development. I can only hope.

I finished a portrait of Roger yesterday and am rather pleased with it. If I was ever to dedicate my painting to anyone, it would be him because of his continuous support, encouragement, and the hours he has sat still so I could learn portraiture. And yes, Metude, I am trying to listen into the silence. Shakespeare got it right—the world is truly a stage, and we are the actors. I am realizing that you and the guides are listening and watching in love, ready, and wanting to help us. Your essence rings true; you are literally the physical proof. I see and hear you! Thank you.

I AM REAL, ASK YOUR QUESTIONS ~ IT ALL FEELS NEBULOUS

On a grey November afternoon, Pam and I are here in the cottage. I came up earlier to set the fire in the wood stove so it will be cozy for our visit. The crackle and fragrance of applewood greets us an hour later. Pam is not relaxing well. The voice that greets me is so weak that I am not sure who it is or if the tape recorder will pick it up.

"Are you Metude?" I ask, slightly holding my breath. *And what if she isn't?* Pam opens her mouth, but no words come out. I continue, "Is there anything I can do to make you feel more comfortable?" She seems to be struggling. I wait, then push a bit.

"Is it all right to ask questions as we do have some people who need your wisdom this afternoon." The rocker begins to move, always a hopeful sign.

She nods then rasps, "Proceed." Her voice is a little stronger and thankfully, it is the cottage woman. *I only want her wisdom—good weird, not bad weird.*

My first question is about Donna, a woman Pam and I have been working with this past year. We desperately need advice, as she is suicidal.

You Learn to Listen ~ It All Feels So Nebulous

"One of our acquaintances, Donna, gets what she calls 'spells' that cause her to cut her arms. How can we help her?"

"It is her pain," the old woman replies. "She must get in touch with her pain."

"We are working on that and the abuse she has had in the past, but she still cuts herself. Are we pushing her too hard? You said I tend to do that."

"Let go of your concern. She is making progress. You learn to listen."

"Yes, you keep telling me that. Learn to listen, but I have deaf ears." *It all feels so nebulous.*

"Much progress. You must see that."

"Well, I do and I don't, but your words are reassuring."

"You ask your questions, and you learn to listen. It will come. It will come. Again, you need reassurance. Reassurance is a good thing. It is good, very good for you."
She is right.

I do need reassurance. I am not psychic. I don't see images, hear voices, or see ghosts, yet here I am talking to Metude, and I am not at all gifted in this area. The New Testament implies the veil between us and the other side can be thin, but mine feels significantly thick. However, I am determined to make it thinner.

The old woman points her hand toward me and repeats, "You learn to listen. You ask your questions, and you learn to listen. It will come." Then giving another little rock, I hear, "We will proceed." *Hmm, not much on Donna, she seems more interested in my learning to listen. Yet, there are so many other important, exotic things I could be learning other than listening!*

However, little did I know how large and how important this listening lesson was to be. It now reminds me of having another pair of inner ears that expands my hearing. It is in the listening that a greater intelligence, a larger awareness, waits to be heard. I was later to learn that silence, stillness, and awareness are its golden, inner companions with its own language, presence, and its own full, juicy aliveness.

Dead Is Not the Word We Use ~ He Has Settled

Returning from my reflection, I continue, "A university student named John has been missing for a year. Pam and I have met with his parents in hopes that we might help. They continue to search, and while they grieve, they insist he is still alive somewhere. Through Pam's images and my sense of it, we feel he may have been murdered. She got an image of his body being dumped in the harbour. Yet, we can't tell his parents that, so is there anything we can tell them to ease their torment?"

Metude pauses; I wait. She nods seemingly to herself, then points her craggy finger at me and says emphatically, "He has settled."

Feeling heaviness in my spirit and being puzzled, I inquire, "What do you mean by 'settled'?" Then it dawns on me. "Is he dead?" *To see the image of his body in one's mind is shockingly different than hearing it from someone in front of you who you know, knows.*

She frowns and states emphatically. "Dead is not a word we use."

I try again. "Is he alive on earth?"

"He is settled," she insists with finality. *I have never heard of dead being called "settled," but intuitively, I'm quite sure that is what she means.*

She continues, "Much needs to be done with his parents. Much wasted energy. They are creating pain upon pain for themselves. They don't let go, but they must." *Metude is right. Pam and I both observe this. They have the pain of losing their son, but also add to their pain by fighting their loss.*

"Is there anything we can do?

"No. They do not hear you."

"We can't do anything for them?" *Yet they are so broken. Maybe if I tell them about this old woman, it will be a comfort. I think she knows what happened to him.*

"No," she retorts, reading my mind and it feels like a command. *Hmm, so no doing anything and no telling them about her. That is too bad.*

John's parents continued to search, but he was never found. And as Metude pointed out, they did continue to "create pain upon pain for themselves." *Yet, I also know that if I lost one of my children, my hope and looking would never, never cease.*

Through later conversations, the cottage woman continued to use the word "settled" instead of "dead." And she also corrected me whenever I forgot and used the word "dead." Obviously, she experienced life's continuation, no matter what form it takes. If that is the case, then death must only happen to the body, which the scripture tells us becomes "dust to dust." So, maybe we do have everlasting life in some way?

Contemplative, a Strange Term ~ An Inner Resource

"I have a question about my minister friend, Tom. He has struggled spiritually, as you probably know. He says he is a "contemplative." Do you have a word of encouragement or direction I can suggest to him?"

"Ah, indeed, he is to continue to seek." She pauses in mid-sentence; I wait. "Contemplative, a strange term." *Oh, she seems puzzled.*

I explain, "Contemplative for us means to be spiritual, as in praying and meditating. I find it interesting you don't know that."

"Ah, yah," she nods with a lilt in her raspy voice. "That's what we call seeking. I like your terms." *I wonder if she means when she was a Swede or wherever she lives now.* I laugh and the corners of her mouth turn up, very slightly.

"Oh, talking about terms, Metude, when Tom asked my opinion about something this morning, I was caught off guard. Forgetting you are a secret, I started to say that I'd check with you, then I stopped myself mid-sentence, and said I'd check with my inner resource."

She pauses, then states as if pleased, "Yah, that is good. 'Tis different.'"

"So, I am going to call you an inner resource when I am speaking of you publicly. That sounds natural, don't you think? People will think it is inside me."

"Yah, I have been called many things, but this is new. Inner resource: 'Tis good." *I am happy about that, too. It's important to find language that protects her and is safe for us.*

I Am Real ~ We Are All Connected

Before she can say "proceed," I ask, "How is Pam doing? Is there anything you want to tell her about her spiritual progress? She's been pretty nervous about you coming through her, but she is doing the best she can."

I feel Metude's energy shift, the rocker stops. Her finger shoots out as she states, "She must become more confident that I am real and a part of her." *Oh, she is emphatic!*

"Yes, I know that now, but it is harder for Pam, as she does not get to see or talk with you. I don't even understand how you are real or how you are connected, other than that you come through her."

In fact, if she wasn't sitting before me, I am sure I would have trouble thinking of her as real.

Ignoring my comment, she instructs, "Keep reassuring her. I am real. I am reality. We are all connected. Proceed." *Hmm, and I wonder how that works.*

We are all connected. I knew this idea was related to the major religions, yet in contemporary-rural Canada, my friends and family certainly felt materially separated from plants, water, and the people we were not acquainted with. However, this ancient woman's sudden appearance in our lives certainly challenged our country road and western perspective.

Listen ~ The Answers Are All There for You

Next, I ask her about my spiritual progress. "This listening, Metude, even though I am trying, I honestly still don't know what to listen for, other than my instincts. Besides, trying to hear when there is no sound is like attempting to find my way in this Maritime fog, which is a fact of life here."

Again, my discarnate friend is emphatic. "To listen, that is your job. To become attuned. This is connected with your centring."

"But Pam's sense-seeing is a lot more interesting. She looks inside her head and sees this image of the situation, which often gives us a clue about how to proceed with the people we are working with."

"It was not always so." *Hmm, I thought she had been born with the ability.*

"Really, Metude? Okay, can she help me learn to see, then?"

"Yah, yah." She answers almost impatiently.

"So, Pam and I will see together?" *I need clarification.*

"You will see on your own," she corrects, emphasizing the last two words. *My turn to say good. Plus, I am glad of the independence.*

Then, I ask, "Am I ready for someone like you to come through me, or should we just do one thing at a time?"

"I think you would be wise to conquer one thing at a time. Conserve your energy. You learn one lesson at a time."

"I can see that's a good idea. Besides, I'd rather talk to you directly, as I do now, instead of just having your visit reported to me after you leave, as happens with Pam."

Metude does not want to drop the subject. "Again, I tell you, you must learn to listen. You will be given your answers. Answers are all there for you. What you sometimes call instincts."

"Well, I know my instincts are real, but listening is so intangible."

"Ah, but listening is real." She points her finger at me and again, adding emphatically, states, "I am real." *Odd, if I use my head, I understand why Pam still questions her realness, but my eyes, heart, and being know she is like a larger real than any real I know.*

I was also learning that the five senses are a good tool, as are logic and reason, but there is more. There is beyond the five senses. I was learning to listen not to physical sound, but to sound in silence, in the unseen, the invisible. And this is where I was beginning to understand that one can develop another kind of listening and seeing. Early in my visits, I kept interpreting it as a physical listening, a physical seeing. However, she seemed to be training me by tangible example to recognize and give weight to this inner communication which reminds me of the Lao Tzu's quote:

> *Beyond what your eyes see.*
> *That which cannot be seen is called invisible*
> *. . . Hear it,*
> *And feel it…*

The cottage woman is teaching me to see beyond what my physical eyes can see and hear, beyond what my physical ears can hear, which opens a reality larger than this dimension.

Much Like Old Friends ~ An Ocean Current Flowing Back and Forth

Wanting to hear more, I observe, "But you are different, Metude. You are real even though you don't have a human body. And somehow, in spite of that fact, I do see you, hear you, and really experience a unique caring between us, which is certainly different than what I have with Pam.

"Yah, 'tis good, we are much like old friends." *And that's what it feels like. Oh, that makes me smile.*

"Yes, very much like old friends, and you no doubt understand that better than I. How come we are like old friends?"

"It is a meeting between spirits, like an ocean current flowing back and forth between two shorelines. I think you can understand that." *Our house is thirty feet from the North Atlantic. I can hear the waves on the rocks as she speaks.*

"Indeed, I can." She smiles slightly. *She is right, there is a sort of love that does seem to flow back and forth between us.*

Then she adds, "There is no tomorrow, no today, there is only now." *Oh, she's just taken a leap. I have no idea what she is talking about.*

Thus, I do not know what to ask her as I parrot weakly, "It's all now, then?"

Metude and I both sit in silence for several minutes. I wonder if she can hear the waves hitting the beach. A question comes to the rescue: "Have we known each other before in some other life experience?"

"No, not in the sense you are asking." Then she shifts in the rocker, her ready-to-leave signal.

I quickly ask, "Is there anything else you'd like to say?" *I don't want it to end here.*

She leans forward stating, "Presence, that which you seek, is there." *Yet even though her eyes are closed, her look penetrates me to the bone. She is reassuring me!*

My pulse quickens. I know immediately what she means. Presence, that love in me that seems larger than me, is what I have been seeking daily for a long time.

"You mean, Metude, that this Presence, this divine spirit that I often experience as pure love is really there?" *And she says it is. Sometimes, I feel it is and other times it is so intangible, I am left guessing.*

"Oh Metude, thank you, thank you, this is so confirming coming from you. I feel it now. I love it." *And there is nothing like having a part of the living proof sitting directly across from me.*

"'Tis good." I feel her observing me with kindness behind those closed lids.

I had practised the Presence that the mystics Thomas Kelly and Frank Laubach (my book friends) did in the early part of the 1900s. They carried on a constant dialogue, developed a conscious awareness and relationship with this larger than human love that permeated their lives, which they knew as God.

Nodding, seemingly at my unspoken reflection, her mouth turns up in that slight enigmatic smile as she shifts in the rocker, saying, "I must go now. An enjoyable visit. Peace to you and yours. I will be back. I am not far from you." *Thank goodness. She knows I need to hear that.*

I thank her for coming and still watch, fascinated, as facial and neck muscles slightly rearrange themselves. Then Pam opens her eyes, raises her arms and stretches. I always have an urge to say, "Welcome back," but don't.

Her first words are, "Well, did we get any answers?"

Oh Pam, you should know by now: Of course, we did. Yet reigning myself in, I respond, "I hope so, my friend. Again, Metude said she is real and that you are to go slowly." *Ah, my impatient self has to remember that, too.*

THE INVISIBLE HAS A REALITY OF ITS OWN - A STEEP LEARNING CURVE

Dec. 13/85 A beautiful Sunday afternoon. I feel tangible love (Presence) whenever I bring my mind to it. Another wonderful visit with the cottage woman. Pam and I are both feeling such a heightened sense of awareness and energy. Understanding this other reality, in which the invisible does not have to be visible to be real, is a steep learning curve. It's challenging, and discouragement comes easily; yet, she tells me, "Much progress."

I wish I could feel this ancient woman's unique presence when she is not sitting opposite me, but I can't. Maybe someday I will experience her when she has not come in the flesh.

THE SPIRIT NEEDS US TO ASK ~ YOU NEED TO BE STILL TO HEAR

When we moved to Seaforth, a young girl named Brooke who lived down the road began to find her way to our door. She was a little older than my children and was mature for her age. She always wanted a larger view of life, which resulted in some good talks. Now, she was attending university in another province. After serious consideration and talking it over with Pam and the cottage woman, I had written to her about this woman's arrival into our lives. She is home now with her family and wants to meet my old friend. Surprisingly, Pam and Metude both agreed.

Thus, I came up to the cottage and set the fire in the stove an hour ago. Brooke arrives, and we have greetings. Pam settles into the rocker. She is nervous about having someone new watch the physical change. It takes courage. I begin relaxing her by talking softly and inviting Metude by name. I watch Brooke as Pam's neck muscles begin to change. I have prepared her for the physical change, but seeing it happen is a different experience. She is not smiling, and her eyes squint as if she is trying to figure out what she is seeing.

As the usual struggles ensue, I ask the cottage woman to let us know when she feels comfortable. After a long minute or two, she starts to speak, but we can hardly hear her. I ask her to speak louder.

"Much resistance in the Person." *I knew it.* Metude shifts her weight to a more upright position. We wait. Then, I hear the usual invitation, "Proceed."

One Must Learn to Speak Without Judgment ~ Firmness Yes, Rashness No

After Brooke introduces herself, I ask the first question in order to give her a little time to recover from watching the muscle and voice transition in Pam's body. I also have an interest in her question. Numerous times, when my young friend dropped in over the years, she would tell me about the sting of injustice she felt when the boys "didn't want a girl" to play in their backyard games. Now, she is most frustrated with the unfairness she sees around her as a young adult. She has tried to educate her family and friends to her perspective, without much success.

So, I ask, "How does one convince people that women and men are equals?"

The rocking chair begins to move. After a pause, Metude states, "The young one must learn to speak without judgment. Must learn to temper it, work with it, and not against it." *Hmm, even though I am happily married, I always chafe somewhat that Roger is supposed to be the head of the family.*

I carried the children for nine months, nursed, cooked, and cared for every detail of their young lives. He is a good dad, but it still does not seem fair that I am not considered his equal by society.

I glance at Brooke. She nods, then ventures forth, "How do I get my point of view across to people without putting them off?"

"By being you," my ancient friend replies with a lilt. "You will have the words when you need them. Not too hasty. Firmness, yes, rashness, no. Must speak with conviction, much conviction. It is the conviction that they will listen to. Never anger. People will learn from your example."

"But it is frustrating."

"Ah, my child, the impatience of youth. You have a lifetime. You will learn not only when to speak, but how. You will learn to speak where you will be heard."

"Will I teach at university?"

"Yah, a possibility. But again, you must choose."

"Well, in the car driving home, I kept coming back to being an engineer. What do you think of that?"

"Challenging, but you must choose, you know your mind." *She does not give black and white answers. She keeps encouraging us to develop our own instincts and maintain independence from her.*

Not wanting to let the subject go, my young friend asks about going into medicine.

"You are not a newcomer to that. Your last life-experience was a struggle."

She continues, "It stayed with you. You must be ready to take opportunities. You have to create opportunities if you are so directed. You are involved with every positive thought you have. We will proceed." *Really? Hmm, she does consider positive thought significant.*

As if having a second thought, Brooke switches tack. "Am I taking too much of your time, Metude?"

"You need not question time, child." She instructs kindly.

Brooke nods, thanking her, then asks, "Is Pam feeling better now about your coming in and talking with us?"

"That depends on her willingness," Metude replies quite matter-of-factly. "The Person still does not believe I am real."

"Well, I am so glad you are." *Brooke is beaming. No nervousness, no doubt now.*

My old friend nods and almost smiling says, "'Tis good. We will proceed."

Spirit Guides ~ A Different Kind of Listening

Brooke's next question surprises me. "I was aware of my spirit guides while flying home on the airplane a few days ago. Do you know anything about that?" *Oh, she is bold; I thought it was just going to be her personal stuff and here she is asking about spirit guides.*

"Yah, you have awareness, but you must call on them. They cannot help you until you acknowledge them." Metude glances my way but says to the young one with emphasis, "You must be still to hear them. That is your lesson too." *Hmm, and listening is definitely my lesson.*

I now realize the old woman's kind of listening means following one's instincts, one's intuition. Plus, she instructs me to listen before I speak or take any action. This kind of listening for that still voice seems to make life a meditation in the moment.

I wait for Brooke's next question. Silence. It is like one of those pauses in a conversation in which people glance at each other and wonder what is coming next. My young friend looks a little uncomfortable. This ancient woman generally will not speak without being asked a question. She has made that clear. So, I begin to excuse the silence, as it is Brooke's first visit when Metude interrupts, saying, "The young one is a bit awed by this. Save her questions for the next time. The questions, they are there. She just needs to relax." *Hmm, yet I am surprised at how relaxed she is.*

"What about names for my spirit guides?" *Brooke knows her questions and here I was wondering if I would have to make them up for her!*

"You will know the names; you will sense them. Must be done in stillness, in that life. Stillness is what you call 'life.'" She hesitates, then adds, more as a remark to herself, "Words are difficult." *Our human vocabulary, I assume.*

She continues. "Reality cannot be contained."

I interrupt, "You mean stillness is life itself? So, the information from our guides comes out of stillness?"

"Indeed." *I wonder if they are as tangible as you are.*

A Spirit Guide Introduces Himself in a Dream ~ "My Name is Sahaad."

Brooke's questions remind me of a dream I had a year ago. I describe it to Metude.

In this dream, I find myself at a dinner party. My good friends, Kate and Hugh, who in real life entertain international students, brought this young boy over to meet me. He was eleven or twelve years old and looked Arab. As we were being introduced, he moved closer to me and said, "My name is Sahaad." The word had an indefinable, throaty sound between the two a's. I must have looked perplexed because he moved toward me again and repeated, "My name is Sahaad." Then, very slowly, he put emphasis on the last syllables again, as if he really wanted me to get its proper pronunciation. I can still see the boy's face vividly. Then I woke. I instinctively knew that he was going to help guide me.

My ancient friend waits for a question. "Why did Sahaad come as a boy, Metude?"

"She shakes her head, "It is not the boy's age necessarily, but others.'" *Oh, maybe she means it's how old I am in this area, not the boy's age.*

"Can you tell me anything about him?"

She seems thoughtful and then this look of delight crosses her face. "Is awesome. Yah, a good word, much wisdom." *Ha! Then it wasn't just a dream!*

"Can he talk to me?"

"In your silence, yah, as one would relate to a teacher. You must learn to listen. You must desire lessons." *Hmm, I must "desire" lessons. That's a stretch. The life lessons I experience often can cause an emotional wallop of pain accompanied by a desire to bury them instantly.*

A Past-Life Experience ~ Fear Does Not Exist if You Do Not Think So

Brooke then interrupts us. "How does one get rid of fear?" Brooke has had a fear that seemed faceless and unidentifiable. We had asked Pam about it one day. She felt our young friend had a difficult last life experience, and she may still experience its residual impacts.

The cottage woman looks at Brooke kindly and responds, "Be open to fear: Look at it, talk about it, work with it, and identify it. Consciousness is a part of it. Fear is lessened when one becomes aware. Do not have negative thoughts. There is nothing to fear. Fear does not exist if you don't think so."

"Really?" Brooke puzzles.

"It will become clearer. We will proceed."

I Can Only Speak as Much as the Person Allows ~ You Are Confused

After several seconds, Brooke asks, "How psychic am I?" *Oh, a good question!*

Metude quips instantly, "How psychic do you want to be?"

"I want to be tuned in."

"Then you will be, young one."

"But Pam is really psychic, and she says she doesn't want to be?"

"No child, she was wanting it. Started to study. She initiated it." *I am not sure that Pam is conscious of that.*

Interrupting their conversation, I reflect, "I am curious Metude. In our first meeting you talked with a Swedish accent, and the voice with the accent said it was not Pam."

"You are very confused." She muses.

"Yes, quite right." I laugh.

"I can only speak as much as the Person allows."

"Then that is what Pam allows?"

"What we both allow." She corrects. *I still don't get it.*

"How does that work? I am not speaking to Pam right now, but to you. So how is it both of you? I know I am confused, but I am trying to understand what is going on."

"Metude is Me." *I instinctively know the Me is spelled with a capital letter.*

"Now I am really confused. Who is this 'Me' you refer to? It sounds like a larger wisdom than even yours. You said before that you are an 'aspect of Me.'"

"You can't understand. It is all part of the one consciousness. When I speak, I come through the other Person." *Odd, she never calls Pam by name—or me, for that matter.*

"Ohhh, yes, I forget that one consciousness is what we all have."

"Ah, now you begin to see. What you call "take on a personality" is but an example. There are many factors. You feared this area. There is no longer any need for a Beat, but that was the thing you needed to hear initially."

"Yes, we certainly did. Even though hearing the Beat thump through the house paralyzed us with fear, we had to accept it as real. We all heard it! It's funny to think that an experience of the 'love of the universe' paralyzed us all with fear, but it did give credit to you, Metude."

The rocking chair stops, and she nods, "The Person (Pam) had lots of questions, but a closed door."

"I sense that. Can she open the door?"

"Yah, she must want to learn, but she has many fears and negative thoughts to conquer, which does create resistance."

"Her family's attitude does that to her by telling her her gifts are crazy or weird."

"She must find other people with positive thoughts. We will try to broaden her acquaintance. Proceed."

Now I need to ask, "Are there any doors to my personal growth that I keep closed that I don't know about?"

"You must give it time. You have enough open doors to work with now."

Brooke looks at me and we both laugh. *How true!*

Again, sensing that the visit is coming to an end, we both thank her for, as Brooke says, a "full-of-wonder visit."

Metude nods, "Indeed, it has been a blessed visit with the young one. There will be others. So, enjoy the rocker." She adds almost as an afterthought. And she is gone.

Then Pam does her usual post-visit, squirm-stretches and is back to herself in minutes. I am in hopes that Brooke telling Pam of her experience this afternoon might help Pam catch more of Metude's essence. So, as usual, I give Pam feedback about the visit, saying, "Metude said there was a lot of resistance today, so she couldn't speak up. I asked her to turn up the volume and she said the Person's resistance (meaning you) keeps it down, and that you still don't think she is real."

Pam sighs, "Well, I am working on my fears. Yet, if I am honest, none of this seems real. I keep waiting to see what kind of answers she gives."

The unfortunate thing, my friend, is it really is not in the answers but in the heart-feel and instinctive range of wisdom coming through her which you only hear about from me, second-hand. However, this person knows another side of living beyond the human.

So, what kind of answers would tell you she is real?" I ask.

"I guess something concrete; maybe if the old woman would give a black and white answer to a question."

"I don't think that will happen. She will not tell us what we should do," I respond.

However, after hearing Brooke's excited and confirming feedback, Pam, I think, is secretly pleased with the visit. After hearing her and watching the cottage woman, my young friend had no trouble accepting her as real. I walk back to the house, thankful because there is so much more to this wise woman than her answers, and I think Brooke caught that.

WE ARE ALL ONE AND THE SAME - BREAK-THROUGH

Dec. 29/85 It was cold the last couple of days, and there is more snow coming tonight. The iced rocks along the beach are wearing little white caps of snow tipping this way and that. Yet, in spite of the cold, we had a beautiful Sunday afternoon, and we had a wonderful visit with Metude. I feel the love of Spirit whenever I think of her, in spite of her emotional neutral-ness. God is keeping my deal of it only having a soul source. Even Pam seems energized from the visits, which is remarkable. (Her home life is a large energy drain.)

What a marker year. The breakthrough with the cottage woman coming to us was the most unsettling, yet greatest gift. Certainly, it is a learning curve. This year is definitely at a turning point—an opportunity to talk to someone who is without her own flesh-and-bone body. I had thought, and was taught, that there was us here and God "up there."

*Yet, now am learning that there are others,
like the cottage woman, and that there is
another side.
What is so exciting is how real and tangible
the "invisible world" is becoming. Metude is
living proof. My perspective and experience
of my "one-dimensional reality" is dissolving.
Metude's kind of listening is also coming.
I may be catching the sound of that deeper
wisdom more. Thus, I continue to sit myself
down in the middle of Love—in the "we"
who are "all one and all connected" as this
old friend states.
I also completed a sizeable body of paintings
for one year, considering everything else that's
going on.*

• • •

The Other Side ~ No Less a Place Just Because This Human Can't See It

The cottage woman is not only deepening my spirituality, but is expanding the essence of an invisible reality and giving it tangibility. I am learning that the other side is a "place" of loving and caring relationship, empowerment, and communication. It is no less a place just because this human cannot see or hear it. Now scientists have instruments that enable them to see energies that are invisible to the naked eye. Even a dog has a hearing range greater than ours, and an owl or a hawk has a greater range of vision by far. We cannot hear or see this invisible reality, but this does not mean that it does not exist.

> *I am reminded of the saying that goes,*
> *"Take note of as much invisibleness as you*
> *can when gazing at a tree, a distant star, a*
> *mountain, a cloud, or anything . . . It is the*
> *principle that beats your heart and grows*
> *your fingernails. . ."*

~ Author unknown

A NEW YEAR'S VISIT ~ LIFE IS A SCHOOLROOM FOR OUR HUMAN LESSONS

January-cold penetrates the cottage. Pam came down early and wants to meet with the cottage woman. Even though I had lit the fire earlier, we can still see our breath. The old wood stove is doing its best to generate meager but welcomed heat, as it gives off the lovely fragrance of applewood smoke. I help her wrap up in blankets. Bundled up like that, she hardly fits in the rocking chair, which starts us laughing.

Surprisingly, she continues to give permission for these visits, in spite of all the stress in her life—Frank's excessive need to demean and control exhausts her. She waits on her children, but they are not supportive of her having time out of the house.

We Will Do Much Work in the Future ~ One Need Not Search for People

Yet, in spite of Pam's weariness, the cottage woman has a surprisingly easy entry. I wait. When she settles in, her first words are, "You have many questions. We will do much work this year. It is easier to work now: readiness." *How different than last fall—from fear to friendship.*

Her observation reminds me again of when the children were small, and we had just moved into Seaforth. I wanted to contribute in some way to the new community, but I didn't know anyone. Thus, on waking one morning, I made a deal with God and wrote it on a piece of paper.

"If you want me to help anyone, you will have to bring them to my door." That afternoon, a stranger drove in our lane. It was the new minister. He needed help with a young people's group. Remembering the note upstairs by my bed, I said yes, and then I invited him for supper. We had hot dogs. From then on, people just seemed to find their way to our door.

However, my first question to this ancient friend is what can Pam do in her family situation?

Metude looks thoughtful, "The body is weak. Must be protected. The situation is also aggrieved by chemical changes in the body. It would be helped by medical attention." *She always knows what is going on beyond the visible! That is a great gift to us.*

"Really? But it's hard to get her to go to a doctor." *And it's frustrating when I know she needs to.*

"Your friend accepts too much responsibility. These family situations are for her to work with, but not to own. Much confusion over loving someone. She suffers from stress and must get rest. She has not learned yet to set aside what is stressful. And because she doesn't, it causes her a great deal of pain." *Yes, and it makes me feel bad for her.*

Stress Is How Lessons Are Fortified ~ She Must Go for Her Inner Strength

Looking to see if this cottage woman shares my feelings, her face is expressionless.

Matter-of-fact, she merely declares, "It is her learning. She must set stress aside and go for her strength. It is inward. She sees stressful situations as pain and pain only. She has difficulty getting past situations, and that compounds the problems. Must learn to pace herself and take time for herself. She lacks discipline, which is much needed. It is the next hurdle she will work on, learning patience with herself and learning there is more to life than giving. She must take time for growth and her needs. She is beginning to see this. Although hard on herself, she is not able to live up to her own demands. Yah, she is quite good at healing herself. She must hear this." *Excellent advice for anyone.*

Unfortunately, Pam is not unlike other mothers I know. I wonder how she will take it. She is so servant-like to Frank. I've already pointed this out to her, but it is not a welcomed observation. I suspect Metude's words won't be either.

I add, "Pam is really stressed about Frank, in particular, which I am sure you know."

"She is learning. As the stress increases, it is how the (human) lessons are fortified." *Everything seems to be a human lesson to her.*

"My land, I never thought of stress working for her."

"Only when the pressure is on will she learn to deal with the situation. Both parties are learning. She is learning to be independent, to make decisions, and she is gaining freedom. However, freedom is not gained without pain. We will proceed." *Imagine, stress and pain functioning to pressure her toward freedom!*

This is a novel thought. Pam and I attempt to work to eliminate her stress. Yet, as Metude pointed out in another visit, my negative thoughts about Pam's troubles could weigh her down. It is definitely a lot harder to find the positive thoughts when watching her in pain.

Your Concern for Him Adds Weight ~ Which Adds a Negative Force

I have another question about a young man I am working with and am concerned about. I tell Metude about him, and add, "He is under a great deal of stress. He is only young, but he feels tired all the time and he can't sleep. Is he sick?"

Nodding, she states, "It is as it must be. When you are concerned for him, it weighs on him and adds to his weariness because you do not see it as positive, but as sick. This adds to the negative force. You must help others to change their perspective. Subconsciously, he knows you fear for his health." *Imagine, can our thoughts be that powerful?*

This is a fascinating concept. My genuine concern can add an emotional weight and negativity to my young friend's spirit. This, of course, applies to Pam and everyone else. If I look at the situation as negative, she is telling me that I add to their weariness. So now, both prayer and thought have plus or negative power depending on how I use them.

Suicide Is Not a Matter of Good or Bad ~ But Learning Now or Later

Changing the subject, I ask about how our friend who has been cutting herself is doing. *Instincts, a natural gift of knowing but not being sure, can carry Pam and me only so far.*

"I know you suggested she is making progress, but she now seems to be in more pain since doing more talking."

Nodding slightly, my old friend states, "She is beginning to feel her pain. It is a critical period."

"Yes, but she is also considering suicide."

"Not a thing to be gained. If she does not do the work now, then she will have to do it again. Suicide is the termination of work, period. She is given a chance to learn; she can take it or she can cut it off. People who commit suicide, they are in control. They are only given the amount of pain they can handle." *So, these decisions must be a part of our lessons, too.*

"But she feels lost and keeps threatening to take her life."

Metude pauses, then nods, "She has lost sight of the light. Each person has the choice to see the light or cut off the work. She must choose. Suicide is not a matter of good or bad, but a matter of learning now or later. An opportunity will come another time, but it just delays the process. It is not a punishment. We will proceed."

In my forty-six years, I had always heard that suicide was a terrible thing to do and that the person probably went to hell, if one believed in hell. To be told that suicide is neither good nor bad, but a learning that can be done now or later was like a lightning bolt piercing a very dark sky. Thus, she seems to be telling me that if I do not do my human lessons now or even in this lifetime, I will have to do them somewhere and at some other time. *I don't like that idea.*

Of course, Metude knows what happens after death ("We don't use the word death.") because she was a watchmaker in a prior life which has given her the transitional experience between this human life and the one, she has now on the other side. Thus, suicide is not the end to all the problems. She is saying our life lessons wait for us. Killing oneself does not make it better and one will only have to live that lesson again, in some other form until one gets it. Apparently, we are given other opportunities whether we want them or not.

Presence is Where You Must Work From ~ Adds Far More Than Mortal Words

Returning to the topic of Donna, I ask, "What can I do for her?"

"Continue your role," she said firmly.

"What is it?" *Oh, I do need clarification.*

"As a listener, she clings to you and hears you. You will be given the words. She has other people she can draw strength from. There is a great deal of energy she can draw from. The choice is hers. Physical exercise done outdoors will help. Confined pain is not a good situation. She must have the outdoors."

"Do I have to call her more often?" *I am not pleased with the prospect. She already calls almost every day or even twice a day.*

"Not necessary. You must be in Presence. That will aid her far more than mortal words." *That's that Presence of love I feel that is almost separate from me, yet exists inside me.*

"What do you mean by Presence?"

"What you are in. She will then automatically be in Presence. Will do much to heal her. Presence is a soothing balm to injury. When two or three are gathered together and focused, spirit intensifies. Don't feel you have to work with her alone." *Oh, how confirming!*

She acknowledges again the Presence I have tried to live in and walk with. Not having up-front psychic gifts like Pam, a lot of my believing is done in blind faith and instinct.

Metude nods. "For you, that Presence is where you must work from. True healing must be on a spiritual level. Spiritual energy must be transmitted." *When working in Presence with Donna, the energy feels like water running through my hands.*

"Haven't I been doing that, Metude?"

"There is room for more. Working in this way will become clearer for you. Spiritual healing will be greater in the future. Must work in the spirit of love twenty-four hours a day. Be constant."

I will never manage that.

"You will work toward that goal. It is healing for others. You will be given more books. Stop seeing life as a reality when it is an illusion. It is not a matter of your life being three dimensions, there is this separate, other side. It is more the reverse. The other side is reality."

We Think of You (Humans) as Being on the Other Side ~ It Is Reality

A rare smile seems to hover as she says under her breath, "And we think of you as being on the other side." *She seems amused at what has to be a very confused look on my face.*

"Really, then where are we who live on earth?"

"You will be prompted to think about it," she replies. "It is what you must hear. It is the beginning of another stage of growth for you. You are ready. This area is developed by listening, which is learning. You will be given more information as needed. We will proceed." *Hmm, I will certainly need it.*

This is like exploring a new world that I would never have considered a reality if it wasn't for the woman sitting across from me. She is here, and she is not Pam.

Death Is Not an Ending ~ Death Is a Matter of Changing Not Losing

And now I must ask, "Metude, how is Mother doing behind her brave face? She has lost several of her siblings recently, and that causes me concern." *Plus, I am always curious to know how this ancient cottage woman sees death!*

She replies instantly, "Much fear. It is aggravated by the situations she sees as negative. Fear. Fear for herself makes her feel vulnerable. Help her to recognize it. What motivates her feelings of fear is what she calls 'the future.' She must come in touch with reality—not what she perceives as real, but her negative thoughts."

"She has just lost two of her brothers and another one is ill."

"Yah, fears losing loves. She must see death as an alternate state, not the losing of her loved ones. She fears being alone. Has much bewilderment."

"Well, all her family is being gradually taken from her. She had nine siblings but now only three are left."

"She must be helped to understand that it is not an ending. We do not use the word 'death.' We would encourage you not to use the word either. It is not a matter of giving up or losing, but of changing. She must see this. There needs to be opportunities to discuss this in a gentle way. She is ready to hear, but needs someone to bring it up. She can't take the first step." *Oh, she wants me to talk to her. This crunches my stomach.*

"You have much fear." *She is observing me calmly through closed eyes.*

"Ah yes, in this area, I do." *Oh Metude, you have certainly read me deeply. However, I would have identified it as a little fear because in most ways, I don't fear her at all!*

My mother and I had a difficult relationship. Yet, she loved me greatly and treated me like an adult. She was my cousins' favourite aunt, our family's source of wisdom, and people enjoyed her forthrightness and humour. In other words, she always had moxie and class. With me though, at times, she was different. When she was young, there was no Google, no self-help books, and no therapist for the abuse she had suffered. Thus, her unhappiness spilled over at times into my childhood.

The emotional messages were mixed and confusing. These opposites resulted in a great love with a mixture of fear and distancing on my part. As an adult, after I had done some of my own emotional work, I tried to do some with her. However, if I brought our relationship up, she was quick to say, "Don't upset me." And, I was always relieved not to.

My ancient friend shifts in the rocker and thrust out her finger in my direction, "Do not be afraid to move forward with her. Much to be gained by venturing forth. You will listen, you will not go too far. It will not stop with conversation between two people. She will pass it onto others like a chain of links. Others will benefit. You have enough to think about." *Oh, do I ever.*

A surge of gratitude and understanding pours through me from this discarnate spirit woman with her head turned slightly to the side. *Maybe I will be able to talk with my mother.*

"I am so grateful for you, Metude." *I could hug you, but you are a bit too awesome.*

She looks kindly, saying with that little accent, "Yah, good, I am grateful for you, too. We will serve one another." *Really, I wonder how I'll ever serve you?*

I have always assumed it is the other side helping me. Yet years ago, I read a little Christian classic on intercession by Reese Howell, who lived a century or so ago. He stated that God needs our help, which shocked me. Sunday school taught us that God was all-powerful and did not need anyone's help. *And now, this ancient woman is telling me that I can help her. Not that she is God, but in the same way, I just can't imagine how!*

As I am thinking, my old friend pauses in the rocking chair, which tells me time is up. She says, "Do not trouble yourself. Peace be with you as you journey through this day. We will now bid you a good day."

I thank her for visiting us and she responds, "I do enjoy, a great pleasure for me, too."

"Oh, Metude, and me too." Pam is stirring.

A WINTER REFLECTION A WEEK LATER ~ A JOURNAL ENTRY

Jan. 12/86 A beautiful sunny weekend, and how nourishing the sun! What a contrast to this winter with its storms, short and cold days, and darkness. A bit like working with the emotional storms and darkness in people this winter.

Plus, how many times are the clothes frozen before I even get them on the line, let alone off it! I average two wash loads a day to keep the family clean. That's a lot of hanging out, hauling in, and drying them above the stove or over the banister.

Later in the day . . .

When I don't have alone-time, prayer-time, walk-time, and writing-time by myself, I have this neurotic child that shows up within me. I talked to the spirit about it. The spirit talked back.

Augusta

"You need to get yourself on firm footing with your spiritual disciplines. Recognize the child inside, know it loses confidence, and talk to it. You have given too much away. So do one of those alone things. Do something that pulls you back in and takes back the power that slips away." Amen and amen. Yes, indeed, I need to recognize the presence of the day and not contrive to seize what is not or is not yet. Humour is essential. My disciplines ground me, give me a base. I don't have to have a lot of moments and they don't have to be long, but they do have to be sweet.

Hmm.

I was told by the cottage woman, "You need to emphasize the need for your space. Do not go too long without free space, or it would be problematic for you. It is a natural need for you to be alone and one that must be obeyed." Well, I agree, but it is the opposite of this passionate, chockablock life I am living.

DISCOVERING THAT REALITY IS MORE THAN HUMAN CONSCIOUSNESS

Snowing out, and beautiful big flakes are floating down as I watch them touch the water, then they instantly disappear. The trees are like snow-laden, snow persons dancing around this cottage. Pam arrives early, and my old friend comes in relatively easily, again. My first question is if I will write a book.

"Metude, it's been mentioned by a few people that I should write a book. My old friend Mrs. Jordan used to tell me that as a child. What will it be about?"

She responds instantly, "What will be written in this book comes out of being centred, because that is your truth. At first, not much written, but as you listen and learn, more will be written. More truth will be visible. One is not ready for it yet. A feeling of being inadequate. Many parts missing." *Oh, so true.*

"Why did Mrs. Jordan mention it even when I was so young?"

"It came from another stream of consciousness she wasn't aware of. We will proceed."

Then, Metude abruptly stops talking in mid-sentence, frowns, thrust her hands out with fingers wide apart. *What's happening? She has kind of gone stiff. Her face is stock-still.*

I wait concerned, then ask, "Can I help you?" *No answer. What's going on?*

Shifting in the rocker, she seems to be struggling to speak. Then, I catch some raspy words about losing the human stream of consciousness. Continuing to wait, she seems to relax slightly, settling back in the rocker.

I then ask, "What does that mean, 'losing the human stream of consciousness?'"

After a moment, she wiggles her index finger toward me stating, "There are many streams of consciousness, like at the lake." *Oh, she was there!*

Several days previously, Pam and I were walking across the lake on the ice. The snow was falling, and ice crunched under our feet. The intricate beauty of each flake etched itself on my eyes as if it were speaking to me. We stopped halfway out; all felt brilliantly different. After a few minutes of just taking it in, there was this odd shift in energy. It was like not being in the body, yet we definitely were. Pam said she felt ten feet tall. I felt suspended. And looking at her, I knew we were both having a similarly beautiful, yet weirdish experience.

Metude continues, "That consciousness at the lake is parallel to the one you focus on here. It is difficult to translate from one stream to another. Your mind is related to certain symbols and words. If energy is not directed, focused, it cannot channel into different frequencies. Yet, it is not what you mean by the word 'frequencies.'

"To receive another stream is a matter of focusing your energy. You must learn to focus and concentrate your attention span to another awareness. It can happen when one is very relaxed, almost like hypnosis. But it is not hypnosis. The whiteness of the snow on the lake switched your focus and you drew information from another stream of consciousness."

Now, I have visions of a river of thought flowing over my head and me trying to stretch my mind up to reach it with little hope of a connection.

"Oh, Metude, this is fascinating stuff, even though I don't understand it. But imagine the possibilities. I probably can't, but just knowing you must be from one of these streams is very exciting." I glance at my tape machine. *This is important stuff. Thank goodness, it is still running, and no unseen hand is turning it off!*

"Pam also started to receive guide information on the ice the other day. Why couldn't I hear any information?"

"But you could, and you do," she reassures me. "It is how one intersects reality. You receive information all the time. You are just not conscious of it." *Interesting. I always thought I was a good listener, as I could recognize the larger wisdom that happened in the moment or emerged from a situation.*

Thus, when my old friend keeps emphasizing that I need to learn to listen, it surprises me as this is what I consider myself to be: a listener. So, I think she is saying I receive information, but I need to be more conscious of it in the moment.

She continues, "However, a combined energy force does offset the human consciousness, so it is easier to shift to another stream. Yet, it is all part of one another. There is more energy in the same spot if two stay focused at the same time."

"So that's what happened with Pam and I. Wow, imagine the implications for prayer, too! The scripture states that where two or three are gathered together, prayer is more effective." *Here is the confirmation.*

The corners of Metude's mouth turn up slightly. *She seems amused that I find this a discovery at all.*

Shifting Energy ~ Guides of the Left Side

Now, thinking of what Metude is saying reminds me of an experience that I had earlier in the fall with Abby, one member of our group. We had been painting and stopped for lunch in Mahone Bay, a picturesque fishing village on the south shore of Nova Scotia. We pulled into a parking lot outside the seafood restaurant and looked over this body of water with a shoreline of boats hauled up for the winter.

We had been talking about everyday stuff, but as we sat there looking at the beauty of the bay, her tone of voice changed. She seemed to be talking more wisdom than I had heard from her before. I was thinking that this might be what Metude meant about shifting consciousness, so I asked Abby casually in case she had shifted, if I would ever write a book. Instantly, she fired back that I would write several smaller books and then a larger one. She also added that it might take twenty-five years before they were read.

I was astonished at the number of books she mentioned. Yet, the rapidity and authority of her reply surprised me. Besides, how did Abby know that? Maybe the bay in front of us had acted as the lake did for Pam and me and shifted her consciousness, as my old friend had been explaining.

I looked at Abby to see if there were any physical changes in her face or neck muscles; there weren't. I asked, "Do you sense anyone else in the car?"

"There are two people over my left shoulder," she replied instantly, as if it was quite natural.

Grabbing a scrap of paper off the dashboard and a pen from my purse, I glanced at her face to see how her Christian fundamentalism was doing. She seemed to be okay. I was afraid she would 'pop out' of whatever 'stream' she was speaking from. So, to maintain her focus, I asked what these two people were wearing.

With her eyes squinted, she replied," Maybe a brown tunic on top and a long skirt." *Hmm, they feel male to me, more authoritative.*

"Oh," she observed, "They say they are monks."

"What are their names?" She turned her head to the left, as if to hear them better. "I hear we can call them the guides of the left side." *That's quite a handle. That fits what Abby had told me.*

She had begun receiving information, seemingly by accident, and the experience came in the form of two guides whom she sensed were on her left side!

Before I had a chance to ask other questions, her 'streamtime' was apparently over. She was hungry and short on patience.

I asked about Abby's guides because they were not like Metude, who often refers to 'we' or 'our' when giving us information and help. So, I assume there must be more than one guiding us. By now, talking and relating to someone invisible is beginning to feel more normal.

Her Guide Voice ~ Another Stream Of Consciousness

I am eager to check out this experience. "Metude, those guides of the left side that Abby identified are not like you at all. Their information seemed more in a natural voice, and they didn't enter her body as you enter Pam's. Abby looks like her natural self when she is guided. Can you tell me what happened?"

My old friend nods, "Another stream of consciousness. She will know her own symbols and reality. Your reality is listening to her guide voice. She will then relate to it and your attention gives it meaning to her. She will know reality is more than human consciousness. Each soul picks a route, a way, and a means of understanding what they can translate from." *Listening apparently continues to be my major lesson. However, it would be most beneficial if I could "see" some aspect of the invisible.*

"So, her guide voice did come from another stream of consciousness?" I say a bit in awe. This is not me imagining it. *Wow, and they are actual guides!*

"Indeed, proceed." *In her simple, matter of fact, straightforward, unemotional way, this cottage woman shifts my world, yet again. So, there must be more beings who help us. Again, just because I don't see them doesn't mean they don't exist. This is such a stretch.*

I feel gratitude. This discarnate friend is sitting before me as a witness to how real the invisible is. They just don't have flesh and bone, which will end up dust or cremated ashes anyway.

Human Consciousness Makes It Difficult to Speak - Breaks the Connection

When we first started talking with this cottage woman, we had some difficulty in understanding the words or terms she used in certain situations. As Pam is quick to point out when she listens to a replay of each visit, "Those are not my ideas. I don't use those words: 'entity,' 'energy,' 'dimensions,' and 'frequency.' " Neither of us does and we don't know anyone else that does in 1986. They were simply not in our vocabulary until we met her, so it is like learning a new language.

I remind Metude that she did point out in the late fall that it was becoming easier for her to use Pam's or, as she called her, "the Person's words." Apparently, she has to do a bit of translating from one stream to another. She explains, "My words are at variance with the Person's. Human consciousness makes it difficult to speak. Sometimes the connection breaks."

"Was that what happened earlier when you stopped talking?"

"Indeed, as one gets on to the human words and symbols, the conversation will pick up speed." *Yes, she seems to be speaking less stilted now. Plus, we know her terms like "energy" and "frequency" better.*

Yet, I share a similar problem with the cottage woman, but in reverse. In some ways, I have both been inventing words these past months and learning new terms, like "transition" or "settled" instead of "death." Also, she rarely, if ever, uses a person's name which sometimes makes it hard to know who she is referring to. And, at times, I am left guessing.

Preparation for a Workshop ~ Keep in Tune with the Stream of Consciousness

Before Pam or Metude decide to end this visit, I need to ask about a workshop that is coming up shortly. Every five or six weeks, I go to a provincial adult-training centre for a long weekend to co-lead programs in interpersonal relations, communication, meditation, and related topics. I want to ask what will improve the program coming up in another week, and I need her wisdom. People have responded positively in the past. But now that I have Metude, I am excited to discuss it with her, as she is going to know what is going on "behind the scenes" with each participant. So, I ask, "Will the next weekend at the Center be successful?"

"You will be heard, but not by all." She replies bluntly.

"Maybe I shouldn't do this weekend because of my business here at home."

She tilts her head slightly as if looking at me from a different angle, saying, "Yet, it's an opportunity to be heard at this time. You must listen. You have fears and reservations.

They will be picked up by others. Even if you perceive negativity and it is not going well, do not give in to it. Remain detached and keep the space to listen. Keep in tune with the stream of consciousness. When or if there is hostility, don't step into it. One must stop and listen, which allows space and this disarms the hostility. It will go how you perceive it. It is a new part of your lessons."

Everything seems to be part of my lessons in this human schoolroom.

And how many times have I got discouraged and felt my energy drain away when I thought the program lagged? Oh, to have known this ancient friend sooner! Her words are so honest and hard, yet affirming. And wow, she got all my issues in one breath! I definitely have fears and reservations because when one is presenting new ideas, people always seem to take issue.

She stops rocking as I hear, "'Tis time to bid you good day." Then she adds, with that hint of a smile, "More enlightenment will be part of our visits."

"Oh Metude, thank you for coming. It is all so helpful for us!" And she is gone, at least, to my seeing eyes.

• • •

Beginning Karate ~ A Peeping Tom

I had started karate a few months before Metude's first visit. Both were like foreign elements entering my life and both were challenging. Oddly enough, she, in her larger wisdom, became helpful for direction with my martial art gradings.

Unfortunately, my motivation for beginning karate was a Peeping Tom who lived in our neighbourhood. The police had received many complaints, but could not catch him. One day, our mailbox contained a notice that karate was going to be offered in the old school a mile down the road, which now functioned as a community centre. Since the police did not seem to do anything about the Peeping Tom, I thought maybe my best answer was to learn to protect myself physically.

The first night, thirty-two young men in their teens and early twenties, plus me in my mid-forties, showed up. The sensei came into the dojo, and I was taken aback. His legs and body were badly contorted. He walked by jerking himself forward. But I did not have to wonder long if he could teach the class.

Although I was in reasonable physical shape, having jogged for years, my body was noticeably jarred from all the contortions he put us through. I went home that night sweating and sore. Over tea, I told Roger that I was good for one more night, if my body recovered. It did. Months later, there were about a dozen of us left in the class. I was still getting lots of bruises, and sometimes I wondered why I was doing this to myself.

That winter challenged me. One of the windows in the school basement had a crack large enough to allow the winds to blow a skiff of snow across the floor. Through the winter months, the continuous bruising and running through the snow in my bare feet weakened my resolve. Yet, what strengthened it in those early months was an incident of hanging out clothes and looking up to see the Peeping

Tom slow his car as he drove by, staring at me. I would not be an unwitting victim.

The Fight ~ A Defining Moment

Then came the defining moment of my karate life. One night, months later, the sensei, in his inexperience and who was just a new black belt himself, put me in a sparring match with a young man half a foot taller and at least fifty pounds heavier. Being white belts, we had no technique or skill worth mentioning. And most of the young guys seemed motivated to prove their physical prowess, whereas my goal was to survive it.

The Sensei signaled the match to begin. Immediately, I recognized this guy was out to prove himself. His technique seemed to be inspired by fights on television, while mine amounted to backing up to keep out of his reach. There were two rules in the ring—we could not hit the other's head, nor could we step out of the ring more than twice. If we did, the match would be awarded to the other person. With a bit of male ego and his peers (which was nearly everyone else in the dojo) cheering him on, he was starting to bruise me.

After several more shots of pain to my body, I felt a strength and anger enter me with the instant knowledge that my survival depended on staying in close, not backing up. "Kia!" I yelled, inches before his face. It startled me as much as it did him. "Kia" is a yell that shocks the opponent, making the attack seemingly worse than often it is and, in this case, it was quite true. I am of light weight and slight build, which in the karate ring was challenging. During those early months, however, I discovered that I was often faster in my responses than the guys. So, I began ducking and crowding him, forcing him backward. Then, at one point, being off-balance, his heel strayed out of the ring. Unbelievable! It was my round.

The sensei signaled for the fight to begin the next round. Again, I waited for an opening. Then, moving in aggressively and yelling "Kia," I shot off a punch and pulled it back just before it hit his face. Ducking back from my punch, he lost his balance and out he went! And the third time his foot went outside the ring, I won the match.

Silence, no cheering. The surprise win shocked everyone and most of all me. Yet, after that fight, even though I had only won by dodging, crowding, and yelling "Kia" (which really did not take any skill), I felt more respect. I still did not know much karate, but I had won.

I could not wait to get home to tell Roger. Relating my adventure rather proudly, I told him the threat of a Peeping Tom had shrunk significantly that night.

YOU DON'T NEED TO SEE OXYGEN TO KNOW IT'S THERE

Several weeks after our last visit, I meet with the cottage woman again. We need some help with Donna, who still doesn't want to live, and I am also eager to find out how the weekend program went at The Center. It went reasonably well, but I want to check to see where I can improve. Luckily, Pam is free. Again, Metude settles in surprisingly quickly.

Suicide ~ Training Her Thought Process to Think Differently

First, I ask this woman, who is apparently as old as time, to check in on Donna's state of mind. She is still calling me in the middle of the night and threatening to commit suicide. Is there more help we can give her? Even the doctors seem to be at a loss.

Metude is quick to answer. "If she can realign her thought process, how she thinks, it still can be accomplished. This could be done through hypnosis to train her to think in a positive way. Hypnosis is merely presented as a possibility. It could launch her across the eddy line."

Living twenty feet from the ocean we know that tidal reference: a current of water that runs contrary to the main current. Looking directly at me, she states, "No matter how loving and how supportive you are, you cannot prevent her choice. You must remember: One must still make the choice of what one wishes to do. Take her life, so be it."

She is speaking so matter-of-factly, but I am in such a twist! This makes me continually amazed at her objectivity.

Yet, I know she encourages me to do everything to prevent her from killing herself, except make the choice for her. As stated emphatically, I must always be for life.

She continues, "The choice is entirely theirs and so is what they choose to allow to happen. It is a crucial time. A time of decision that rests entirely with them, a path they wish to follow. They choose. A great weariness is within her. Her friend would be wise not to move into negative feelings around the issue, but think that it is a free choice. One is not to view it as a negative event, but as a choice. Do not be confused. Her responsibility is for her own growth and learning. One must recognize the human emotions that are involved in such decisions. Pain and sadness for her."

The cottage woman shifts in the rocker. I wait. She continues, "Helpful to arrange a time, early morning for her to run. Those hours are best for the friend to run and best suited to her needs. Watch her breathing in her jog. Breathe in purity, breathe out the negative emotion. To be done very consciously. In with the freshness, out with the pain." *Oh, what a good exercise for any negative thinking.*

It's so easy to get caught in emotions, social energies, thoughts, and patterns that are not even ours. And sometimes, they are almost impossible to identify.

Ending One's Earth Lessons ~ One Will Continue Learning in Another Life Experience

Metude turns her attention to me, again.

"Watch the amount of tension (in you) that builds up. Relax the physical body; a great deal of stress held in the jaw, upper back. One is deceived in thinking that stress is not held just because one feels in control. Such is not the case. You only need to be loving and supportive. One does not have to have the answer to another's choices. You only have to be supportive to the extent the other has a choice to make. We will proceed." Oh, thank you Metude for your wonderful wisdom. *I certainly have accepted the responsibility for Donna if she kills herself.*

This wise old woman is telling me that this choice is not mine to make. There is no right or wrong to it. No judgment at all. If one chooses to live, then there are options to help one grow and learn the lessons we came here to learn. And to allow Donna to make such a choice is even my human lesson. If a person chooses to take their life, end their earth lessons this time, then they will be given opportunities to continue learning in another life experience or another lifetime.

Therefore, if I don't do my work now, deal with my issues, learn my lessons here, they wait for me in the next dimension or on the other side. I do not like that idea, but that is what this ancient woman is telling me. Calling me back from my revelry I hear, "We will proceed."

"Oh, thank you Metude, that is such a help for me to hear."

Feedback from the Workshop ~ We Prepared Each Participant before They Came

Now, I need to ask about the workshop at The Center this past week. As she said in the last visit, I would be heard but not by all.

She starts to rock nodding, "Much was done. We worked and prepared each person before they came." *Imagine how caring her world is and how invested in our learning it is.*

"Wow, so that is why it went so well!"

"It was good. You have the beginnings. You listened. It is the spiritual-psychic area which so clearly you heard. It will keep coming to you. You will listen until it becomes clarified. You have been doing your work. It will expand and be built upon. Much was done." *I'm relieved. This is high praise from her, but most importantly, I must be listening better.*

"How did Pam do?" It was her first time at The Center and being away from her family.

"Yah, indeed, did well, yet merely a beginning. There are other opportunities. Public encounters are a drawback for her. She perceives the public in a negative way. A lessening of resistance, but there is no need for her to push back so far. It would be good to continue bringing her to these sessions. It is coming."

Pam doesn't get to do many outside family activities.

Getting Caught in Everyday Dimension

"Were you with us, Metude?" *I turn my mind to her often, but when she is not here physically and as hard as I try, I am never sure if she is present or not.*

"Yah, very well handled," she hints a smile. "You don't need to see oxygen to know it's there." *Ha, she caught my thoughts. She was actually there! I think I sensed her, but her world is all so invisible.*

Then, referring back to the participants, she adds, "They heard the truth in the words. One will improve with exposure."

Metude continues, "You must take time to move the focus from your everyday reality to the other stream. That means stepping back. You have a saying, 'practice makes perfect.' You must practise," she states emphatically. *She often says, "You have a saying . . . ," then I wait until she uses my own words to help me understand some concepts better.*

"Oh, but I think I did connect to that stream with my co-leader in our planning session. Initially, it felt like we were disconnected, so I pulled back, centred myself, and then felt more connection and Presence with him. Is that what you mean?"

"You get caught in an everyday dimension rather than perceiving how out of touch you are, and then you begin to work with it. By remembering with your heart, you begin to move into another stream of consciousness. You use the energy to transfer it to the other person. It happens in stages. Then, he becomes aware and moves into it, although not necessarily aware of the process." *She is right. I do feel his energy shift. Our mood changes. We enter a more meaningful and creative space.*

Metude interrupts my reverie. "He is more aware of the depth in his being than his connection to the stream. His being and every living soul are not isolated. Physical reality is not total reality."

Reality Is Merely How One Thinks ~ Remember with the Heart

"Oh Metude, it is so neat that you know what happens. Often in these committee meetings I do pull back to feel Presence, then I can notice a similar shift in the committee's energy. I didn't know that was happening but as you say, stepping back, remembering with one's heart is such a simple thing and yet, it does change the energy in the room. And because of your feedback, I am getting better spirit-eyes. Now, when I think something is happening, I know it is happening because you confirm it and, most importantly, enlarge it. Even my meditation feels meaningful and deeper. The invisible world is becoming more of a concrete reality."

"Yah, indeed." Then she reminds me, "Reality is merely how one thinks." *How can that even be possible?*

This reminds me of Carlos Castaneda's old shaman, Don Juan, who observed that there is no reality, but only perception. If I could really believe reality is merely how one thinks, then the implications are immense—my prayer for another person could be as real as a physical hug. Yet, at the same time, that niggling, negative thought about someone might have the weight of a physical punch.

However, this is a big leap. I know she is not lying to me! She just sees from a much larger reality than my little brain encompasses. The idea of my thoughts being as concrete as physical things is not logical. She seems to know when she has stretched my mind to the limit. And this is often when she states, "We will proceed."

The Spiritual-Psychic Area Will Keep Coming to You ~ Listen

"How is our counselling work doing?"

"Watch for opportunities. They are coming. It is time to broaden the area of work. There will be more knowledge, people contact, and you will be given more areas to work with. You have been doing your work. The spiritual-psychic area will keep coming to you. You will listen until the area becomes clarified, expanded, and it will be built upon. Remember to step aside. Do not fear missing an opportunity to help. It will come in another way." *But I just feel so dense in this area at times.*

"It is coming, my child; it is all coming. I will be with you. A lot more readiness with the Person. You will sense me more. Mutual meeting, loving, and love meets. We will proceed." *Oh, I hope so and her words warm me.*

Although, she does not use the word love that much, just about everything she tells me is about caring and compassion in one form or the other. Plus, the invisible side which she refers to as "we" seems to be helping too, even if I can't see them.

Meditation ~ Wears a Path to a Magical Garden

Every day, I start supper for the family around three or four in the afternoon. The kids often say they can smell the bread, cookies, or other baking as they come up the lane from school. Normally, the table is set for six. During the summer or holidays, it is often more.

Ever since they were in pre-school, the children were given chores, which were rotated daily. That left me free to head for my prayer spot in our bedroom after supper. In the winter, Roger would likely watch TV. I would sit on the floor facing the east wall, legs crossed, eyes half-closed. Initially, I could hear the dishes clattering as the children did the supper clean-up. Yet, over the months, I heard the clatter less. Eventually, by breathing and clearing my mind, the feeling of love found its way in the quiet. Sometimes, if I could be present enough, I would just be still and hold others in what I trusted was healing light.

Thus, my next question to my ancient friend concerns my daily, spiritual routine. "Does prayer help me enter the stream of consciousness?"

My old friend responds quickly. "Yah, each individual has a spot that gives the body more energy. Spots vary; see what is best for you."

"I think I have." *It's interesting, the spot or place is not only geographical but also there is a place inside I now go to, that seems to be more alive with Presence than say, my knee or foot.*

Landscape Painting, a Form of Meditation ~ Expands the Energy Forms

I also think of my landscape painting as a form of meditation. "So, Metude, should I give painting more importance in my life?"

I had been studying drawing and painting informally since university and have had a series of good art teachers. Yet, it always seems to be my Cinderella child, and it is left in last place as far as time and energy are concerned. However, at the end of the year, I am constantly surprised at how many paintings I paint, and some are even sold.

My ancient friend nods, "Art is a balance in your system. You will learn from it because you make your own reality."

"But I only have so much time, and I can't decide if I should be working on portraits or landscapes." *I would like to drop portraiture as getting a likeness is unforgiving.*

"You will use both, one for balance, one for investment and earning. You must choose, and that you will know. You must allow for a certain readiness and then you will be ready." Metude smiles slightly, adding, "The outdoors is a very essential part of your being. It allows you to expand the energy forms. One cannot expand when confined." *I understand what she means and feel myself expanding just listening to her.*

"Oh Metude, you give so much meaning to the seemingly ordinary things. I do love the outdoors. Painting landscapes allows me to sit in beauty for hours and study it."
I am also growing to love this old woman in Pam's body. How weird is this?

The afternoon is drawing nigh, and I always have more questions, but I know Pam does not have the time. I reluctantly end the visit. My ancient friend bids me peace and then is seemingly gone. *And indeed, as she stated, we don't need to see oxygen to know it is there, nor do I need to see Metude and her invisible "we" to know I am not alone here!*

• • •

My Art Story - A Gift of Balanced Energy and Beauty

Three years ago, I went to my first week-long outdoor-painting workshop. I took a little tent and discovered landscape painting. Until then, I had concentrated on portraiture, having taken private lessons weekly for four years. My teacher had been trained at the Royal Academy of Art in London for eight years.

I discovered painting and camping made a perfect fit, and I loved it. It took me outdoors and brought balance to the intensity of my work at home. Life was just me, a little tent, easel, paints, sky, trees, beaches, and ocean. It was a eureka discovery, a little slice of life that was mine.

Two summers later, Abby decided to do the art workshop, too. She stayed with a friend, and I stayed in my little tent. That was the beginning of our on-site, landscape painting trips, which continue to this day. Painting moved me into another world—a meditation space that offered me a significant balance to my emotional work with people.

• • •

The First Mini-Training Session, Floating Ten or Fifteen Feet above My Head

Two weeks later, dropping in at Pam's for Saturday tea, I asked if she would help me connect to "another stream of consciousness."

After tea, we walked down the railroad tracks, as we often did. The air was crisp. Through the years, with the scrub spruce on one side and the icy Seaforth River on the other, we often got insights. However, this Saturday we had to concentrate on our feet, as the snow was boot high, and we kept slipping off the railroad ties. Pam, not knowing where to start either, suggested I try to pull energy into the top of my head by drawing my breath in and pushing the energy up. After several attempts, the top of my head began to feel shaped like a cone or a dunce cap, and it ached a bit.

Then, I seemed to be floating about ten or fifteen feet above my head, although both feet were still on the railroad ties. Snow must have heightened my awareness. My face felt down there, and my being felt up and separate from it. I remember thinking, *I hope I don't drool down there.* In this floaty-ness, I had had enough, and we headed back to Pam's house having had my first planned stream of consciousness training.

Witches and some shamans wear pointed hats. I wondered if those hats are symbolic, and whether they had originally represented another stream of consciousness. My inner head did feel somewhat pointed. Then, on my way home, I had an anxious thought: What if someone else from the invisible realm did come to me? What would Roger say if he thought I was setting myself aside so a person without a human body could come and talk to us? Thank goodness, he did seem fine hearing about the cottage woman. He seems to recognizes the cottage woman's wisdom, but when it is his wife, he might not be as easy with it. Plus, my children may not understand; after all, I hardly understand myself. These relationships are very, very precious to me. Thankfully, they are all off at university so they don't need to know right now.

Little wonder Pam is concerned about Frank and her children finding out. I realized that need to appreciate her position more!

PERSONAL PAIN WORK LEADS TO THE MOST HONOURED HUMAN STATE

March is snow, fog, and rain in Nova Scotia. After the long winter months, it feels like spring will never arrive. There are certainly no signs of it today. The ocean is only a hundred feet from the cottage, and it cannot be seen for iced rocks and crusted snow. There is low hanging fog. This poor old, wood stove from the early twentieth century does have to struggle and today, it's doing its job.

Pam came down. The fire is burning nicely, and she wraps herself snuggly in the blanket. I always seem to anticipate the visit in some awe, as it's rather like meeting this cottage woman anew, each time. Again, face and neck muscles rearrange themselves, and then the rocker begins to move. With greetings, her presence and the fire seem to warm the cottage.

Reality Exists as Each One Sees It ~ How Each One Thinks

Now my first question this afternoon is to ask if karate is still okay for me. I needed to know if it was doing any significant damage to my body.

Metude is quick to answer. "Reality is how you see it," she replies. "If you think it is beneficial, it will be. View it as good and it will be. If the situation is seen as negative and dark, then you will move into that. Thought is reality." She leans forward and points her finger at me, repeating, "Thought is reality. It is how each one thinks reality is. That is how it goes. Reality exists as you see it. If one perceives life after death, then the transition is not difficult. If one thinks hell, then hell, but one is given people to help them toward a new perception. Reality: It's of your own making." *I'm guessing she is talking about more than me getting hurt in karate.*

Apparently, how we think, feel, and conceptualize our life helps create our human reality. Then we must create our own reality. Hmm, maybe that was what happened to Aunt Nell all those years ago.

After Death ~ One Is Given People to Help Them toward Another Reality

My aunt, my mother's sister, was like a second mother to me. I lived with her and her husband during my second year at university. One day, she came into my bedroom and showed me a lump under her arm. Four months later, she died.

For years after her death, her face came to me in my sleep. It was always unhappy. Often, the dream woke me, leaving the room filled with sadness. Even in my early twenties, with my limited, conventional-perception and insecurity, I wondered if it was really her and if she was stuck somewhere. It never entered my mind that I might be able to help her. After four or five years, she never came back again.

Later, I found out my uncle had been in love with another woman and had been having an affair for years. My cousin told me that my aunt's fear was that after she passed over, my uncle would marry the other woman. He did.

I dreaded her coming to me because her unhappiness suggested that maybe there was a kind of hell after we die. I asked the cottage woman about it one day, and she responded, "But one is given people to help them toward a new reality." This flooded me with comfort. Of course, my grandmother would be there for her daughter. Since this cottage woman must have died (a watchmaker in Sweden in another century) and has come to help us, then why wouldn't my grandmother come to help her beloved daughter? Besides, how comforting it is to think that even after passing over, one is given people to help them out of an emotional stuck-ness. From my observations, most people seem to be emotionally stuck somehow or with someone. My mother and I certainly were and are.

Then, Metude says her usual line: "We will proceed." *Oh, but I have more questions.*

I had been working with Fran, an acquaintance from the city for the last year. I was attempting to help her release some emotional pain around her mother. The latter not only favoured her older sister, but seemed out to destroy the younger by devaluing her at every turn. Fran dreaded her mother's dragon tongue that had burned her like acid many times.

A few months ago, Pam had an image of their relationship. In her mind's eye, Fran was shuffling on deformed feet behind her mother. It seemed to be an insightful picture of the painful damage that had been done to Fran. Then, last week, I asked Pam for a current image of their relationship. She saw a wooden stake sticking out of Fran's chest. Instinctively, I knew I could not grab and yank it out, even in my imagination.

A Wooden Stake in the Chest ~ A Relationship

Thus, I ask Metude about the image of the stake. "Much held back," she replies sagely.

"Are there specific ways we could help her deal with her mother in this upcoming visit?"

"She is not open."

"Really? She's asked for help. Yet she is not open to it?" *Being open is so important to doing any of our human lessons.*

"To the situation." *Oh, it's too painful for her.*

"Then how can we help her?"

"Yah, you must continue to show her that questioning is good. She must want to move. She has much fear. She can't be pushed, but needs encouragement. Wait and listen. It is timing. She must be ready herself. Much fear."

"Oh, so right. She is not ready to tackle her pain, but she is bravely struggling to engage it anyway."

Uncovering Different Layers of Pain ~ A Breathing Process

"As you know, Metude, I am using this breathing process with her that I read about in a book. It's about helping people work through their pain. Is it working, or am I causing her more pain? Most times, it seems like I am, yet it often leads her to some insight and emotional release. When she touches these painful places, I encourage her to slow down her breathing and then imagine breathing the pain out. After a little while, I suggest she speed up the breathing which seems to loosen the pain. She hates the process, but it seems effective. But I don't know what else do to, and I really need your kind of seeing."

Sitting in her rocker, my ancient friend looks thoughtful, then nods, saying, "It is a way of uncovering different layers of pain. As each new layer is approached, much resistance, but one can't grow in layers of pain. Peel them back, but do not push. Better to encourage. Each one knows their own rate of uncovering their pain and they must be ready. Proceed"

"Thank you, that relieves me."

Images and Information Are Subject to Our Human Interpretation

Fran and I had been driving back from shopping one day. She talked again about her painful relationship with her mother. Then, working with her pain, I did exactly what Metude told me not to on more than one occasion. I tried to force her to see a situation that I later realized was too painful for her to process. She became hostile. I backed off immediately. As we drove along, an image of us flashed in Fran's mind that suggested we could have a bad car accident. It scared us, so we pulled off the road and had supper. Later, somewhat fearfully, we continued home.

Now, a week and a half later, I need to ask Metude what really happened, as I am guessing Fran's image was not about a car accident. My old friend nods, "In this incident, it would be a valid warning but interpreted through the imagination, seeing pictures with her inner eye." *So, it was a warning and the images of a car accident act like symbols which point to a deeper meaning.* "You were told to exercise caution. You thought it was about the car. It was a warning for something else."

"We sort of figured that out over supper. I had pushed her too hard in her pain work."

"Precisely, in part. One must learn not to be ready to accept the other stream of consciousness at face value—the human element. One is over-eager." *Ah, she means how we interpret it.*

"You are right. We were really afraid that we were going to have an accident."

Pointing her finger at me, she advises, "It does hinge on not accepting the image at face value. Sometimes, it's in trying too hard. You need to be ready to question rather than accept. You are given valid information, yet before it is fully given, it gets interpreted. It is coloured with one's own imagination rather than coming from the stream. Again, look at how the information ballooned in the situation. The idea got fixed in the mind. Lost objectivity. You must look at the fact."

Oh, is this good advice. Learning to work with images is like learning another language, a spirit language.

Our Human-Lesson Work ~ Leads to the Most Honoured Human State

My ancient friend continues, "However, she is making good progress. You must not relent pressure. You must be steady, no backtracking. She has not come to terms with her pain. Bitterness is there. She says, 'Why me?' It would be well for her to say, 'Why not me?' The opportunity to do our personal pain work leads to the most honoured human state." *Doing emotional work does not feel like the most honourable state.*

Just this past weekend, I had to work with a feeling of injustice and self-pity which instantly flooded and sank a very happy me. It took me a while to work out of "poor me" to arrive at a place of acceptance, non-judgment, and finally, as always, waiting for me, was a loving, compassionate Presence.

You Dwell in a Stream of Consciousness ~ Even When You Sleep Is Work Time

Changing the subject, somewhat out of frustration, I state, "Pam is still questioning you, Metude." *She keeps asking me if this wise, old friend is real, and I know she knows she is.*

"Ah, indeed. She does not know yet that she need not take responsibility for me. She need not own it. She feels failure if things do not work out.

"I am a part of a stream of consciousness, and each stream has its own vibrations. There are psychic centres in the body that relate and correspond to particular streams. She has a fear of moving forward. Work is in progress."

"Oh, so there are different streams. Well, the one I want to tap into is a stream for service to others." *Imagine, being able to say that! Six months ago, I didn't even know there were such streams.*

"Yah, there are streams of consciousness and each stream has vibrations. You add to them." *Oh, how interesting and exciting. As service of helping others with their human lessons will enlarge and add to that different energy/consciousness in the world.*

She then changes tack. "You look at your need to control." *Whoa, where did that come from?*

"Is this information for Pam?" *She might mean me. I hope not.*

However, braving my resistance, she continues matter-of-factly, "Some is for the Person, but it is mainly for you. You must learn to look at fear. You dwell in a stream of consciousness and even when you sleep is work time. Remain open acknowledging your fears and reservations; if you do, then they become less real. Progress is good."

Not considering myself a fearful person or a controlling one, it's puzzling. I'll have to give it some thought.

It's Not by Chance We Are Together ~ The Cottage Woman Is Learning, Too

I move to the next question. In spite of her lessons on Presence and leadership, I always need more wisdom. So, I ask, "How will the spiritual-development program go next week at The Center? I am feeling better prepared." *She always knows beforehand, which is a comfort.*

"It will be a good session. You have much to offer; a role is being groomed for one. Will learn the lessons of stepping back. Must not fear. You have the tools. Only when you get in your own way will you have a problem." *I wonder what role or job I am being prepared for?*

"What more can I do other than listen and be present?" *That just doesn't seem enough.*

"One thing at a time. Your area of work is given to you now. This is the area of greatest need. It is your listening. You are well-guided. It will be made known when the need arises. Each situation dictates its own moves. You will know whether to speak or be silent. It is coming as it should."

"But Metude, the area of greatest need is listening, yet I have said before, listening to a disembodied voice seems so nebulous, so invisible when you are not here in the flesh. I need something more visible, a little more obvious than guessing what you and the spirit guides are telling me when you are not sitting across from me." *If I am being groomed for another role or purpose, I need to hear in a deeper way.*

"Ah, my child, but I know." She nods, saying, with a tone of finality, "Listen, it is not by chance that we are together. Learning is situational. Many faceted and absolutely mutual." *Yet, I love that it's not by chance we are together and that she is learning, too. I know she's real, but somehow it makes her more human-real if that is possible.*

A Friend Who Had Passed ~ Has Settled and Is Learning a Process of Evaluation

Several times a week, I walked up to the edge of the bluff which is about a quarter of a mile from our house. Many storms, in winter and summer, had me leaning like the trees against the wind to keep my balance as I viewed the frothy, grey seas of the North Atlantic. Plus, it is wonderfully effective in cleansing my energy.

I had been thinking of my friend Dee, who I suspected took her own life several months ago. She had been depressed. One winter afternoon, I was trudging back down the hill, soaked from salt spray and frozen snow. I could not wait to get home to the warmth of the kitchen wood stove. Halfway home, I passed an old, gnarled tree that I had passed a thousand times before yet, this time, something caught my attention. I was not thinking of Dee when suddenly the sense of her presence stopped me. She was in her early thirties and mysteriously went to sleep one night and never woke up. She had talked of suicide numerous times, but her family never released the medical report.

Drawn by her presence, I trudged through the snow to the tree which was about fifteen feet off my path. I put my mitts against the tree, then shockingly, I felt more caring and concern for her than I had when she was alive! My friend felt so real that I came home and told the family I had met Dee on the road. They listened without comment other than a couple of curious questions.

Love Summons Her ~ Those in the Other Stream Are Very Aware of Your Thoughts

Before meeting the cottage woman, I would have second-guessed this encounter with Dee. Now, having a discarnate friend, I can ask about those who are on the other side. Being able to take these experiences back to her for an explanation just makes life more meaningful and relatable. *Besides, her past life as a watchmaker in Sweden surely shows that we continue to exist.*

I tell her about my experience with Dee by the tree. The corners of her mouth turn up slightly as I ask, "Was that my imagination or was that really Dee?"

"It was real. Yet, when one connects in thought, it is not your friend coming to you."

"Really? I don't think I thought of her first." *I am sure I didn't.*

"You had summoned her." She insists. *I wonder if it could be like when Pam didn't think she gave permission for Metude to visit initially. It must have happened at an unconscious level.*

My old friend continues, "Yah, she is settled and learning a process of evaluation." *Hmm, settled is what she said about the young man who was missing and his parents are still looking for him. So maybe he did pass over.*

"Can I help her?"

"Loving her helps her. Love is that which summons her. Thought is a reality. Those in the other stream are very aware—of what you call your thoughts. You are learning to rely on other streams."

Through the years, my old friend's words have become indelible. Mother has passed over, and so has my father, Roger's father, my aunt, and others I have loved. They have come to visit me at different times, be it in dreams or just sensing them strongly. Then, I find myself in a love that tangibly seems to love me back.

Many Negatives Do Not Exist ~ Trying to Get the Blinders off

Now Metude, about my friend who is negative, I need to ask, "How is Ellen doing, the one who you said had blinders on as she blamed others for her unhappiness? I am trying to get her blinders off, as you suggested last fall. Yet, she is still thinking other people are against her, when really, they aren't."

My old friend has a stern air about her as she states, "She must be willing to let go of her interpretations, viewing them as injustices and making them important. What she must do is see them for what they are—misinterpretations—and let them go. Show the path she has been given. She has an opportunity to see it in the Entity. When she sees how the Entity handles her situation, that will help her."

Then, she leans forward and observes, quite matter-of-factly, and seemingly out of the blue, "This one has much resentment of you." *Oh, you pick that up. I didn't know it was that bad! My guess is that she blames me for not being attentive enough, and she interprets it as non-caring.*

"Why does she resent me, Metude? I really do care for her."

"She believes you and the family have a perfect situation, and therefore feels you can't understand her situation. Many of her negatives do not truly exist. She holds to an ideal of a situation and then sees it as a reality that nothing can measure up to.

"Yet, you do have a part. You are a sounding board with both of them." *Oh, she is speaking of both Pam and Ellen now.* "It is not by chance when we are brought together. You must be available to both parties. Time will be made available. You will know when to move." *As she said, it's not by chance she and I are together either. However, I still don't know how that works.*

"Do I need to call Ellen more often?" *This is one of her complaints.*

"When the need arises, it will be made known. Listen." *That's a relief. I don't have to feel guilty. I guess I am not to call until I listen to my intuition or watch for a sign of some sort.*

As Breath Is to Your Body ~ Each Day Your Reality Becomes Larger

"Oh Metude, I do have great confidence in what you say. You set the crooked straight and are a wonderful balm when

I start second-guessing myself in situations like this one with Ellen. When she blames me for her unhappiness, I have to analyze myself to see if it is true, even when logically I don't think it is. You are so affirming in your wisdom." *And I feel relieved that you don't think I need to feel guilty. Some people you just can't make happy. That's probably a human lesson of mine. Maybe people can only make themselves happy.*

Looking kindly, my old friend nods, "As breath is to your body, it will become an integrated part of who you are. Each day your reality becomes larger." *I am going to hold you to it, my old friend. Your words are often like water in a desert of doubt.* She leans forward in the rocker, "And now I must go. I will continue to be with you. You are never alone. All that is needed is to go into silence. There is a vibration for a different stream of consciousness. It is always there in silence. Merely go to it. You already do it, but not fully aware of focusing on it. Now, within you, it will grow." *What a lovely thought. I suppose one stream of being aware is just living an ordinary life. Another stream of consciousness is when I pray. The energy in each feels different. Maybe that is what she means when she refers to "the vibration of the different streams."*

My ancient friend shifts in the rocker, "And now, I must leave. Peace be with each of you and enjoy your community."

"We are enjoying it. It is a blessing for us."

"Yah, a blessing. Take a good joy in it, a grateful joy. To enjoy the simplest things of life is the greatest gift, indeed."

"The simplest things, oh yes. Thank you, Metude, it is lovely being with you." *And so, truly, it is.*

Muscles are rearranged, and Pam is back.

Images and Dreams Are a Language

> *The true sign of intelligence is not knowledge but imagination.*
>
> *- Albert Einstein*

Images were becoming a major tool that cast light on puzzling situations and generally offered a larger understanding of their underlying challenges. They also told me when I was off track. For example, when Fran got an image of us having a car accident, we initially interpreted the image as a real accident when it was really a sign that I was pushing her too hard and too fast in her pain work. Also, the image of the stake in her chest gave me an idea of the pain she had experienced as a child and what work we needed to do.

Images are available to each of us. We close our eyes and can easily see a car, a chair, and a road. However, we can also see images that feel independent of a situation and act like symbols that point to a larger, inner meaning like Fran's wrongly interpreted car accident. When I first started using images as a deeper source of information, I quickly learned that it might not make sense on the surface, but seeing a stake in someone's chest might certainly tell me the level of emotional pain they were in. These images held deeper insight and guidance.

Then, if I could not get an image, conjuring seemed to open the door for a deeper level of images that became independent of my guesses and biases. For example, an image of a bear trap certainly speaks of entering a situation, or possibly an upcoming encounter, with caution. It is not to judge the image too quickly. Also, it's to be aware that one's own bias or emotional response can misinterpret the image or write it off as, "Oh, it's just my imagination."

This cliché certainly is a misnomer. The imagination and images are a medium for insightful meaning. They offer significant depth and guidance into human lessons. Imagination is dynamic and multifaceted. The universe never leaves us orphaned. Thus, we can be thankful Einstein did not dismiss his imagination, or we would not have his unified field theory: $E=MC^2$. This theory began in his dreams and has turned into one of the pillars of science.

Predictive dreams also are made up of images and symbols. And they can become an alert or a warning. I became aware of how important this type of dream was a few years before the cottage woman's arrival.

The importance of observing my dreams was made painfully obvious when Dev, our youngest, was eleven. I dreamed he was hit by a car. The ditches were filled with snow. I struggled but could not seem to reach him. When I got to his side he was bloodied and unconscious. I woke from the nightmare with fear that nearly stopped my heart.

Ten months later, when I was co-directing a program at The Center one night, a call came from Roger. Dev had been hit by a car and was in critical care, unconscious. With my breath suspended, I was hearing about the accident as it had been presented in my dream months earlier. I replied quietly, "I know." Apparently, he had been coming out of a friend's driveway on his bike and did not see the car driving by. When Roger got to him, he was unconscious in a ditch, fifty feet from where he was hit.

The nightmare continued now in waking life because The Center was a hundred miles away from the hospital. The night was dark and there was a fierce snowstorm raging, a kind of intensity of weather one can see in the Maritimes that time of year. A friend volunteered to drive with me. Keeping the car on the road and keeping it moving against the weather made the journey extend to four hours instead of the normal two. The dream told me it would be a struggle to reach him, but I would get to him while he was alive.

Arriving at the hospital, I was taken to critical care; Dev was unrecognizable and still unconscious. We waited by his bed. Five days later, upon opening his eyes, he told us a joke. Roger and I looked at each other, both of us caught between a laugh and a sob. He had no memory of the accident.

> *"Don't ignore your dreams, in them your soul is awake…"*
>
> *~ Neel Burton*

Dreams Are Teachers in Our Human Schoolroom ~ Guidance

That day, dreams ceased to be meaningless fluff. Yet not all dreams are predictive like the one about Dev. Some are visitations, like the one about my aunt, and some are like guide information for my inner and outer meaning. In other words, they sometimes act as teachers in my human schoolroom; they inwardly correct me. Not long ago, I dreamed I was visiting this summer cottage and was in a changing room. Looking in the mirror, I see an image of myself wearing a nice new outfit with a flowery blouse on top, like Frida Kahlo, and shorts on the bottom. Although new and bright, something about this outfit did not feel good. Frida could wear it, but not me.

In parsing the dream, the clue was the changing room. There were some behaviours I had changed recently that didn't suit me and clothes are how we present ourselves in public. I pondered it for several days, then identified that I had decided I needed to smile more in social situations which did not suit me because they felt fake. Such human lesson dreams still have me asking periodically, "Who am I really, today? I may not be the same person I was yesterday." They do call me to be authentic.

The First Spring & Summer

The supernatural is the parts of the natural that is not yet understood.

SPRING AND GARDEN

Every spring, I love the prospect of working in the garden. The wind off the North Atlantic is a wonderful, salt-smelling, hardy treat. Yet, there is hardly a day during the summer when we do not wear a sweater. And, every year, the garden has an almost fifty percent success rate. The spring enthusiasm for working the garden wanes by August. Aside from the cold, the root vegetables have a hard time in the rocky soil. The peas and string beans are the best crops, mainly because we can eat them right from the vine. Yet, regardless of the failure rate and the neglect, the garden gets planted every year, and we eat what we can.

MRS. JORDAN DIES AND EASTER

April 19/86 Mrs. Jordan died yesterday. We'd had a wonderful, long friendship. We met when I was ten years old while visiting my aunt. I became friends with her daughter Julie, but she was never ready to play when I arrived. However, her mother was always baking in the kitchen, and we had meaningful talks while I waited. She was a wise woman. As the years passed, I saw less of Julie but more of her mother.

This loss plows my heart tender, leaving me feeling vulnerable and making me appreciate my remaining loved ones all the more. I can hardly believe it. She was going to go to hospital yesterday, but died while coming down the stairs to have breakfast. Thirty-eight years of friendship. This page is getting wet as I write. I am crying because of how much I will miss her being on this planet. Yet, I am not crying for her. Her faith is strong enough that she'll be walking on water over there. I wonder if she is where Metude is. I must ask.

A week later . . .

April 20/86 What an Easter. Mrs. Jordan was so much a part of it. Dev said it coming home from church. "We've been celebrating resurrection every Easter, but do we really believe it?" Yet this year, when we were singing the hymn, "He lives, He lives..." we looked at each other and knew—Mrs. Jordan lives! What an astounding awareness. It was a tangible and exhilarating experience. Now, isn't that something! Thank you, Metude. The invisible becomes more visible again because of you.

• • •

Meeting My Father after His Funeral, a Happy and Joyous Laugh

My first inkling that there may be life after death happened the afternoon my father was buried eighteen years earlier. He was fifty-seven, and I was twenty-eight. Being brought up a Protestant, I had accepted by word of mouth that there is "life everlasting." My acceptance was too shallow to have anything to do with belief, and it certainly had nothing to do with experience.

For months, before he died of a brain tumour, he disintegrated before our eyes and his own. He went blind within weeks and lost his bodily functions, which embarrassed him greatly. Shortly after that, he lost his ability to speak. It was horrible, and his death was a relief. My mother, his devoted younger brother, and I had been traumatized merely watching his dying. I could not imagine what he had been going through, and his speech was not clear enough to understand him.

Coming home from the cemetery after the funeral, I started to go upstairs to change my clothes. The children were outside with Roger. As my foot took the first step, I saw my father before me on the stairs. He was laughing. Shocked, with no time for disbelief, I watched him, captivated. His head was thrown back, and he continued laughing. His face was full—not skeleton-like, as it had been for months.

He kept on laughing, a happy, joyous laugh, as if he was just making a great discovery. Then, after what seemed like minutes of me staring at him, he disappeared. As I climbed the stairs, laughter began to gurgle in my stomach. His fun and joy were contagious. As I reached the top, I was laughing out loud. I could not believe it. Here, this joyous laughter was juxtaposed with the grief, pain, and darkness of the past months. The graveyard feeling an hour ago was now being transformed. My awestruck spirit felt pixie-light for the first time in months. I knew my father was fine. In my core, I just knew it.

WHAT I AM LEARNING FROM WORKING WITH THE COTTAGE WOMAN

April 30/86 I was thinking tonight: I have no need to prove that Metude is real. Even if I could, who would believe me? Thankfully, for the few who visit with her, her presence speaks for itself. Also, the less said the better in most situations. Besides, telling anyone that the tape recorder goes off when any question is asked about physical healing might sound gimmicky; however, with Metude present, it seems rather natural. Maybe in the cottage woman's case, seeing is believing.

For me, she is becoming a real friend who just doesn't have her own physical body, but seems to be intact in every other way. I'll say this: She is certainly wiser, more human, and more healing than any human I have met. And as she states, divine Presence is more healing than mere words and doesn't her presence and words heal us.

> *However, I wish for her kind of listening, not necessarily for spoken words, but for an inner feeling of direction (which seems to be my main lesson), as uneventful as it feels.*

• • •

The Second Training Session ~ Clearing the Conduit

After the first training session a month and a half ago, when Pam and I walked the railroad tracks and I felt the top of my head become pointed like a witch or dunce hat, I wanted to try again to shift my stream of consciousness. Pam came down and, at her instruction, I concentrated on gathering the energy in my head. Then that cone-shaped feeling came again. I began trying to stretch my mind-energy up further and further. Knowing Metude was probably helping us, I felt safe and asked her to guide me.

Nothing happened. Then, in my mind's eye, a door appeared. It opened, and I found myself going through it. Looking around, I waited. Again, nothing. Then I was drawn backward energetically as the door closed in front of me. I heard, "Not today."

The next day, encouraged by the door and hearing something, we tried again. Pam said she felt considerable energy in my chest. There seemed to be pressure at the top of my head again. The door appeared without me trying hard. It was wavy at first, but finally, it took on a more solid appearance. I was looking at a barn door-like handle. Encouraged by Pam, I reached to open it, then found myself in a sunny field of blowing grasses. I felt part of the field.

Pam continued encouraging me, "That's your field, hold it. Now, look around." Then I heard my name, so I walked toward the voice. I first saw rubber boots and a man's work pants. He was walking about ten feet from me. Then Pam told me to look at his hands. Oddly, they seemed long-fingered and not roughed up by farm work. I waited and nothing else happened. After a little while, Pam suggested I come back through the door and into the cottage. Not quite believing the experience, I still felt a little pleased. And best of all, we had Metude's coming visit to check it out.

Third Training Session ~ Joe's Third Visit

Before meeting with Metude for the next visit, I had another training session with Pam. We used the same technique. After relaxing, I attempted to bring the energy up in my head and beyond. Then, in my mind's eye, it felt like I was flying and came to rest in the same field where the same man was standing in the training session, a day earlier. The location had a New England feel to it.

When I got my bearings, I asked if he had a name and where he lived. It took time, but I thought I heard "Joe." The last name was muffled but sounded like "Martinique." Pam felt that he might have lived on a farm in New England in the late 1700s. Nothing more happened, but strangely enough I really felt a part of that field with its grasses blowing.

Now I was excited that I even heard a name. I could hardly wait to ask the cottage woman about him, as I was totally second-guessing myself and struggling not to write the experience off as "just my imagination."

EXPOSED TO A REALITY OTHER THAN THE HUMAN SIDE

Even though it is May, the air still has a chill to it. Pam is bundled up in the rocking chair and our old friend enters easily. I think Pam is more relaxed and is always eager to hear what Metude has to say. It's more like we are now on this adventure together. We talk about her with an ease and as our old friend. I truly think Pam has more confidence in the wisdom she offers.

We both are curious and a bit excited about my training exercises and what will happen. However, whenever I have any time distance on the experiences, I begin to feel like they are merely my imagination. Thus, the first question of the visit is, "Is Joe just my imagination and if not, will he be a guide for me?"

"Neither" she states flatly. Then gives a little rock and that index finger moves towards me as she continues, "It is a learning experience for you so you can better understand this area. You must have patience. The training session was about practice. The Person directs, but you can do these exercises on your own. These exercises are so you understand how hard it is to accept that which you do not know. Reality is as you perceive it." *She keeps repeating this, but she knows I don't really get it.*

"But Metude, I don't understand. Do you mean the concrete kind of reality we live here?" She frowns, as if puzzled, so I explain, "I mean, we humans consider reality anything that is solid like our bodies, the rocker where you are sitting, and the wood stove here—anything we see with our ordinary eyes and feel with our hands. But you are different; you don't have a solid body. Yet, you *feel* solid. I know now that you are definitely real and are a part of our reality, but you belong to this other reality that isn't a reality by our human definitions." *Ah, a hint of a smile.*

A Lesson for You ~ Imagination Is a Much-Abused Word

Metude nods, rocks, and continues, "These training exercises are just that: They give you exposure to a reality other than the human side. You will give it some thought. If an opportunity is presented, then take it, but don't make an opportunity. This is a lesson for you. Do not fear letting your mind go. One must not be quick to discredit. Imagination is a much-abused word. Yah, much good work and progress. We will proceed."

I saw Joe only four or five times. Our meetings did not seem to go anywhere. Even so, a friend of mine went to the university library and looked up his name on a whim. Later, she dropped in at my house, excitedly saying that she had found his name in some New England document from that time period. A coincidence, probably, but I am learning to give more weight to my imagination.

Working with Another's Defence Mechanisms ~ One Must Be Protected

Changing the subject, I continue, "Metude, working with Fran's pain takes a lot of energy, even on the phone. Her mind is brilliant, and so are her defence mechanisms, which makes working with her a challenge. I need some direction on how to keep myself from losing energy when she challenges me negatively."

My old friend leans forward, "Watch that. Monitor the call. Pull back to a neutral area. She has a strong energy. One must be protected. One must remain alert. Watch for the shifting of energy. Redirect it to neutral. You will understand this. Watch your energy level. You've been given your direction. Much good work. There is much clearing away so more can be done. Continue and hold true to your course. That is your role. She is more in tune with having a sense of readiness. You must play your role: listener and monitor."

My role must be to guide Fran through the pain of that early period when her mother was vindictive. Thus, after several months of working with the pain by using the breathing process, I ask Metude to look at the imaginary stake I had seen in Fran's chest to see if we had made any progress. Also, the pain work seems to be dragging on. Thus, I ask, "Is there a faster way to take the stake out?"

"It can't be taken out all at once," she cautions. "Help her to focus on the pain and letting it go by breathing deeply. The stake is to come out inch by inch. There is the dark around the handle. It is not fresh blood. She is in a lull, gathering her forces. More work to be done. Raw pain needs time for healing. One cannot just pull the stake out with both hands. Blood on both her hands. She is trying to pull it out, but it is not ready to be moved yet. A lot of pain takes longer in healing before one can put it to rest. You must keep bringing it to the front of her mind. Something she has to own."

I am concluding that most humans have a metaphorical stake of some sort in their chest that needs attention. And I might add, how helpful this image is for my understanding of the process.

Light Comes Through but Is Not of You ~ You Are Merely a Vessel

I continue, "The other day, Pam had an image of a light beaming from the middle of my forehead toward Fran's stake. I guessed that is a visual representation of me concentrating spiritual light on her emotional wound."

"The light comes through you, but it is not of you. You are merely the vessel. There are different streams of consciousness, and drawing from these streams provides the energy. Focus on the pain, focus on light for healing. Again, you are merely the vessel. Your energy is connected to Fran's when you work. It will help her to process it. Watch for bleeding."

Having no idea what she meant, I ask, "How do I do that?" *It's all invisible, but I know it is an important caution. Did she mean symbolic bleeding?*

"Gauge by the pain. Use your ears; listen. Hear it. Do not back off but temper the pain as she breathes out."

"Anything else?" *I am still not sure I know what she means by listening to pain.*

"Follow her lead. Let her set her own pace, releasing the pain rather than letting you lead her. Follow through. You will work with her by listening." *Well, that tells me how important listening is. It's like my eye-ears. And where would I be without them?*

Fears ~ When Listed, They Become a Reality and Can Be Dealt With

My next question is how Fran might handle a telephone call from her mother. She called me earlier in a panic. Her mother, whom she has not seen for years, was coming to visit a friend who lives close by. She left a message with a mutual friend that she will call Fran when she is in town. "How can I help her prepare for the phone call?" *Imagine visiting a friend who just lives down the street and not staying with her daughter. I can't.*

Metude pauses, then instructs. "List the fears, then they become more accessible. Panic is in the fears. That way they are faced. When listed, fears become a reality, and then they can be dealt with. One must have a proper foundation to work from. Step back. One must learn how to step back. Control breathing, much value for facing fear. Breathing provides space, protects one from panic. Key is getting fear identified on paper to see what is real and what isn't. What is in one's mind becomes magnified." *Hmm, good advice for anyone.*

I also need specific, concrete strategies for Fran to implement in the moment of stress when she hears her mother's voice. So, I ask, "What should she do when directly talking with her mother on the telephone?"

"Has to avoid panic. Must provide herself with breathing space that will help her not panic. Make an excuse to go in another room to get something or hold the phone at arm's length, breathe slow and deep, and then go back to the conversation. She must have distance. She could say, 'Excuse me a minute.' And again, hold the phone at arm's length, breathe, and get distance. It is in the breathing, then talk again."

"Metude, her mother seems to be a very unhappy person. Can she help her mother?"

"Cannot love before one is ready. She must free herself. One cannot help another in life until one is fully alive oneself. Truth is in the freeing of oneself. Life is only found in freedom."

"Is there anything else on handling the fear of her mother?"

My old friend pauses, nods, then reiterates, "Put the fears on paper. More effective, more tangible when one sees it, rather than elusive where it grows larger. When they are in the mind, solely, fears loom larger. Can work with them on paper, they are concrete on paper."

She's right. These suggestions apply to any fear-driven situation. My fears do tend to multiply if I don't deal with them.

"Indeed, we will proceed."

Protecting My Energy ~ A New Lesson for You

I change the subject to my own schedule, which is my next area of concern. It feels too intense. I must learn how to live this better. Thus, I observe, "Metude, I am down on energy, and the work is still draining me despite your wise counsel."

She nods with a slight smile that indicates: *I am reading your thoughts.* She continues, "Until one concentrates on that spiritual aspect, so much is missed. As one turns on a light then one sees very clearly."

"Oh Metude, you are right. I have missed a lot of spirituality in this area."

"Yah, indeed, it is why it is given to you as balance."

"Yes, I see. Hmm. All this I have gotten myself into, all these projects on top of an already overflowing life."

She looks at me with understanding and says nothing for a little. Then she observes, "You are feeling like you are standing under a waterfall." *Oh, so true.*

Laughing at the truth of it, I respond, "You've got it. I am hoping it will even out, won't it?"

"Yah, indeed. You are already in the process of sorting it out."

Then she adds, "Don't walk into a crisis full tilt. Gauge your energy output. It is a new lesson, another aspect of listening. Also, go outdoors, walking, painting, and isolate yourself. Painting is a type of release. Very good, very good, find yourself some wharf, provide your own isolation. Less counselling work. Painting is healing, re-focuses, re-channels energy. Painting changes your direction, shifts focus for you. Most imperative to listen to this advice. A command call. It will come. Do not worry." *Oh, I am to do less counselling. That's actually good news.*

"Thank you Metude, I will."

Mrs. Jordan on the Other Side ~ She Got a Lot of What She Was Seeking

Now, before my old friend leaves, I really want to ask about Mrs. Jordan, who by that point, had been gone for a few weeks.

"Metude, how is Mrs. Jordan doing on the other side?

After a short pause, my discarnate friend shifts forward in the rocker and spritely replies, "A lot of energy. Very happy. Ah, yah, like a kid in a candy store. She received a lot of what she was seeking in her time on earth."

Oh, my land, I can almost feel her joy! "This is so encouraging. She had a wonderful faith, yet so much of it feels intangible. At times, she wondered what was real and what was not. And I couldn't help her out with that."

My old friend nods, "She got a lot of what she was seeking. Yah, indeed, a lot." *I am so happy because that is such a confirmation of her faith and the way she lived her life. She always felt there is a larger life after death. Yet, whoever knows for sure. However, you do, Metude, with your other-side-eyes and experience.*

"May I ask a question to Mrs. Jordan?" *Ah, I see a hint of a smile.*

"If you can hold her down long enough. She has real eagerness to communicate with her child. Her daughter will sense a physical touch on her shoulder, right hand to the right shoulder. It is early evening, and the sensation will be strong. She will look behind her, but she has a lack of awareness."

"Do I alert Julie?"

"You are not to say anything yet. Right hand on right shoulder, but her mother is on the left. The daughter sits in a kitchen rocker, wooden—her mother's favourite spot. She will look back because of her mother's touch, but she won't believe it." *Yes, that is a big stretch for us, but I know the rocker.*

"What is my role in this situation?" *I ask with some trepidation as my guess is Julie will react vehemently to this information and think I am nuts. She was always challenging her mother's faith, which created tension between them.*

"To nudge her. It has already happened and will happen again. The daughter may contact you. And now we will proceed."

Julie never did, at least, not about her mother. And when I saw her, I never felt she was in a space to bring it up. *And, oh dear, what we miss when we close our minds. Julie would have loved to feel that touch from her mother.*

A Young Father Dying ~ He Is Not Isolated, Physical Relating Is Not the Total Reality

A week ago, I visited Philip, a young father with inoperable cancer. A friend asked me to see him and possibly work with him. I had no idea how to help him. He could still look after his children who were pre-school while his wife worked, even though he was already debilitated and knew he would only become more so. His situation was desperate, and he felt isolated and alone. I didn't know where to enter that kind of suffering. Yet, I had Metude for eyes and wisdom. As I look over at this cottage woman sitting so peacefully in the rocker, I ask about his situation. And I feel her caring as she speaks.

"Darkness when you begin a visit, but by virtue of the visit, light lingers after. I will be with you in moments of despair. Time to move more in light. The father will hear you. He will become more aware of the depth in his being, his connection of and to the spirit, his being, and every living soul. He is not isolated. Physical relating is not total reality. Indeed."

She raises that finger, saying, "And for you, one thing at a time. Your area of work is given to you now. This is the area of greatest need. His soul can't attain peace until he learns. He has the readiness to move. It is your listening. You are well-guided. It will be made known. Visit when the need arises. Each situation dictates its own moves. You will know whether to speak or be in silence. It is coming as it should."

Oh Metude, you are a Godsend, literally. Ah, and again I am to live in the sea of another's pain.

"Ah my child, but I know. May you both walk in light."
Oh Metude, I love you and so feel loved. I have come a long way from fear of you to loving you. Although, you are not emotional and feel somewhat detached, I still experience your caring.

Seemingly ignoring my sentiment, she continues, "It is also an initiation for your friend Philip into learning to use his other senses to access streams of consciousness between one and the other. You are meant to work with him, and it provides a bond between the streams. It leads to meaning and relating. Watch those areas that are ready to move. He is not ready to relate in a personal way, until safe.

"Be encouraged to see that he can work in these areas as well. Help him to see how real the other streams of consciousness are. He was given a glimpse of his role, now it must be backed up. It is not to be dismissed. Do not allow him to do that. Let us proceed."

Then his role, like mine, is to see nothing as hopeless. There is only change (not death), and everything is larger and more than meets the physical eye. Hmm, we will be treating more than a brain tumour.

How to Communicate with Guides ~ The Only Boundaries Are Those We Create

I ask another question from a young friend who asked me, with much enthusiasm, how she can communicate with guides. "What would you suggest, Metude?"

"There is a beginning awareness as the young one begins to seek. As she has the willingness to seek, she will find the answers. Must learn to settle oneself; only in stillness one can seek. Must be still to hear. Her enthusiasm is a good thing in its place. If moving constantly not the room for silence. One needs to learn to be calm inwardly, as in this stillness lies her seeking. She will be given her name for her guide. She will know it. One first feels the essence and then comes the name. She knows her names. No one else can. And they cannot help until you acknowledge them."

"Well, Metude, Pam and I are more aware of you."

"Yah, indeed, I am also more aware of you. But work to do yet. That will come, listen." *Oh, she is not completely aware of us.*

That's surprising. Yet, maybe it's because she has more things to learn, as she says. I like that we are not the only ones learning and somehow it makes her more human.

Most of the time, I have to wonder how Metude ever came to us and how we will ever hear and see as she suggests. Reading my mind, her answer is instant: "Oh, how closely in touch we are with one another. One will learn more about this as we move along. The only boundaries are those which we create." Then, she shifts in the rocker which tells me she is leaving. I thank her for coming.

She nods, "Yah, it has been a pleasant visit. You will have further questions, but we now bid you a good evening. Peace to you and yours."

"And indeed, to you, Metude. Thank you, so, so much."
I am beginning to feel love and a real kinship between us.

• • •

Light comes Through the Cracks in Our Pain ~ And Our Healing Happens

The cottage woman was right—Philip was not ready to be personal. After visiting with him for weeks, he remained stalled. He enjoyed the social visits, but I couldn't seem to take him where it counted. It felt like we were dragging him along. I wrote in my journal, "Understandably, Philip wants a surface encounter, as it involves less emotional pain, yet he also wants inner healing. Light comes through cracks in the pain. As Metude says, "It is in and through our pain that we get our freedom, that we can heal, and that light enters. The time is for his pain, the cards are to be put on the table as you would say."

Eventually, with more visits, Philip did break through the pain-wall and eventually light entered. After a number of social, surface visits, I think he began to trust me. Then, he became open to the questions I asked about how he really felt about the situation. He began sharing his fears, the seemingly stark reality of his situation, and the losses of his young children, his wife, and his very life with his coming transition (death). He allowed his emotions a release or better said, could not help himself after a while.

Philip was a mild-mannered man who found anger, despair, grief, and eventual acceptance within himself. We talked about love, shed more than a tear and eventually "somewhere on the way" he was healing. His perspective did shift as I shared Metude's words and mine. She would not allow me to tell him about her so I just inner-listened as she kept teaching me to do and did the best I could.

He managed to make it down to our house several times for supper and music. Having him in our home got him out of his usual surroundings. With the family table talk and the music after supper he could feel a different energy than his home offered at that time. We also had become friends and that is what friends do. We walked and talked together on our journey for two years before he passed over. And those two years did make a difference.

> *"More than happiness, love wants growth,*
> *widening, deepening of awareness . . .*
> *Whatever prevents that causes pain. Love*
> *does not shrink from pain.*
>
> ~ *Jack Kornfield*

BEING OBSERVED AS I WRITE ~ A PLEASURE FOR THE OTHER SIDE

July 18/86 Because of my disembodied friend, I now know that I am being heard and observed as I write this, and that interestingly enough, there seems to be a pleasure in it for them on the other side. I like that and there is certainly no end of pleasure for me.
I also like that Metude seems to be quite independent of Pam. She tells me she likes our hoedowns, at times, even when Pam is nowhere around or might even be in a crisis at her home. Obviously, she does not need Pam's body to be present in our house. Thus, just because I can't see her doesn't mean she is not there. It is like she knows what went on in a conversation, say, in my living room before I tell her and when Pam is nowhere in sight. So, I wonder if I can conclude, the invisible must be occupied by more wonderful spirits that are like our ancient friend?
"You are so right, Metude, you don't have to

see oxygen to know it is there."
Another thing I am seeing more clearly is that Roger's mother's Alzheimer's is getting worse. It reminds me of Albert Cullum's line, "The geranium on the windowsill died, and the teacher went right on talking." She has left us already, and we just go on our way, seemingly ignoring the fact. Why aren't we crying? Where is our sadness? I want people to yell and cry a bit when I leave, whether it is before the physical demise or after.

Back to painting after a month! If I listen, I will be told how to paint better. My inside voice agrees. Felt much stronger doing the landscape painting of North West Cove yesterday. I also got another portrait of Roger started on canvas this a.m. He has much patience when it comes to my art and sitting for hours. And the cottage woman is right—painting is healing and balancing.

LIGHT COMES THROUGH BUT IS NOT OF YOU

The spring sun is finally helping to warm the cottage. Even the smell is different. The green growth of the spruce trees rubbing against the outside wall gives off this tangy, spruce-gum odour. The wood smoke from the winter has gone right into the walls and is always present, whether the fire is lit or not.

Pam came down earlier than expected, and the cottage woman settles in easily. What a contrast to those earlier visits when I was so scared of her. Now, it's more like a personal friendship, but still a little weird. Both Pam and I have some questions ready, plus, one Fran gave us. We did work with the stake image, using the breathing process. Fran somewhat managed the stress during the phone call from her mother by following the cottage woman's advice. She held the phone away from her ear and excused herself when she felt too uncomfortable. It apparently worked, as she felt it gave her a feeling of control and strength that she had not experienced with her mother before. Also, aside from the breathing-out-pain exercises, it apparently created distance which helped her become an observer of the situation.

Separation for Identity and Independence ~ Casting of What Is Not Ours to Carry

"Fran needs more help with her mother because she is thinking of going to university but fears her mother's sarcastic put-down. Can you suggest a strategy?"

My wise friend rocks, then leans forward saying, "Separation for identity and independence. They each must own what is their own truth, casting off that which is not theirs. Mother is left separate and detached. They are not coming together, not even blending—side by side like equals, but individuals." *That sounds like they are getting their personal identities mixed up.*

They need to be true to who they are, separate from being a mother or daughter.

That certainly feels like it will take time.

"How can I help?"

"Hold your ground. You identify the wires connecting that relationship so she can see. Do not increase the pressure or relax it. Hold firm." *Hmm, Metude knows she can get testy.*

"I understand but what ground can she hold with her mother?"

"Hold her own identity. Keep it up front. Her identity must be as a banner, a flag. Hold true to her own identity. Maintain space. There must be space, firmness, and determination. We will Proceed." *That is a challenge. However, I actually find this advice healthy and helpful in separating and holding my own identity—not only with my mother, but in other personal relationships.*

Surface Talk Is Much Like Self-Preservation ~ A Camouflage

Another situation was bothering me. Our regular group, composed of Pam, Mila (another good friend), Fran, and Ellen meet regularly to share and discuss any meaningful events that happen to us during the week. However, Fran often dominates these conversations and seems to need the attention of everyone in the room. She also wants to convert us all to her fundamentalism. Yet, her creative mind has a deep understanding of life when she allows it to think freely.

I need to find a way to make some space so others can offer their perspective. I instinctively know this surface-talk is somehow associated with her pain, so I ask Metude, "Has the stake moved?"

"No," she replies. "Both hands are down at her side. She gets in her own way. New issues coming up. Continue to use your breathing process so she does not become surface. Her pain is much like a wound that must be drained. It must be kept open. Breathing allows one to talk from a new level. Breathing allows her to get past herself. It's the healing—healing from the inside out." Pointing her forefinger at me, she directs, "You remain in control. Do not allow surface talk. When one is allowed that level of talking, such issues are used as camouflage.

"Surface talk is much used, as what you call a 'red herring,' as a means to give one self-esteem. Such talk is a straw she is hanging on to. When she feels a lack of importance, surface talk is much like self-preservation."

My old friend tilts her head my way and directs, "Ask her what the real issue is. Is this really how we are meant to spend our time?" I can almost feel her direct gaze at me with her eyes closed. "You choose how to spend the time. You control it. You are in control." *This style of leadership sounds more upfront than I am used to; I am more a questioner than a teller.*

"Thank you, Metude. That is such helpful guidance."

Deliberately Switch to Light ~ You Are Too Quick to Allow Dark to Overshadow

Two of my friends, Sue and Mary, are becoming closer friends. A few days previously, they had gone on a trip together. In the past, we had gone as a threesome, but they didn't invite me this time. I feel left out, resentful, and hurt. I need guidance on how to handle these miserable emotions.

"Metude, the old adage that three is a crowd is resonating with me. I feel left out among my two new friends. I can keep my feelings buried, but I don't like the negative thoughts arising from feeling left out. I need your help to handle the situation."

Sitting in silence, I wait, vulnerable and ashamed about such feelings. Then she states rather matter-of-factly, "What one interprets as negative thoughts are given for a purpose. One must sort and classify before filing away. Re-examine what happened. The interpretation is wrong and thus, one misses something." *She's right. I just want to stuff negative feelings in a corner and not think of them again.*

"Really? Is my interpretation wrong?" *It feels dead-on. Hmm . . . So, negative feelings can have a purpose! Well, this is schoolroom work for me, I suspect.*

"Reassess the negative interpretation. One jumps to conclusions. You've coloured it yourself. Back up. Your interpretation has distorted the message. You trigger the feelings of being left out. They come from another (previous) time period. It's to do with the situation. One situation has become over-shadowed by another."

When I was a child, I often felt left out or unwanted. I was an only child, and I lived with adults who mostly talked to each other. Metude must mean that this current situation triggers those old feelings, and that I superimpose these feelings onto my two friends.

"Learn to recognize when you do it and identify where you have done it in the past. Analyze what happened in that instance, how you interpreted this situation, and how you reacted. Recognize your role. Learn to recognize the situation. You failed to look at the other side as light." *I think she means I am not being "dumped." Even logically, I know that is not true, as they both do care for me. My problem is that my negative feelings give me another message that feels like the absolute truth.*

She interrupts my reasoning. "Deliberately switch to light. You are too quick to allow dark to overshadow. Should remain detached and balanced. Your own personality overshadows. You will learn to work that. Must look at how you handle it. Do not put it out of mind."

Again, she stresses, "Your interpretation is wrong. Balance your thoughts. In situations where there is positive and negative, light and dark have to do with personal experience. Overshadowing throws off your balance. Rid yourself of feelings that are still hanging on. Detachment is positive. You will enter the relationships freely. Burying it was not freeing oneself."

Metude continues telling me that I need a corner, a physical spot, in which to do my negative thinking and feeling work. "It (feeling not wanted) will come at you in different ways, so you can become free of it." *Hmm, I probably will.*

As she says, if we don't get it the first time, the opportunities will be given again. I know why she is pushing me. My negative feelings are an old wound that falsely colours innocent situations in the present and leave me with these emotions I don't like.

"Thank you, Metude. I had not heard about overshadowing or superimposing the past on the present. That is very important to identify."

"Yah, and now we will proceed."

A Negative Thought ~ Given for a Purpose

Often, she repeats her instructions just to make sure I understand. Thus, she continues, "Identify that in which you get caught up in. Be prepared to handle the things you get caught up in. Work with what is given. One must sort out and classify before filing away. Re-examine, take it out, and look at it. What one interprets even as a negative thought, you are given for a purpose. You interpret it as negative thoughts, but look at it again. Pull it out, re-examine what happened. You interpreted it wrong and missed something. Re-evaluate, reassess your negative interpretation. The end result is that you jumped to conclusions. You've coloured it yourself. Back up. Your interpretation has distorted the message." *Well, at least she is forthright! And I am learning important lessons.*

"Why do I draw the parallel between the past and the present?"

"It's to do with the situation. One situation has become overshadowed. You triggered it. You see the shadow of one circumstance (the past wounding experience) overshadowing the present situation. Work with it. Learn to recognize when you do it. Take note of it for your own development. Using your terms, when you feel tweaked, it is a red flag. A warning light goes on. That is working with it. It is a step. The way will be cleared. There is a positive in every negative. And now we will proceed." *And as my old friend says, her "we" will make us humans uncomfortable when necessary. Apparently, all part of the lessons.*

Several decades later, reading *The Power of Now* by Eckhart Tolle, I was reminded of Metude's wisdom and all the work we did identifying how past wounding emotional situations can overshadow the present, and can be mistaken for it. A great learning.

Loneliness Needs to Be Understood ~ Aloneness Is Different

My next question is about Pam's situation. Frank is becoming alarmingly depressed, which makes him more difficult to live with. She has spent weeks trying to get him to see the doctor and is now exhausted from weathering his dark moods. The more growing she does, it seems the lonelier she feels in her marriage (a fact that is often articulated by my other friends, as well). Being worried, I ask the cottage woman how Pam is really doing.

She responds, "The Entity is physically and emotionally tired. Drains the will to live." *Ohhh, it's that bad!*

"What will help her?"

"In some sense, a crucial time for your friend. A great loss in her energy, she is now on reserve. Reserve energy was spent pushing the Body to get medical attention. Her reserves are very low. Great emotional drain exists even yet." *It is indeed a wonder that she even allowed a visit with Metude.* "She has yet to deal, to face inner loneliness. It is not fully and totally examined. Must be faced and let go of. It is merely that which is needed in the physical realm. Once one lets go of it, inner loneliness will no longer exist.

"There is another way to fill her need. Yet, she seeks it from the human realm, and it is not where it is to be found. Much energy is used for physical fulfillment. Loneliness needs to be understood. Aloneness is different. It is coming. Even as we talk, she is hearing and working." *Oh, that's news. She hears it even though she has no memory of what is said when she comes back after Metude leaves. At some level, she must be learning from the visits without my feedback.*

Hanging On to His Pain Greedily ~ It's Where He Wishes to Be

Well, I continue, "How is Frank doing?"

"Much pain in him. He hangs on to it greedily. He is where he wishes to be." *Sometimes, Metude shocks me.*

I always assume people want to get rid of their pain, yet I instinctively know what she says is true. Everyone jumps to his wishes when he is in his dark mood. This type of power he can experience without challenging himself, and it saves him from facing fears or his own lack of value.

She continues, "He is not able to hear, and the Entity has no energy left. One must let go of the struggle. Opportunities have been given to him. He has not taken them. Much pain in him but again, he hangs on to it greedily. He sees it as part of his whole. He must change, the Entity can't do it for him. Until he reaches that point, not much to do. We will proceed."

"Oh, thank you Metude. She is worse than I thought." *She is right, yet saying that Frank is greedy would feel unkind or inaccurate to me.*

In other words, if Pam won't let go of his problems, it is dangerous for her. I hope she is listening to this at some level. Besides, he has been given a million chances to live more creatively.

You Cannot Swish Through Prayer ~ Each Person Must Be Given a Space

Before Metude leaves, I need to ask about my uncle Ned. He is my mother's youngest brother and is somewhat estranged from the family due to their lack of acceptance of his homosexual partnership. He lives in Florida with his life partner, Tim. Unfortunately, Tim is possessive, which dampens my uncle's resolve to visit. However, he often told me on the phone how much he enjoyed our family talks the previous summer. Ned had recently been diagnosed with throat cancer. I started praying for him. I want to encourage him to come up this summer for a visit. I really need advice.

Nodding, my wise friend instructs, "You must continue to give him energy if he is to visit again." *Good, then my praying does help him.* "You still have an opportunity to work with his pain this summer, if he chooses, but he must be given the energy to do that. You just listen. If his energy drops low, you will pick it up. Prayer is not effective if you swish through it." *Oh dear, I know she is referring to my on-the-run prayers.*

"Each person you pray for must be given a space and a time. A mere second is not a fact. Effective prayer is individual space given to each person. Scanning is not the same as focusing. Take each person in their own turn. Prayer does not look tangible, but it is real."

"Well, I am feeling uncomfortable about not praying as much as I should."

She bends closer and a wisp of hair falls past her ear. "Good. We are watching when you are uncomfortable. That awareness of being uncomfortable, knowing that we are here—and then we are getting your attention. That awareness is listening. Effective intercession does not depend on time but on attention. Your focus is what counts." *Well, feeling uncomfortable is not always negative and may have a larger meaning than we are aware of.*

She smiles enigmatically, "The person has the need-to-know love. At this point, he needs to talk, feels isolated, misunderstood, and not seen or heard."

"Who can really help him?" I ask.

"In part, the person who feels so moved. Each can send love in their own way. We will proceed."

In 2005, Gregg Braden, a theorist who weds theology and science, visited Tibet. In his book titled, *Secrets of the Lost mode of Prayer*, he asked a monk why they chanted. In essence, the monk replied that the words of the chant itself are not the goal. They chant to create the feeling of the prayer in the body. This is the language of healing presence. The feeling is the prayer.

Little wonder my old friend says that the person who is so moved is the one who can pray.

There's More Than One Way of Seeing

I so often forget Pam's eyes are closed when I am visiting because I feel Metude looking right at me. So, I ask, "Can you see me?"

Ah, there is the hint of that enigmatic smile again as she tilts her head to one side. "Yah, that is important for you. There is more than one way of seeing, even as we are here. It pleases you. It is all a means of linking minds, thought, and communication. A person's being may unite physically without being aware. Space is not a barrier. I am real. Do not be inhibited by the body when the eyes are closed."

Well, I'm not; somehow, even with your eyes closed, I know you are looking at me and seeing right through me.

She shifts in the rocker, a sign we have visited long enough. "Oh, Metude, I so appreciate your coming."

"Ah indeed, we continue to work and be near you. Learn to monitor your energy. We are never far away and would contact you. What you don't get one way, you will get another. And now I must leave. We bid you a good afternoon." *I think she means if I don't get my human lesson one way, they will give it to me again in another way.*

"Again, we thank you so much for visiting."

"And to you my child, we will continue to work with you and be near you."

Pam is beginning to stretch.

• • •

The Spirit Needs Us to Pray ~ The Language of Healing Presence

Thirty years later, Metude's words continue to expand, taking on a larger and larger meaning as I read about the latest scientific findings. Quantum physics now tells us we are energy, and not concrete matter. We don't have to move flesh to get it healed, just lovely weightless electrons held in the divine embrace—as Richard Bartlett, the creator of matrix energetics, points out:

> *You are composed of electrons, which can and do behave differently depending on the*

> *observer's perspective or set of expectations.*
> *Knowing this, you can begin to understand*
> *how a physical pattern or condition*
> *could change if you chose to congruently*
> *observe that condition or problem from a*
> *quantum perspective.*

In prayer, as Metude said, the divine light comes through a person. I don't create light, but I position myself for it to flow through, emit, glow, and heal. Prayer is a relationship not only with this light, but also to oneself and the person one is praying for. Indeed, we cannot swish through these relationships if they are going to have substance.

VISITS ARE HANGING BY A THREAD - A NEW STRENGTH

August 2/86 Sunny today, and a warm breeze blowing my "Spirit of the Day" tree (a poplar under which I often sat when looking at the ocean). My pretty new flowered-blouse and white skirt are dancing in the sun. The warm breeze against my skin gives me exquisite feelings for life.

Pam has changed significantly in these past few months. Still, doing her own growth work is paying off. A little self-value is like gold. Also, I think Metude's presence is giving her a new strength. She is now working on her high school equivalency, so she arrives after supper with her math books. Then Roger helps her for an hour or so, which they are doing right now. Takes a lot of courage for her to do it when her family is not supportive.

However, it makes me sad. She has lost

her youth, her naivety, her tenderness, her eagerness, and her laughter. I sense soberness, an emotional defeat, and a sadness, too. Life is just too raw and too hard sometimes. I am so thankful she still allows Metude to visit. She now recognizes the wisdom the cottage woman gives her. I also think she knows she is real, more than she admits. Yet, that permission for those visits with us hangs by a thread, and it depends on what is happening with Frank and her family in the moment. He resists every independent move she makes. I just keep praying.

Three days later ~ a missing boy

August 5/86 Pam and I had a hard day yesterday. A little boy named Tom has been lost in the woods for several days. Search teams had come from other parts of Nova Scotia and were looking for him. Search and Rescue showed us the map of the area. Pam could see an image of him and thought she had an idea where he might be. So, we joined the search.

Following the images, we tramped through brush, swamp, and dense woods in the rain for eleven hours: wet boots, stumbling over countless dead logs, falling down, helping each other up, calling his name until we had no voices left. But he never answered. We came home exhausted and feeling defeated. Roger got us two buckets of water to soak our feet while we told him our sad tale. We had to peel our socks off gingerly as the blood from the rubs stuck to them.

We both felt the little boy was alive this morning, but that feeling was gone by this evening. The search covered miles, and we were so sure we had been looking in the right spot.

Two days later - repercussions

August 7/86 Tom was found in Tasley Meadow this morning, curled up under a tree. The daily paper showed his location on a map. Heartbreakingly, he was not alive. We guessed he was about a hundred yards from where we were looking. We were so close. This knowledge leaves us hollow, very sad, and a bit lost in ourselves.

Our searching is having repercussions. Pam told me she has no confidence again. I pointed out that we did have the right spot, considering the miles the search covered. We just did not see him. It is desperate to think his life might have been saved if we had. We were so close.

Now, Pam does not want to let the cottage woman visit, and she tells me she has no more confidence in her images and information. I have to let it all go. I feel a bit orphaned. People like Donna are still calling, and they really need more wisdom than I have. Now, I know why this cottage woman instructs, "You must listen." How utterly vital that is; I dread the day I won't be able to visit her. It all seems to depend so much on Pam's family's dysfunction. It is devaluing and takes her confidence.

Next week, I am staying with Mother. And now I can't ask my wise, old friend for any extra advice on how to help my visit, which means I will really have to listen. I am also recognizing how valuable that ability is in the moment

A week later ~ I thank my mother

August 14/86 I am staying with mother and Jim, her husband, about a hundred miles from home, for a week-long art workshop. I must stay current with my feelings about her. Maybe that's another form of Metude's listening. I should heed what I feel today, not what I felt about her in years past. When I look at her, I love her. She has always been so with it, smart, and wise with a ruthless integrity, which I have always appreciated. Must tell her that is how I feel more often. I certainly do shy away from anything personal, though.

Last night, I told Mother about searching for the boy, Tom. I was very aware of the guides being present. The energy rippled in my hair and up my right side. It was especially active physically when I touched on certain points of the experience. This physical sense of the guidance seems to be developing. Plus, for the first time this morning, I heard, "You are listening." Oh, I love that.

Two days later ~ I am not sure she can hear me

August 16/86 It's hot enough that the sweat is running down my cheeks and behind my ears. The week is flying, and I am wonderfully looked after by Mother. Full days of painting and trying to make colour sing. I must develop a larger palette. There is nothing like producing something with one's hands.

I thanked Mother last night for what she gave me as a child—the feeling that I was special and loved. What a priceless gift that was. I also told her that I would rather have had her as a mother than any of my aunts, as nice as they are. However, I am not sure she can hear me.

Home again . . . a greater awareness

August 19/86 Good to be home again. My, what an exquisite summer it is. Metude, you instruct me to have greater awareness. I am learning that one can love more than one thinks possible.

My body is worked out—karate, biking, swimming, and standing outside painting all day. In karate tonight, we did front rolls, back rolls, and cartwheels. Imagine, cartwheels! I couldn't do them as a kid, and still can't! My gi was soaked with sweat by the end of the session.

Then, getting out of the car about ten, I could hear the waves lapping at the edge of the lawn. Went down to the beach and checked our house and the neighbours' houses. All were in darkness. I stripped down to what I was born in and went for a swim. The moon's reflection was almost full and shimmered a half-inch below my nose as I swam toward it.

IMAGES BECOME A THIRD EYE - AN IMPORTANT TOOL FOR SEEING BEYOND THE SURFACE

Donna is doing terribly. She is back into threating suicide. We might lose her yet. Pam is right. It is beyond us. Other people we work with can improve, but her depression seems unmovable. We called the doctor on her behalf, to alert him that she might need to be admitted to the hospital. Apparently, he wants her to go as well. However, she is still resisting, as she thinks people will think of her as insane. This is untrue and so unfortunate.

Thus, I need to consult with the cottage woman and Pam agrees, thank goodness. We are at our wits' end. She has experienced abuse in her younger years, and her brother committed suicide in his early twenties, which does not help her outlook.

Metude settles in, and Pam's muscles are rearranged into what is now a familiar face. We certainly have come a long way from those early months of strangeness and the scary Beat that she told us was really universal love. Since then, the world has shifted somewhat on its axis for me—new eyes, new ears, new understanding, and a new dimension. The rocker moves, a signal that my discarnate friend is ready.

Kindle a Spark of Life by Blowing on It ~ A Process of Healing

I tell Metude that Pam has had a vision of Donna in a fetal position with her fist in her mouth, her eyes wide open, and that we are feeling a bit hopeless again.

My old friend listens, then she moves slightly forward in the rocker, "You and the Body (Pam) are standing there but can't get near her. She is in a bubble and needs nourishment. She must summon enough energy to take nourishment. You can kindle the spark of life, blow on it. Mentally encourage her to get up, mentally call her back. Call her back." *Maybe sending her love and energy through prayer is nourishment.*

I've never thought of either as nourishment, nor have I thought that I can kindle a spark of life by blowing on it. That's rather exciting. Plus, she also said the same about my uncle that has cancer—we can actually lend people energy through prayer.

Images Become Our Third Eye ~ Blowing on a Leg in Daily Prayer

Ten years ago, I had an experience of blowing on a wound. A serious accident had resulted in numerous operations. I had asked for an image of how to heal a foot-long femoral artery incision, as there was a concern for infection. The image I received was of a healer in a cave standing over me.

He was blowing on the incision, so I blew on my leg in a daily prayer. Then, one day when I asked, the healer was gone. The incision had healed.

Again and again, such images continue to be an important tool in our work with people. We are learning how to use and interpret them more accurately. Again, they continue to offer us a larger understanding, and thus a more creative direction. They are becoming like our third eye. In later years, I was struck with how similar this instruction was to some shaman-healing work done in the southwest.

Pain Unfolds in Layers at a Time ~ As Does Understanding

Interrupting my reflection, I ask, "Metude, Donna's doctor wants her to go in the hospital, but she is against it. I agree with him but how can we encourage her to go to what she calls, a psych-ward?"

My old friend leans forward, stating, "It cannot be forced. She must be ready. Better if she sees it as going for a rest. She must be made to see the naturalness of her illness. Perceive it as a rest rather than treatment. She needs to talk, talk, talk, and you listen. She needs to get to the root." My old friend then pauses and suggests, "Understanding comes in layers, series, and sections. Pain unfolds in layers at a time. We are working in depth. Fears are not clear yet, but it is coming. Yah, good, getting closer to the root of the pain."

Hmm, so we must be making progress. She does a lot of withering in pain when she allows herself to open up and that is what makes me second-guess myself.

Metude continues, "The other aspect of understanding is how people will perceive her. If she will appear insane then her worst fears would come true. She is not insane, yet that is how she would feel if she falls apart. Then she would have to admit she was insane, which is not the situation. Talk to her. Rest rather than treatment translates as being the same."

"Can I tell her about you?" I venture hopefully.

"No, it is beneficial for her to know that you are just being guided. In one sense, my resources are your guide. It is merely for you to point out by saying, 'I am being guided.' She must hear that." *Ohhh, she has resources, too.*

"But do I tell her what you say?"

She shakes her head. "Watch the timing of your sessions with her. It is of key importance. Space allows time for healing." *Good point, even a cut on the finger takes a few days.*

Next, I need to ask about Donna's dream this past week. "Metude, she still dreams she kills herself. Does that mean she will do it?"

"Again, suicide is not to be seen as a threat, but an option, one that is being considered more seriously than ever before. The dream is her subconscious way of bringing it to the forefront. You are merely to remind her that she does have options to live. There is not only one way out. Get another year behind her. When the moment is negative or bad, help her see tomorrow or beyond the moment. She holds moments rather than lets them go."

You Must Always Be for Life ~ There Is Always Hope

With a shortness born of weariness, I then ask, "But sometimes, Metude, I wonder if it wouldn't be better if she did end her learning, which is what you say suicide is, and start a new life experience. This life seems such a torture for her." *Oh, I just got a shot of energy up my leg.*

This ancient woman raises herself to the edge of the rocker, points her finger and states unequivocally, "You must always be for life. You must always be for life." *Oh, she's emphatic. Hmm, I'm not bringing that up again.*

"Oh, I will, Metude, I will." *Yet, I really needed to hear her say it because it's easy to think when Donna is in agony that she might be better taking her life. We need to choose life.*

I had also dreamed last week that Donna had committed suicide, and I had felt very sad. So, I ask Metude about the dream.

A little rock and a pause, and then she answers, "We are not in control. It is a possibility of what the dream is about. You are doing what must be done. Each has a responsibility for themselves. You are doing well with listening. A valuable key to the other stream of consciousness. Whatever path one chooses, listening is key."

"What more can I do?"

"Support, calm, and soothe." She responds, ever serene.

"How can I give her hope?" I persist.

"You can't," she says, simply.

"Is there any hope?"

"Yah, indeed, indeed."

"Where is the hope?" I sigh, not being able to see any myself at this fraying point.

"In her knowing all things can be changed. In knowing we each have our own role. Nothing happens without reason. She is where she needs to be. The hospital is an opportunity for a good rest. We will proceed."

Our Human Schoolroom ~ One Never Sets on a Course of Learning Alone

Brooke drops in. She had called earlier asking if she could come over. This summer, she is working in a small fish plant to help pay for her education. The owner has been difficult to work with and demeans the staff, no matter how hard they work. Brooke wants to ask about quitting.

My old friend, with a hint of a smile, says almost as an aside, "The young one has set on a course of learning. Would be wise if one would relax." *Oh Metude, you know this job thing is tense for her.*

"How long will this course of learning take?" Brooke asks, not too happy. *She just wants this job to be in the past tense.*

"One cannot set time limits. It depends on your own rate of absorption. Ask what you wish to know. One does not see growing as positive. You must not fear. One is never set on a course of learning alone. If you don't get it, it will come back again. You try hard preparing and the preparation is part of your growth." *I suspect her preparation has been checking out her fears and their consequences.*

Brooke is silent. We wait, then she states, "I am giving up my job." *Oh, she is making the decision right now.*

Metude shifts in the rocker and with the hint of a smile suggests, "That will be a lightening of the load and a new sense of self-awareness." *Oh, that has just turned the negative into a positive. Brooke is smiling.*

"Will there be another job for me this summer?" *She is worried about school finances.*

"You will get other offers, but you must choose for yourself." She then adds, "Soon, an easing of your way, a leveling off from a rough time, a new plateau. There is much progress, and soon you will see that."

"Oh Metude, thank you." *Relief floods her face. Maybe this will lighten her summer.*

Dreams, a Lesson Tool ~ They Reveal Our Pain

Then Brooke asks how dreams work as she found her latest one disturbing.

"Dreams reinforce what is already known. Your dreams are a valuable tool for you, a reinforcement. Wise to relax more. You would benefit from walking, a solitary time to think. You respond quite well to sailing. The breeze holds much for you. When troubled, walk and much care is blown away. When you don't have answers, you set it aside child and come back later. Nothing to gain when one can't see clearly. Yah, set aside, find something else to do. Space is more beneficial. You must not be troubled. Must learn to consciously recognize when swamped, flag it, using your term. It will be dealt with. There will be other opportunities."

Changing the subject somewhat, Brooke asks, "What causes pain, Metude?"

"My child, what you perceive as pain is a combination of one's own human nature and how one interprets a new learning. It is also a part of the human experience of reaching forth. Pain gives the opportunity to bring past experiences out. We do not ask what you can't handle. For you, there is a life of great opportunity, much advancement. You will do much seeing in your lifetime, seeing that brings recognition.

"You will be given that which you need. You must not fear missing an opportunity. What you don't get the first time will be provided for the second time.

"Yah, 'tis good, we will proceed." *She is always adding if we don't do our human-lesson work now we will have to do it later. Again, apparently, we have to work on it till we get it.*

I know our visit is soon ending, but Pam needs more support. I ask Metude if anything new is coming up for her. She also wants me to ask about Frank and the rest of her family, as her spirit and energy are still at a low ebb. She is also concerned about her health, and so am I.

"Indeed, her suffering and life are at a low point, yet there are other elements to enter the picture. A new friend. Possibilities do exist, although met with fear rather than eagerness. They are perceived as adding to the burdensome relationship. She has merely to be open. Tendency to say no to people, a fear, and a defence mechanism. What can't be reached can't be hurt. Not based on fact, but fear. It has to go."

Metude bends her head, as she continues, "Your friend is at a low point in her life. Weakness of the physical body is evident. Operation, beneficial. The difficulty is in her environment. Lacks sense of value. Suffers greatly for not being recognized, seen, or valued. A difficult choice was made long ago. The choice had great obstacles."

Hmm, Frank was twelve years older than Pam, and from the age of fourteen and she is thirty-seven now, he met her after school every day. They married several years later—child bride marrying a jealous man. A rugged choice…Or was it even a choice?

Living with Pain ~ Is Not What We Have in Mind

Continuing, I ask Metude, "What else would be beneficial for her?"

"The Entity (Pam) is not getting rest. Much emotional suffering. There is much suffering caused from the relationship—isolation, loneliness. Aloneness is the next step. Great deal to learn in one life, but of her choosing." *Imagine, she chose it. It seems so uphill.*

"How can I help or can I?"

"Although you are close to her, she alone must make her decisions. She sees the solution as learning to live with pain. That's not what we have in mind, but that she should live a full and valuable life. It is basically what she is willing to accept, what she is committed to. She feels committed to 'your word is your bond,' but that is not necessarily so. The relationship leaves much to be desired. She is not willing to hear that at this point and not willing to discuss it. You need to give her space." *Oh, you so get it. And doesn't everything stall without a readiness.*

I know when Pam is too energy-depleted to continue the visit. My old friend shifts in the rocker saying, "The body is restless. I now must bid you a good day. We are open to you and present. Peace be with each of you and yours."

"Oh, thank you and the same with you and yours, Metude. I will pass on what you said." My old friend's presence shifts, and Pam is back.

As the cottage woman said, the path to freedom is so often pain. Yet, these human lessons lure us to engage them, reminding me that more than happiness, love wants growth.

A HEALER MUST MAINTAIN LIFE-GIVING BOUNDARIES FOR HERSELF

August 23/86 Donna's situation has significantly worsened even though we are working with her, and her doctor has had her on meds for the depression, weeks ago. She finally consented to go to hospital once it was framed as taking a rest rather than being considered crazy. And what a relief! They changed her medication, but it has not started to work yet. Now she says she feels like she is imprisoned. If medication can't lift this, what will happen? And how long will they keep her in hospital?

Also had another dream of Donna last night. The fire is on her hospital floor, and she's in a wheelchair. I panic and run down the stairs before they get clogged with others trying to escape. When I get out, I remember she is left on the top floor and can't make it out on her own. Then it hits me; it is no good saving myself if I leave her, but how will I ever get up to the top floor again? So, I start into the building, but the fear thumping in my chest wakes me.

The dream suggested that I was operating on a fear of history repeating itself. Dee, my young friend who had come to me by the tree in the snowstorm, had threatened to kill herself many times. I did not believe that she would, yet she did. Afterward, I wondered what I had missed, what I didn't do. Now, here is Donna. In spite of what Metude tells me, it feels similar.

However, at times, it's as though if I give Donna every minute of the day, she would just want and need more. Thankfully, she is under professional care in hospital and I am re-evaluating the situation and the other responsibilities in my life. My lesson is that no matter what, I must maintain life-giving boundaries for myself.

And I should have known this lesson, having taught classes on personal boundaries at The Center and trained hospice workers at the hospital. The airlines have it right—the parent puts on the oxygen mask before the child. Plus, I can't give away what I do not have.

A week later - a quarter of a century gone into child-rearing

August 28/86 I am up before the sun. I went out here on the cement to observe this "sailors take warning" with this red sunrise coming up over Potato Island. One waits and waits and if one blinks, it's missed. How like life. I haven't blinked, and here are those magenta, purple streaks threading the sky. The gulls are also seeking the shore for shelter. When Roger and I sat out here last night, there were some ducks' heads bobbing up and down, like notes on a music sheet. A quarter of a century has gone into child-rearing and parent-rearing. As a parent, on both accounts, I am satisfied with the job. I developed alongside the children. Dev leaves in a few weeks for the west.. He is our last child to leave home. Haley will be leaving soon, too. Callie has already left. Our two youngest, gone. It is a good thing we don't feel the full impact, as life will be duller without them. And Doug is more gone than ever. He says, "I am coming to your home." The emphasis being on "your." We feel utterly blessed by these children of ours and oh, how we are going to miss them!

The Second Fall & Winter

We Are Being Brought into an Awareness of What Is Only a Dim Reality to Humans.

THE SEAS ARE HIGH ~ AND THE SAILBOAT MOVES IN HARMONY

Sept. 20/86 Saturday night. The smell of baked beans is wafting up from the kitchen. Roger is napping, and we are the only ones home in this wonderful noon-time storm. He just finished putting the winter wood in the shed yesterday. Cotton cat is sitting here on the sill, looking out the window and seemingly watching the Spitfire (our thirty-two-foot sloop) strain against the mooring. Like the old guy at the wharf said the other day about sailing: the sea and the sailboat have to move with each other in harmony. Pam also told me yesterday, "You are one of the great gifts of my life." That makes me feel bad; my lack of tolerance for her constant state of crisis frays me.

I encouraged her to take the family on a camping trip last week. I thought the vacation might do them all some good. However, it was their first and now I expect their last. It rained all the time. Yet the good news is

*that she is eager for a visit with Metude.
Maybe that is what my ancient friend
means when she says the negative can have
a purpose.*

DEATH IS BUT AN OPPORTUNITY TO STUMBLE INTO A LARGER REALITY

Fall Melancholy ~ A Universal Transition

Maple trees at the end of September in Nova Scotia offered landscape painters a brilliant harvest of red, yellow, and orange. Abby and I go down the shore to a little fishing village, set up our easels on the wharf, and paint for a few hours. One morning last week, halfway through a painting, I felt a sudden surge of sadness. I was so overwhelmed that I thought maybe I was going to die.

The experience of sadness stayed with me the rest of the day. I am not a moody person. The emotion was unexplainable—definitely a question for my discarnate friend. And thank goodness, Pam needed to have some questions asked as well.

The Pulse of Nature

My old friend settles in easily. We have greetings and she is, of course, already aware that I need to talk with her; she nods in her all-knowing way. *I feel her compassion, thankfully.*

"Metude, what happened on the wharf?" *She needs no further explanation.*

"Indeed," is her instant response. "You were fine-tuned and receptive, much like a clear channel or frequency. The experience was not bidden." *No, it surely wasn't.*

"Does the experience refer to my coming death?" *As death is what it felt like, not Metude's seemingly lighter version of "passing over."*

"Your understanding is not fully clear. Go back over it. Your own emotion divorced the information. Your interpretation, but not necessarily a physical death. Again, emotion coloured it and cut off the real information." *Oh, this is what she told me when Fran and I misinterpreted the car accident image. Our emotions distorted the message.*

Without pausing, she adds, "Another word for death is transition." *Hmm, but sometimes it just feels like death.*

"Then why was I sad on the dock?" *I felt like crying.*

"One moved into a general stream of consciousness, a universal transition. One moved into melancholy. Don't think person, think a universal transition, summer to fall, a universal stream, melancholy. You were without awareness. You chose it as your own or thought it was your sadness when it was the pulse of nature. To everything there is a season, which in this season is interpreted as melancholy, a general wind-down in nature. You are susceptible, sensitive to universal vibrations."

This wise, old cottage woman continues her instruction. *And I am loving it.* "Death, your interpretation, is but an opportunity to stumble into a larger reality. It was done through emotion. Yours is a limited scope of understanding. One needs to develop scope-vision in order to see the interplay and connection. That is how all are a part of one. Each is in tune; all things are in tune with the same vibrational frequency. You panicked. There is not the adjustment to what you term as death."

Oh, she's right. I have no wish to leave those I love or this beautiful world, no matter how much faith I have that there is "life after death." I want to stay right here.

She nods, and I feel her caring as she observes, "It is a progressive journey—leaving what one has known. You melded with another frequency on the wharf. Each has its own vibrational frequency, yet all one and the same, simultaneously. A higher learning. It is as one expands that there are new learnings and a new knowing. One has but to reach."

Is she saying the trees and the fields on the distant hill feel the life changing in them for the coming winter? Is this the universal emotional vibration that I stumbled into?

One Does Not Grow Overnight ~ It Is in Your Seeking

"How do you reach and what do you reach for?" *I ask, knowing I am out of my depth.*

"That altered state. They (enlightened beings) live that altered state, again what you call death. Reach out with your mind. Information is given as you are ready."

"How does one get ready?"

"Let the mind go. Allow one's being freedom to fly. One might deliberately listen to silence, to nature. Allow one's being to move in tune with freedom in the silence, much as in meditation done outdoors—outdoor space and universal vibration. When outside, that allows the freedom of being. Then the universal frequency is more attainable."

"Do I go out daily?" *She pauses and is looking at me with compassion or possibly sympathy for my limitations.*

Then, she quietly states, "One does not grow overnight. It is in your seeking. It does not happen by chance. Rigidity of structure closes out opportunity for other learning. You have been given a glimpse. You have enough to assimilate."
Thank goodness, as it's a struggle to strain for some glimmer of understanding. Again, it feels like another language.

"Yah, indeed, we will proceed."

Ah, my turn to say, "good."

Pam wants me to ask about her health. It is still giving her trouble and we are running out of visit time.

My ancient friend is quick to reply, "To do with the lining of the uterus. A specialist has the ability to listen and hear. Wise to rest. Avoid fatigue. Will feel more up and down. Use the mind positively. Wise to watch blood levels—blood count drops lower. Need not to be alarmed. Doctor will suggest removing uterus." *Metude must have been waiting for this question.*

I interrupt. "Can we do anything to heal her uterus?" *I'm thinking about prayer.*

"Will not prevent the ultimate outcome—removal of the organ." *She is emphatic. Interesting, how come she doesn't tell us to pray for the healing of it?*

When I told Pam what our old friend had recommended, she was quiet, then nodded and said okay. She continued to put off going to the doctor. She ignored her symptoms until it became a crisis just before Christmas.

In a Coma ~ the Person Is Weak, Thus the Prayer Can Transfer Too Much Energy

I continue to the next person I need her wisdom for. "Metude, Tom, my minister friend, called this morning, asking me about a woman who was hit by a car yesterday. She is in a coma. While he was holding her hand and praying by her bedside, she became restless. The machines she was hooked to started to beep so loudly that it scared him, and he stopped. He wondered if I might know what happened. I am not sure why he felt that I would know, but I thought it might be a good question for you. What did happen to the machines?"

I love being able to ask her what goes on behind the scenes. It seems such a vast trove of knowledge.

"It was a transfer of energy."

"Was the woman aware of him praying? Was it good?" *Praying is always good, I should think.*

"The person is weak. He must be careful." *Oh, I never thought of being careful. Can I pray too much? I have always prayed as hard as I could—squeezing God like an orange to extract the last bit of healing.*

Needing a little reassurance for my own approach to healing prayer, I ask tentatively and hopefully, "Tom's energy is good, though. He needs to continue praying, yes?"

"Yah indeed, but he must put more distance between them."

"Then he shouldn't take her hand? Can he be in the same room with her and pray?"

Metude, being a woman of few words, states plainly, "More distance." *Now, what does "more distance" mean?*

This is probably what she means when she states I have to apparently listen to that "small, still voice" inside me that is so hard to hear. Most times I can't. I wish the spirit, or someone, would say the words out loud in my head instead of me having to sense the answers.

Was this ancient woman there in the hospital room? She instantly knows what Tom was referring to. I bet she even knows what the woman was feeling. Maybe he shouldn't have assumed that she needed prayer, or to have her hand help. Plus, he needed to listen first and sense what was really needed. Maybe he was sitting too close to her and Metude literally does mean distance.

Besides, how does a transfer of energy work? Our prayer really must have power if it can affect machines and people! Describing prayer as a transfer of energy seems to make more sense. Just normally, if someone comes in the room in a bad mood, others feel it. So why wouldn't focusing healing-light on someone be felt? I know she is not going to answer these questions this time.

Presence Must Be Called Forth, What to Humans Is a Dim Reality

Next, I ask my usual question, "What do I need to do to increase my spirituality?" *She must get tired of me asking this, but always seems glad to respond.*

We sit in silence, then she nods as she starts to rock, "Yah, indeed, practise the Presence." She smiles enigmatically. *But I already do that.* "It is not that you neglect or devalue. It's the attention. Presence must be called forth, honoured, given dimension to fit with one's values. It must be given dimension to be made tangible. Presence is a love reality." *Yes, I know this faceless love that permeates my days, the people around me, the sea, trees, and birds.*

"Encourage and call Presence forth, rather than it just being in you or you for it. Love it, glory in it. Do it with your being."

"Well, how much time should I give it?" *I feel let down as I already sit twice a day. That, apparently, is not enough.*

She leans toward me. "As you wish. Presence must be called forth. It is not enough that one would contain it within themselves. Presence must be given tangible witness; thus, it gains full value. You gain. To contain it is not enough. Must be given tangible expression, felt in love. Rejoicing provides a needed aspect. Rejoicing, moving, sharing, that's the combination—is one and the same." *Although somewhat reserved, I do celebrate Presence in my being.*

Again, nodding, she continues talking. "Expression will come. You have done that in the past. You are merely being brought to a more concentrated knowledge that it is good to bring it out. Give love recognition. You are being brought into awareness of what to humans is a dim reality."

Yes, no matter how much love I experience, I cannot seem to break the barriers to a less dim reality, except for this cottage woman who sits before me. My veil is just too thick.

"So how does one live from all dimensions, Metude?"

"All one and the same. Not necessarily verbal. A physical calling. Hold Presence up front, rejoice in it, honour it, recognize, and expand it. Not enough to live in it or be of it. Call it forth. Give it that recognition, hold it. Presence is much larger." *There must be a subtlety I am not getting, but as she says, one does not grow overnight. Quite true!*

"We will proceed." *Oh, she is not going to tell me. Probably I need to develop more before I can understand it.*

Increasing a Bond After Passing ~ What You Call Times of Learning

Switching to my next question, I ask, "Abby's father died when she was seventeen. She was close to him and now finds herself thinking of him a lot. What is going on there?"

Metude nods, "A bond, one of increasing awareness, one may promote it by turning one's thoughts toward him. Must realign thoughts of death. The father is not removed from her."

Yes, and even though I know there is life after death and this cottage woman is sitting right before me, I still feel my grandmother is gone.

"What about my grandmother?"

"With her being, she is very good. That is what counts." *Hmm, that sounds qualified. I wonder if there are other parts of her that might not be as good? I don't like the thought.*

I was also concerned about our finances, as the cost of living was increasing and our budget was stretched. So, I ask Metude what our budget looked like from her side. She shifts in the rocker. "What you call a time of learning? No need to struggle or fear. No need to worry about what you call finances." *Maybe she means that I need to put my trust in a larger spirit in the invisible to handle it. Oh, that's easy to say yet, hard to live, at times.*

The rocking stops, Pam must be ready to come back. Then, feeling filled with gratitude just sitting before my wise, old friend I say, "I am so thankful for you, Metude."

And with kindness, she offers, "You are not away from me. I am with you as you walk, and in your silence as you sit. There is not a barrier that exists between. And good is your listening. Notice Presence outdoors. Peace be with you and yours. The body is impatient."

Again, face, neck, and hand muscles are rearranged, and Pam opens her eyes. With a good stretch, she is back. She told me later that when she got home, one of her children had just been dropped off by the school bus earlier than expected. So, that must have been why she ended the visit sooner than we had planned.

NATURE HAS FEELINGS

Sept. 29/86 Every day is more awe-filled. I understand now what happened on the wharf a bit better. I can tune into the universal frequency vibration. And imagine, nature has feelings! Oh yes, I need to let my mind go, as I am beginning to understand: We each have our own vibration, and so does everyone and everything else. Plus, physical death is what Metude and those like her call "transition." I'll think about this more.

Yesterday, driving to Mother's, I looked at the trees with a new awareness. I tried to let my mind go into them. They looked a little different. Yet, I did feel the impact of the colours and texture of the trees slightly differently.

A day later . . .

Sept. 30/86 Graves Island. (a provincial park about twenty miles from home.) Just set up my easel. Sun, wind, beautiful fall colour. Roger has gone off to buy a bluenose sloop, which he has wanted for some time. I am here till dark, painting, reflecting, rejoicing, and journaling. What a gift of time. I love sitting here with the sea breeze flipping my hair, listening to the lap of waves, smelling the salt, with nothing else to do but paint. No one will interrupt. I have another hour of light.

Pam was in a lot of pain yesterday and said, "This is the core of it. He doesn't love me. How far does that fact go back?" I never see her cry, even with all she deals with, but she did when she articulated that. Personally, I think he does care for her, but in a crooked sort of way, as much as he can. Anyway, it took a metaphorical battering ram to get her in touch with as much as she did. Metude stayed way back. We each have our own human-lesson work. And even though our invisible friends can help, they can't do it for us.

• • •

A Past Life and How It Seeps Through ~ An Experience

When Pam dropped in for tea early in October, we talked about our children as the kitchen woodstove fought the fall chill. At some point, I began to feel the energy in the room change slightly, like a ripple of electricity over my body. The cat, which was sleeping on the mat before the kitchen sink, erratically streaked for the dining room, slid on the turn and skittered on to the living room as if having a fit. It disappeared under the sofa. I came back and looked at Pam as she said (exactly what I was thinking), "Weird."

We both laughed, nervously—it was like having two dimensions to be aware of and having one foot on this side in our humanity and three toes in the other one, something I couldn't understand. Yet, in spite of the fact that the cottage woman is a part of the latter, her companionship is a strength and comfort. At least I can talk to someone about these things after the fact.

Then Pam suddenly stopped rocking. Looking down at her hands, she began talking.

"I see a young man in candlelight, writing. His hair is long and falling over his collar. The suit he has on is not what men wear today. I see this big floppy tie."

She paused between sentences, as if she was taking her time observing him and seemed in another stream of consciousness. "He lives alone, but the loneliness is okay for him. He loves to be outside, to walk, and be at one with whatever is. He has dark hair, brown eyes, and he is very thin. There is sadness in his eyes, but not for a physical reason. There is soulfulness in his sadness, yet a wholeness. He writes constantly about everything he lives. His entire being is in his journal which is much more than a diary."

Suddenly, she looked straight at me saying, "You know, this person feels like you, like your essence." Then, in what obviously was an altered state, she carried on, "I see journals, books with leather covers. One has a green binding with a burgundy spine. He is writing in black ink. The lines are narrow." She paused, "Oh, 1783 is in a copperplated script on the cover of a book."

"Really! Where are you? Can you hear or see a name of a place?"

She cocked her head as if trying to make it out, "Leon?"

The only Leon we knew was my art teacher who lived down the road.

Then it dawned on me. "Do you mean *Lyon,* as in the city in France?"

"Yes, Lyon, but I think I am in the 1700s." She says slowly, staring off at a past unseen yet seen.

Not satisfied, I probed. "Who is this person? Does he have a name?"

Struggling, she said, "Mart-ess, no, I think Marcus. Now he is walking back and forth, book in hand, before a classroom of young men. However, he is not understood, which causes him a great deal of pain."

"What does he talk to them about?"

"Has not the freedom to discuss what he really wants to talk about. The philosophy of the textbook stifles what he knows in his seeking. He knows there is so much more than what is in the book. He is not allowed to expand, that is his biggest pain. And he knows there is no time." Her voice was agitated.

"What do you mean, no time?"

"His nose bleeds a lot, and I can feel his chest." Pam's hand went to her chest and frowned. "There is like a weight sitting on it. He's cold, even on the nicest day, always cold, always chilled in the dampness. I think he has consumption. He is putting his pen down. All his energy is gone." It was like a sadness entered the kitchen.

My friend paused, sighed, and leaned forward. I waited. Her voice caught. "Oh, he dies alone in the little room." I felt her emotion for him. I waited and then asked her if she saw anything else. After another pause, she nodded, "A gravestone." She took more time, then states, "October 1783, 24 years. There was not a lot of pain, but he was very tired." And almost under her breath, she added, "This is inadequately put by me."

We talked a bit afterward, but we really had no insights. The cat wandered back in the kitchen. However, I couldn't wait to check this Marcus out with the cottage woman.

A Past Life Experience ~ Rather Than a Past Life

I ask in the next unplanned visit with the cottage woman if we really had stumbled into a past life? Smiling slightly, after a pause, she nods saying, "I am aware." *Hmm, I think that might be a yes.*

"If so, what happened to him after he died?"

"A convalescent time, a time of absolute rest. Then analysis, missed points, and deciding. Remember, there is but one life with continuous life experiences." *So, all our lifetimes are really just experiences of one larger life. That's an interesting perspective.*

Then I ask about his writings. After a moment, as if she has to go somewhere to get the answer, she nods again, "They still exist, but are neglected and undiscovered." *Does paper even last that long? Hmm, yes of course, in libraries.*

"Are his writings of any use?"

"Historically speaking, a record of one man's journey. However, we refer to it as a life experience rather than a past life."

I ask, "How can we experience our past life experiences?"

"To re-experience, use your own mind." She instructs. "Vibration of emotion is what lasts the longest and is the strongest from another life experience. Very few moments last. Life experiences are short but seemingly long according to the experience itself. We refer to it as life experience rather than past life as a continuous learning experience." *Of course, I cannot learn every soul lesson in one lifetime for sure. Odd though how we might naturally think that.*

The visit is brief. Her words don't lend a lot of clarity, yet our experience of Marcus added more weight to the possibility of past-life experiences.

• • •

A New Name ~ You Were Brought to It

For the last several years when saying my name, I would think, "Something is missing. My name doesn't feel complete." The feeling was becoming stronger, so I started testing out different surnames for myself: my father's name, my grandfather's name, but none of them felt right. Then, after months of living lightly with the question, yesterday I wrote, "This morning when I woke, looked at the sun streaming through the window, and eureka! I knew. My new name will be Augusta, my grandmother's name. Well, what an astonishing surprise! How did this happen? Yesterday I had one name, now I have another. I am amazed at how belonging it instantly feels."

Later I wrote, "When Roger came in the door for supper, I announced, 'I have my new name. Can you guess what it is?' I gave him a hint. 'It is not a surname.'

He paused, then looked at me with a twinkle, and I got my second shock of the day as he replied, 'Augusta.'

'How did you know?'

He laughed and shrugged his shoulders saying, 'I don't know.' I assured him I was not changing my surname, but merely adding 'Augusta' to my married name, as I didn't want him to think I didn't like his. With a grin, he hugged me and asked when he could pick up the papers to make it legal. I was delighted, relieved, and thankful. Plus, I couldn't wait to ask the cottage woman what she thought of it."

YAH, A GREAT BOLD
A ~ A NEW NAME

Pam drops in on her way home from town. I inquire if she has a couple of minutes to ask the cottage woman about my name. She is as curious as me, and our old friend enters with relative ease. As soon as I hear "Proceed," I excitedly announce, "Metude, I have a new name. It's Augusta." *She probably already knows.*

"Yah, a great bold A. It is done." She retorts spritely, then adds, "It was already changed." *Oh, interesting, I wonder if she means on the other side. She seemed amused at my announcement.* "You were brought to it—integrity and firmness based in gentleness, love, and strength. You do not just teach—you enlighten." She lowered her head, then pointed her finger at me saying, "It is hard, a hard role." *I feel her gravitas. Hmm, I wonder why.*

Then she adds almost as an afterthought, "Your name goes a long way back." *Is she telling me, before my grandmother?* I can't ask her as Pam doesn't have time so, thanking her, the energy shifts, Pam opens her eyes, and I am thankful for even the drop-in visit.

During the years since, in working with others, I have often had occasion to think of her words about how hard the role can be at times. Yet, I am aware of the privilege of doing my own growth work and of walking with others in theirs. Light has a way of burning dross, those unhealthy ways of thinking and being not only in others. It also can burn the hand that holds it and certainly has, at times, as it exposed my own spiritual dross, my own need for more emotional and spiritual development.

Also, taking on a new name was a significant starting point for living "the rest of my life." Little did I know it was a precursor to my subsequent spiritual-feminist journey, but also a "firming up" of my walk into a larger universe of experience, an awareness of invisible helpers, and just how present and how caring those on the other side are.

Space, Water, and Gods ~ Here, I Am Home

> *Oct. 16/86 I have not seen Doug, our oldest since summer, and I was missing him. Roger could not get away, so I am here in Quebec for a short visit with him myself.*
> *Doug had some work to do today at the university. We walked in old town last night. Streets are narrow, old stone buildings, and some were built more than a century ago. It's great seeing him; one-on-one time is always special. We had supper at a Greek restaurant, and then we had a good talk. He likes my new name. Thank goodness. Now*

everyone in the family knows and seems to be more than fine with it.
He and a friend live in two rooms, almost in the rougher part of the city. In comparison, Seaforth feels like paradise. So much space, silence, land, house, cottage, and the absolute oceanic beauty we live in.
We had a great visit. So good just to spend a few days with him on his own. Heading home tomorrow, back to live more gracefully and to learn more about how to do that, to paint daily, and to have enough space to practise the art of wonder in the morning. The latter, though, is a bit optimistic.

The next day . . .

Oct. 17/86 Arrived home. How soul-satisfying. I went for a long walk along the shore. Space, water, and the gods. Here I am. However, I was dead tired and dead asleep when Donna called at 12:15 a.m. She is on the edge again. After I pulled myself awake, we talked—or rather, she talked. This feels hopeless to me. I also find Pam unhappy, with a bad crisis between her and Frank. Her shoulders were slumped when walking across the field to go home.

THE OTHER SIDE IS SEPARATE, BUT MUCH THE SAME AS YOURS

Coma ~ She Feels Her Family's Despondency, It Takes Her Energy

Pam drops in for a visit that I arranged earlier. The cottage woman settles in nicely. I am always so thankful to see her. My first question is from Tom, who had previously asked me about the woman that was in a coma because of a car accident. He called again this morning after several weeks, telling me she is still in a coma. The family is losing hope.

Tom sometimes comments on the wisdom he receives. When he wonders where the wisdom comes, I tell him, "It's got something to do with the Spirit we hang out with, an inner source if you like." We both laugh, yet he seems to accept that and acts on it without further explanation.

My wise friend is silent. *Maybe she is going to the hospital room herself to assess the situation.* Then nodding her head, she begins, "The one is aware. Touching her, she is aware. Must have positive thoughts or it takes her energy. It also lessens her will to live. Touching her superficially does, too. It suppresses her to have negative feelings in the room. They may not be verbally expressed, but she senses the discouragement of others. Got to touch her, brush her hair. For that woman, your community can help, too. Crucial. She is aware. Going to lose her when they don't have to. That woman knows. She feels, senses the despondency. It doesn't have to happen. Only touch her when they are feeling positive."

Metude is emphatic, "She is in trouble. She is giving up. Touch her only when centred and not despondent. She hears even though she is way back. She would respond if the right person is centred. It is like she is saying, 'Listen to me. Come listen to me.' Give her that energy. She is aware, we needn't allow this to happen. Disappointment in the room has to be changed. She doesn't have to die; she's got a chance." *So, the other side needs us to pray or, as Reese Howell would put it, God needs us to pray.*

"Oh, thank you, Metude. This is such important information. I'll pass it on."

I then ask, "What does the coming year look like?"

"You will be given broadening areas that you will perceive as new. One does not need to search (people) out. Proceed." *Quite right, and that I never do.*

Presence ~ Masters from All Parts of the World Know the Techniques

My next question for my ancient friend is about my progress in practising the Presence: the daily or more constant awareness of this divine spirit I am immersed in.

She responds, thoughtfully, "Yah, 'tis coming. Again, just a gentle reminder to call it forth. It's taken away when one struggles. Merely call it forth. Live it. 'Tis coming, a new awareness. There is much to be offered yet. Must be content for the moment. It is yet to be fully settled into. When one needs to call it forth, that will come."

I still did not really understand what she meant about my "rejoicing" needing more attention. So, I looked the word up in the dictionary, which did not enlighten me. However, instead of sitting silently in my joy, I am trying to be more active. I did a little two-step here and there when I felt it, but I don't think that is what she means, as it feels fake. I ask, "How is my rejoicing coming?" *I expect it's thumbs down.*

She looks slightly amused. "'Tis coming. Utilize your breathing. Do it more often. Be aware. Must be much centred. Masters from all parts of the world know the techniques. Must be aware of being loving. *Odd, when she says this, I always think I am. Plus, it's interesting that I need to connect rejoicing more with Presence.*

In light of Pam's family stress, her uterus problems, and the emotional strain of Frank's continued resistance, I ask, "Are you well, Metude?" *How can she be when she enters Pam's body, and it is in such turmoil?*

She nods, "Well is more of a state of mind. Yah indeed, I maintain a good state. Same thing happens here in human life. The space occupied is much as yours. Not as you understand, but our life is much the same. It merely exists on a different frequency. We will proceed." *Hmm, she is not going to discuss it further, probably because she knows my limits.*

A Guide Is Assigned on the Other Side to Each Person ~ Do Not Let Mistakes Cripple

This reminds me of the human development program at The Center next week. The focus will be on interpersonal relationships and meditation which does happen at different frequencies. And, as always, these programs make me nervous beforehand. Yet now, thank God, I have the cottage woman to consult with.

She is quick to respond, "Do not be afraid to make mistakes. Don't let your mistakes cripple or destroy your effort. Do not let mistakes cripple or destroy your freedom or joy. Take your time. All of us, we are ahead of you already." *Really? Oh, I love that. How blessed are we who know we have helpers in the invisible!*

"How does that happen, Metude?"

"A guide/helper is already assigned on the other side to each person. The participants have been dealt with. They come prepared. Expect it." *Oh, they are prepared before Dave (the other leader) and I even meet with them. Imagine.*

"You are to remember you are in leadership. Must feel it, lead into it, hold the tension. Must have confidence in yourself and walk with assurance and love. People are ready to make significant moves. You must be very aware of being loving. Walk in love. You do not do these things by yourself." *How many times have you told me this?*

However, it is different hearing about it each time. It is shocking to realize how much help they give us humans and we are not even aware they exist for the most part. God just simply has been too far up in the sky.

She continues, "Be alert to each section, to each segment, each person. Know they are fledglings. You are a bit like a mother bird. Every moment has meaning, every step, every breath. Be very sensitive to air, light; it engulfs and enfolds you, even the touch of air. Every raindrop has meaning." *I love what I am hearing. And this applies to my human lessons, to daily living, and to everyone I meet.*

You Are Like a Child Growing Wings ~ There is Another Side That Is Not Separate

Then I ask about a meditation technique I call "walking awareness," which I do to relax and centre myself in between sessions. It is downtime and inward time. I ask her, "Has my walking awareness improved?"

"Make every step count," she confirms. "Breathe. Every moment has meaning. One is very sensitive to air, to the light that engulfs, and enfolds one, even to the touch of the air. Every touch of a snowflake, every raindrop has meaning." *I love this spirit woman.*

She continues, "Turn inward, great joy, abundant joy awaits you. Resign yourself to the lot that has been chosen for you." *Is she referring to my wishing the reality of the other side was more visible for me?*

So, I ask, "What do you mean?"

"You'll know," she assures me. "Be aware that the accessibility is there. Shift positioning. Remember and it will be back. Not necessary to let joy go. One does not have to be positioned; one must only remember." *That there is another side, another reality that is not separate from us humans. Hmm, that's hard to realize.*

Metude stops rocking, I check my watch. Pam has an appointment. I thank this wise woman for coming and I certainly feel like a fledgling myself and hopefully am growing wings to take flight. *I'd hug her if she had a human body and was more on my level.*

Then on a flood of feeling I hear, "Yah, indeed, love and joy to you and yours. We will meet again soon." *And she is gone. Thank God it's only for the time being.*

THE MANY-ING AND ONE-ING OF GOD ~ THE COTTAGE WOMAN SEEMS TO BE ONE OF THE MANY-ING

Oct. 20/86 I have been in Presence since waking and it's seemingly a more constant state, thank goodness. Presence is truly the gentleness of calls and the turning "in" to this loveliness as I write this. Thomas Kelly, the Quaker, continues to speak to me in his little book, A Testament of Devotion: "The horizons I have wanted to break through have been breaking and showing me wonderful vistas. There is as much mystery to the many-ing of God, as there is the one-ing . . ." And Metude, you resonate with this depth of understanding. You seem to be one of the many-ing of the One he refers to. And imagine, I can meet with you in the flesh. Well, sort of.
Thought of Dev most of the day. His first time away. Hope he could feel it. Roger and I were in a fun energy at supper and had the

best conversation. I told him about Metude again. He likes to hear about her, but still is not ready to see her.

Pam is learning about the psychology of being an abused wife. We didn't even know there was such a concept until recently. Men just naturally ruled, and women obeyed. The knowledge itself is painful for her. Having met Frank when she was fourteen, she has always been under his thumb.

I don't know why he allows her the freedom with me, other than the fact that he likes both Roger and me. Yet, aside from his demons which we don't see, we like him. He always comes across as a nice guy. However, I know too much and quite frankly consider him possibly dangerous. She stopped the physical abuse a decade ago, but he is into guns and, at times, even I keep looking out our driveway! I trust that Metude would warn me if necessary.

A week later ~ Roger's first boat, the mini Augusta

Oct. 27/86 I walked the beach in the first snowstorm of the season this afternoon. The wind was fierce. It's rattling the windows as I write. The grey storm clouds hovered on the horizon. The snow cut into my nose and cheeks. The gulls were huddled down on the rocks, facing into the blizzard. Then, suddenly, there was a white-out. I did well to get back to the house. Oh, but that new sheepskin fur hat with its side flaps wrapped right down around my chin did the trick. At least my head was warm.

I could feel Roger loving me last evening as we were sitting watching TV. It has been with me all day. This morning, it was so explicit I called him at the office to tell him. Too often those "ten thousand things" can keep me from feeling the feel of it. We do have a wonderful mutuality.

He wants to build his own boats, little ones at first. Seaforth Boat Works is the name he has chosen. A sign would be a good Christmas gift. Iron might weather better than wood. He says he is calling the first boat, "the Mini Augusta," a two-station rowboat. We both had a laugh. And he would!

A GAUGE OF INTUITION ~ AN OPENING TO A MAIN AREA OF WORK

Waiting for Pam to arrive for our visit with Metude, I glance out the cottage window and am brought to stillness—sun setting, banks of snow, indigo-blue water—all absolutely motionless in its own beauty, so vivid in this late, velvet-dark, afternoon light. All of it strikes me in mid-moment with an acute feeling of this love which holds everything.

Metude comes in relatively easily. We exchange greetings. I need her assessment of the workshop at the Center. I was disappointed with parts of the program. After all the excellent advice she gave me in our last visit, I fell short. *Good thing she told me not to be afraid of my mistakes.* After she settles in the rocker, I lament, "Too many times, I didn't listen to my inner voice, and too often lost the feeling of being in Presence. Thus, parts of the program felt flat and uninspired."

A Matter of Listening and Sense Feeling

I wait. She sits in silence as if pondering my conclusion, then shifting slightly in the rocker and pointing her forefinger at me, she states, "Not as it appears. Must have trust and confidence. It went as it should. You worked well. A matter of listening. When you feel doubt, go back to listening immediately. Go immediately to listening. Sound it out through listening. Much as in checking the gauge, the gauge of intuition. Rely on the instruments and instruction given to you.

"The gauge of intuition is a connection, as in listening. Stop and check it. Have confidence. It is not always what the human eye perceives. Trust that you give your best efforts, then the program will proceed. You overreacted and didn't check it out. Listen, sense-feel while working with the participants. Hone these areas. You are understanding now." *Sometimes I wonder if I ever will.*

Your Energy Gauge Is a Tool ~ One Must Practise for the Tool to Be Utilized

This second gauge I was given before Metude entered our lives. For years, after a heavy program at The Center or even counselling, I felt lethargic. One afternoon, I had asked Pam for an image of my loss of energy. She saw a temperature gauge divided into three sections. The lower third, which was in red, was where my energy level was that day. The guides, talking through her, told me, "You must control your energy. Do not let it drop into the lower third of the gauge for that is a dangerous area."

I ask Metude how I am doing in that area. "An area you have almost conquered. Your energy gauge is a tool now. Your energy will increase by conscious breathing and walking. One merely needs to practise for the tool to be utilized. There is an opportunity for more awareness of one's lack of sense-feeling and over-reaction. Continue learning in the midst of struggle. Stop*,* sense-feel, much like getting directions. When you feel you are off, stop, pull back, and sense-feel for direction. Your energy is good. Does require work, but you will work in freedom. You are being well-led."
That I am and she's referring to more than just the program.

Go Back to the Original Pain ~ Other Areas Will Follow

Fran had also attended her first human development program at The Center last week. She met someone she knew from the private school she was forced to go to as a child. Somehow, it brought back the pain she felt from the years of abandonment and attacks by her mother.

Apparently, every long weekend, she would pack all her bags, wait by the side of the road and hope her parents would not send her back after the holiday. They always did. Now, years later, meeting this woman from that school, she was so emotionally upset that she could not continue the program. The pain she experienced was exactly like the raw pain she felt those nights she was driven back to school. This pain was overshadowing the present, as it did with me several months ago with my friends who went off on a day trip without inviting me. I ask my wise old friend about Fran's extreme emotional reaction to this woman she hardly knew.

"It is an opening to the main area of her work, which is connected to the other areas you have been working with, such as self-worth and relationships. One must explore the area. It is a new area of intensity, but key to many areas." *Ah, I suppose it is referring to the image of the stake in her chest.*

Being anxious to help I ask, "What can I do?"

"As a mother to a child, you must go back to the original pain. Other areas will follow. Be alert and see the connections as they are brought up. You are to call forth that which has been opened. In the private school, she got the true feeling of its pain. Find where the pain originates. Have her identify what type of pain: fear, loss, rejection, or abandonment. Don't allow her to shut it off. Call it forth. Identify the pain."

"Can I do that? She has made it plain she doesn't want me asking questions in this area, so I am a little leery."

"You are ready." My old friend assures me. "Your friendship will carry it. Be assured that you are listening and getting the moves." *Thank God for the lesson in active listening because this could be rough for both of us without it.*

Then she shifts in the rocker, adding, "Much was accomplished at the workshop. Yah, 'tis good. Many doors have been opened; many lives have been touched." Then, she tilts her head toward me and cautions, "One must not neglect the role of those left at home." *Hmm, well, my kids sure don't need any more of my time, but I wonder about Roger.*

Roger loves to hear about what we all do, and I also tell him about Metude and my work with people, as much as privacy allows. He is always interested, encouraging, and gives insightful comments. However, he is clam-like about his own emotions. And it is not that I haven't asked. He seems to live through the children's and my life, but does he live his own? I wonder. Family activities are an integral part of our life. Living on a country road we have been basically our own entertainment.

Often, when I ask Metude about him visiting her, she reassures me he is growing his readiness. I could feel that she always thought he was special. Last week I asked again, and she assured me, "Ah, as his readiness develops." At least, that was encouraging. Yet, I am still puzzled about her comment.

Set Up a Regular, Rhythmic Pattern of Prayer ~ The Other Will Set Up to Receive

Bringing my attention back to the visit and remembering Tom and the woman in the coma, I ask if my inner visit while praying for the woman was real and if the community praying was helpful. Tom had passed on Metude's information from the October visit to her family. Whoever visited her had to become more positive, as their heaviness was making it harder for her to come back.

One day, while praying for her, I had a different experience. I seemed to be in a liquid, and I felt myself swimming down-down which took considerable effort until I reached what I felt was her. She was just lying there, which reminded me of a dead fish floating at the bottom of the ocean. Yet, I sensed her as being aware of me. After trying to stay down where she was, an indescribable light and caring gradually seemed to join us. I proceeded to talk with her in what felt like liquid love—encouraging her to come back into life and rejoin the people who love her.

I relate my experience to Metude. She is quiet, then nods, "The Entity is benefiting and receiving more energy. Listen, other opportunities may arise. You have no other role except the calling forth of energy. As you would term it, the praying worked. Beneficial if you would get over your own reservations. Relax, be receptive. Set up a regular, rhythmic pattern of energy rather than unexpected surges. Human body will set itself up to receive. When one is centred, it is intensity rather than time. We would proceed."

My old friend's words were also an important confirmation for me for another reason, the last time I visited my father was the day before he died. He was in a coma. I was going to speak at his funeral and, among other things, I would say that I believed his life would continue.

Yet, I needed to tell him privately while he might have some possibility of hearing. He lay comatose, without sound or movement. I was nervous. As I talked to him, he began to stir, becoming more restless and uttering sounds I couldn't understand. I left the room wishing and wondering if he had heard. Now, I think that maybe he did.

Then she adds, "And now there is much impatience to get on with preparations for the holidays. I did enjoy the visit and will remain with you in your hearts. Light and joy be with you and yours. An enjoyable visit." I thank her, and Pam begins to stretch.

The Cottage Woman

• • •

Attempting to X-ray the Physical Body

The family of the woman in a coma apparently responded well to Tom's suggestions, or rather Metude's, about changing their energies before visiting her and even touching her. The woman came out of the coma not long after. Relief and affirmation flooded through all of us. A year later, I heard she was living a normal life in another province. I expect she has no memory of our "visit in liquid," but I will never forget the experience.

A week later, Tom called about his ill brother. He asked me to scan his body and apparently assumed I could! I told him that I was not gifted in that area. Being rather desperate, he encouraged me to try.

After we had hung up, I struggled to see inside of him. I tried to ignore the voice within me that said that I couldn't do it. After several tries, I started with his head and scanned downward. It all looked like a person-shaped cloud. After a time, there seemed to be two areas cloudier than the rest of what I assumed must be his brother's body. Not believing it could possibly be real, I tried again later and saw the same locations. So, I passed on the information with repetitive cautions that it might be just my imagination.

A week later, Tom called to tell me that the hospital test had detected cancer in those two areas. I could hear Metude pointing out that we often don't know what we can do until we try. As she said, "If you need proof, go for proof." I still felt it was somewhat of a fluke, so I only scanned a few more times.

In relation to the gauges, the inner energy gauge became very important. I would still get myself overbooked, yet the gauge in my mind's eye faithfully revealed whether my energy had slipped into the red, lower third, much like reading a thermometer to see if you had a fever. I found I could raise it with concentration or getting more rest. Eventually, it dawned on me, after a few years, that I rarely felt tired and had no need for it, except on rare occasions.

Grandmother's Ring Arrives ~ A New Name and a New Ring

A few days later, I walked along our maple-arched lane to check the mailbox. A little package was there. I opened it. Wrapped in Kleenex, inside a folded sheet of paper, was my grandmother's wedding ring. She had worn it on her finger since 1898.

As I fingered the well-worn rose gold, memories flooded me. When I was little, sitting next to her or on her lap, I played with the ring on her finger many times. I loved her hands and her ridge-ripple old fingernails. (Now, I have them.) Often, I thought about how I would like the ring after she passed, but with all the children and grandchildren, I knew there were too many people in front of me wanting it as well. When Grandmother died at one hundred years old and six months, she left the ring to her youngest of ten children, Ned.

Here in my hand, was the ring I had never told anyone I wanted. I was shocked when my uncle said he wanted me to have it, months earlier. He, too, considered it a treasure. His note explained that he felt Grandmother would want that. He told me how important it was for him that I had taken his mother's name.

Pam had a tear when I showed her the ring. We celebrated the event over tea. In another mini visit a short time later, the cottage woman informed me, "Yah, indeed, you have your ring. Good. It has come full circle, and it is where it belongs.

"It goes further back than your grandmother. The ring is for the work you do. The ring symbolizes a coming of age, growth, and a seal of approval. You carry on the work she did not have the opportunity to do. You have walked where she was unable to go." *How interesting. She must mean my work with others. I didn't know that about Grandmother. Grandfather would not have let her, if he knew. Thank God for Roger.*

My old friend continued, "She wishes to give it to you. It's a symbol. Now is the time for it. Was done through one's uncle, but nothing to do with him."

Really! He must have been prompted by the other side. Now that's caring from our ancestors, even though our society usually ignores them.

I thanked this wise woman, realizing there was more to the ring than just being a present or my uncle's sentiment. It now felt almost like it marked a rite of passage from my grandmother. As I write this manuscript, working from these original notes and tapes, I see the light flicker off the rose-gold ring on my wrinkled finger. Also, a little note from my grandmother came with it; she had written it for her youngest son, my uncle, decades before. She knew his homosexuality was an anguish for him. How he must have suffered, and she must have, too, in that ancient time.

Later, showing my daughter Haley the note, she said, also with a tear, "Every word is so full. One can feel Great Gram saying to her youngest, 'See you in a better world.' This world certainly was harsh to both of them."

CHRISTMAS PREPARATIONS ~ ARRIVING FOR CHRISTMAS

Dec. 18/86 Looking into the candle last night, I felt its resonance, its vibration. How naturally I adore this reality called God. I hear, "Walk in the silence. Carry it about your person. Breathe it. All is holy ground. Listen with your breathing, listen with your flesh." Is this not a balance to all the outer stuff? Indeed, as Metude would say.

The house is decorated, and our young adults have been arriving home, one at a time. Tonight, the four kids plus one of their friends are now in the beds upstairs. What a marvel, and what a wealth of humanity for Roger and me. We do love it and feel overwhelming gratitude for it all. And yet there is always a fragility to it.

They are growing up and challenging life each in their own creative way. Bringing home new ideas for me to ponder, as well. Callie and Dev are both taking gender classes and introducing new perspectives for

*this traditional wife to ponder. It's a bit of
an eye-opener. Women are not considered
equal and, of course, I see that, but I wonder
why. This needs some thought.
Doug thinks he might paint over the
holiday. He will be home for three weeks,
with no papers to write. He is staying a week
longer than the others. Other Christmases,
he was out of here as fast as he could go.
Metude told me in one of her visits he does
nothing without a reason. How true. Oh,
my old friend, keep me listening.
The kids and Roger played Trivial Pursuit
at the dining room table all evening. Fun
hearing them joshing one another. I am
sleepy—much laughing from downstairs.
Such a Christmas feeling in the house.
Dev observed, "This house has incredible
presence." And it does, but how wonderful
he feels it.*

Several days later...

*Dec. 22/86 Snowy and am listening to
the Messiah as I write. The tree lights are
on. Dev and I just checked to see if the six
stockings under the bed were full enough, to
make sure "Santa" will make it Christmas
Eve. It's a big job, and I panicked a bit.
We talked long at the supper table tonight.*

It was nice hearing where they each are. All adults, now—even if still students.

Mother and Jim (her husband) arrived yesterday with the car loaded to the roof (literally) with Christmas baking and presents. Yet, she is suffering from osteoporosis. I don't know how long she will be able to keep coming. The kids will also start being away in their adulthood. What an adjustment for two parents that will be. This Christmas may be one of the last of an era; that makes me sad.

Pam has her uterus operation tomorrow (the problem that the cottage woman identified months ago). I reminded her several times of the need, but it seemingly fell on deaf ears.

A Crisis on Christmas Day

Dec. 25/86 The phone rang. Pam was in crisis. She called this afternoon, almost whispering, "I think I am in trouble." By her voice, I heard the pain and panic. I ran at top speed up to her place. She was in agony. Her bladder had been blocked since she came home from the hospital. Frank wasn't home, and she didn't want to call anyone because it was Christmas Day.

I called the doctor. He told me not to move her by car or ambulance as her bladder

*could burst if I did. The pain was so severe
she kept moving even though I tried to hold
her still. What a scary time it was until
the doctor came; he seemed to take forever.
I tried to keep her mind off the pain, but
it was no use. We started counting from
a hundred backward to see how far we
would get, then we started over again. It
was awful.*

*Finally, we heard the doctor's feet running
up the steps. I am terrible at the physical
stuff, but I had to help him put in the
catheter. It relieved the pain significantly.
When the doctor left, Pam and I looked at
each other and started laughing—probably
tension releasing. We both agreed that we
have been through enough stressful adventures to be bonded for this life and beyond.
Frank came home from the woods later.
Lucky guy, he missed it all. Anyway, he said,
"I think Dr. Augusta sounds nice." Pam was
all smiles when I left. Thank you, God.*

The next day . . .

*Dec. 26/86 I love the earthiness of living.
The light playing on my toe. Sounds funny,
but it is an exquisite moment that is such
a counterpoint to the ordinary. However,
I wonder if there is any ordinary in*

ordinariness; there is nothing more ordinary than my toe. And it is so diffused with light, not so much the chairs here or the kitchen pots, but the natural world—my toe is a part of that.

The tide is as high as we have ever seen it—must be a full moon. Gram (Roger's grandmother) died at one 103 years old this afternoon. Her daughter and family asked if I would give the eulogy. We felt Gram was always going to be here.

Several days later . . .

Dec.29/86 I finished Gram's eulogy yesterday, and it felt like completing a good painting. She was not only a 103-year-old woman—she was all her ages, as each of us is. I am the Me that looked out these eyes at three, sixteen, thirty-three years, and now at forty-seven. And does this not beg the question: Who is looking out of these eyes, the child, the young adult, the middle-age woman, or the Me that never changes and is always changing?

What a wonderful privilege to give the eulogy. Roger played the violin. The procession to the grave leaves a memory—the casket, six daughters walking behind the coffin, arms linked in pairs. Then Roger and

I, our children and his sisters, all with faces like roadmaps of their past experiences of Gram as we watched the coffin descend into frozen ground.

• • •

New Year's Reflection ~ Compassion Is the Foundation on Which Life Is Based

After talking with the cottage woman for a year and three months, I continue to learn. I have learned that there are such things as streams of consciousness, spirit guides, other realities, and past-life experiences, that life is a schoolroom, and that death is not the word they use on the other side. I have learned that there even *is* another side.

My understanding of reality is becoming multidimensional. We are not alone. We each have helpers, and this knowledge is changing my life. And most importantly, I am learning that reality is no less real just because I cannot see it. Through the developing friendship with this cottage woman named Metude, I am also learning about the invisible world's great compassion for us humans. Their life is, as my old friend says, "very much like yours." Every hair on our head seems to be counted, and indeed cared for, in mysterious ways. This experience of recognizing there is life after death did not come through a sermon or lecture, but through this cottage woman who has had the experience. As she points out, "The transition or change is but an opportunity to stumble into a larger reality."

My New Year's conclusion is that I have been brought up on an extremely limited view of reality. In fact, the seemingly material, solid human form is hardly what we could call *total* reality at all. There is indeed an invisible world beyond our eyes, ears, and emotions that we can relate to and that relates to us—beyond our five senses. Metude is real, has had a human history which we refer to as "past life" and she refers to as "a life experience." Her understanding is beyond our community's limited perceptions and experiences, and that information certainly was not covered in my years of university, decades ago.

My perception and relationship with nature also has changed this past year. I had felt the melancholy of the trees in the fall to the point of tears, which shocked me. The experiences on the lake, where ice and trees began to expand into a less-than concrete form, as well as our training sessions giving me the experience of other streams of consciousness, is changing me.

And finally, I am also starting to understand why listening is so important. Pam, Abby, Brooke, and I are becoming more sensitive to that larger, inner voice, that deepening intuitive, guiding voice that is apart from our own. Every human possesses inner direction, intuition, and imagination.

Images are a language that continue to be vital in our own personal growth and work with others. They come in symbolic form, but they allow us a larger understanding of the situation and the bigger story under us. In fact, they are becoming one of our major tools. Yet, this does present us with a problem, and that is the interpretation of what the images actually mean. Thus, any information or predictions received rest in the area of probability or possibility.

THE SECOND NEW YEAR ~ A TIME OF REFINEMENT

It has been several weeks since our last visit with the cottage woman because of Pam's operation. Rather surprisingly, she feels well enough to welcome our old friend. Snow is banked against the space under the cottage, which actually makes the floor warmer. Again, the wind off the Atlantic is challenging the woodstove. We see our breath even though I set the fire several hours before. Pam wraps herself in the blanket and settles into the rocker.

The cottage woman enters relatively effortlessly. I am so glad to see her I want to hug her. However, her demeanor, which feels somewhat reserved, always dissuades me. She must be progressing in her experience of being in a human body as her use of words seems more fluid, plus, her eyes (or Pam's) seem slightly open the odd time. Trying to look closer without being obvious, I am not sure she has human-sight, but as she says, there are other kinds of seeing. After our greetings, I mention that Brooke is here, as well.

"Ah, the young one!" *I watch my old friend's face. As usual, my ancient friend seems especially pleased when a young adult comes to visit. In fact, whenever Metude herself enters,*

243

the cottage seems to be filled with an almost tangible loveliness of spirit.

This year, a Time of Refinement Not Advancement

I am wondering if there are new areas of work this coming year, so I ask her.

Pausing, she nods, observing, "It will be a time of refinement rather than advancement, a broadening. Your primary areas this year are listening, receiving, and evaluating information."

"What kind of information, Metude? Do you mean like last week, when I was putting on my skates down at the lake? I looked up and everything—the ice, trees, and houses across the way turned into squiggly light-rays of energy. That was a little scary, but it was a neat experience. Immediately, it came to mind that it must be one of those streams of consciousness you tell me about."

"Indeed," she responds readily, "A direct display of physical energy. It is not the first time it's happened, but it has not been noted." *Do I ever need to pay better attention if I really am going to see beyond the ordinary?*

"I also remembered what you said about my needing to rejoice more. So, I skated around the lake with my arms spread, as if I were a bird, flying. I loved the feeling of being at one with everything. How can I encourage it to happen again?"

"Merely requires one to be open," she muses. "It is not a matter of seeking, but of recognition. Open to it. Merely be open to it. One's physical mind refuses acceptance."

"Oh, thank you." *That is an interesting distinction. I am always seeking as I assume I can't see.*

Changing One's Name ~ An Opportunity Earned

Changing the subject, I ask, "Pam is thinking of changing her name too. What do you think, Metude? She feels she isn't the same person she was ten years ago, plus now she does not want Frank's surname." *She wants her father's name as he was always the person who loved and supported her.*

My old friend pauses, then nods, "Indeed, much like a nautilus moving from one home to another. A name she will live into. Connected with coming home and growing. Transition is not yet complete. It could be still set aside. Changing a name is a journeying forth." *Who would think there is so much to changing one's name? Sounds like we need to grow into it. Hmm, so I must have grown into mine or completed my transition.*

My discarnate friend is reading my mind as she corrects me, "Again, we would say one must make their own decisions. Is one totally who they say? Is a person living into total being or into their highest potential.

"Oh Metude, then there is more to this name changing than just feeling I was missing something. How interesting that it might be connected to my development."

"Yah indeed, let us proceed."

Next, Pam wants me to ask how she is doing in her own personal development? *And she rarely asks that.*

"The person is reaching another stage. Fear and struggle, the final remnant of a low self-image. This channel must be cleared. Still the remains of a block. Lack of self-confidence. More exposure coming, being led back to lesson-work. She perceives our visits as an end to work, which is not the case." *The cottage woman's visits are apparently one of the tools that are being used for Pam's personal development, too.*

And yes, when she gets free, she will have a treasure chest of healing gifts that she hasn't or doesn't want to recognize yet. Wait till she hears there will be more exposure of her special gifts. Interestingly, I just told her that a couple of days ago and she objected.

Metude continues, "The Person must go back over the information given. There is a lessening of one's barrier to this work, a gradual eroding of barriers." *Oh, thank goodness.*

Even though she is still somewhat reactive, she seems eager to hear what this ancient woman has to say. Taking the advice about standing up to her family and not being a doormat is helpful, and she recognizes this even though it is a hard lesson. However, as my discarnate friend points out, Pam wants to grow deep down, but she does not yet have the readiness to tackle certain areas.

"Can I help her in any way?"

"Perseverance," my ancient friend states with finality. I expect she knows of what she speaks. *I need it, too.*

A slight smile plays on her face as she adds, "You are responding to motivation. Proceed."

Energies From a Past Life ~ Confuses the Present Situation

A friend's daughter Sally was in the process of separating from her boyfriend, Harry. He was extremely needy and would not let go. She was at her wits' end. I ask the cottage woman how to help the situation and guessing, ask, "Is this about a past life experience with Harry?" *He hangs on like a drowning man.*

"Yah, indeed. The situation was not resolved then. She has been given another opportunity to work with the issue.

"What issue?" I ask.

Metude's head turns toward me and her eyes or Pam's are closed again. She continues saying, "Her son's dependency." *But that doesn't make sense. She has no son. He's a boyfriend.*

"But Sally doesn't have a son," I point out.

Then, my old friend shifts forward in the rocker, raises that crooked finger, turns her face directly at me and states, "She has a son." *Oh, I get it.*

"You mean Harry was her son in a former life?"

"Indeed, now known as her boyfriend. His dependency is the issue. A great need for approval. He has not learned who he is." *Hmm, so he was Sally's son in a past life experience! Really, it seems unbelievable, but Metude is sitting here telling me it's true!*

"The young one must hold her own identity. Keep it up front. Her identity must be as a banner. Flag it, as you would say. She must hold true to her own identity. Must maintain space, firmness, and determination." *This reminds me of what she said about Fran separating from her mother.*

How important it is to maintain her own identity in spite of what her mother wants. This advice is also helpful with my mother or any other personal relationship.

My old friend continues to reiterate basically what she told Fran a year ago. "Separation for identity and independence. They each must own what is their own, casting off that which is not theirs. And they must separate and detach. They are not coming together, not even blending, but side by side like equals but individuals." *This is fascinating.*

They now have the opportunity to do some emotional detachment work they apparently did not finish then. So, in this human school, apparently the things we miss in this life we get to try again in the next. That's motivating, as going through it once is often enough.

My old friend shifts in the rocker as she continues, "This young one must think with intuition rather than the heart. She knows what she must do. Her intuitions and feelings must be listened to. It is part of a lesson she is to learn. She must identify what is her job to do and what is not, what fears are hers, and what is another's. She will understand this, and as she does, more work and opportunities will be given to her."

"Thank you, Metude, I will tell her this."

The Missing Notes ~ They Will Be Brought to You

With time, I realized that taking notes during the cottage woman's visits was not an efficient way to record the details of her wisdom. Thus, my next question: "As you know, Metude, I write down what you and the guides say. Unfortunately, I have lost my notes." *I can feel her frown.*

She lifts her head again and looks directly at me through those closed eyes. Leaning forward, she instructs, "You must keep more complete records. It is time. Learn how to keep them because you are entering a period of intense training. Keep two sets of records, one on tape."

"Right, but I am worried," I confess. "My notes being lost makes me realize just how irreplaceable some of the information from you and the guides is."

She pauses, then nods, "These will be brought to you. Losing it was not without purpose. We will proceed."

"Really?" *I wonder how that happens. Yet somehow, I know it will.*

The loss of my notes was a sharp lesson for me. And it was more mystifying when the notes turned up several days later on the coffee table in the middle of our living room. The family and I had searched and had passed that table numerous times. There had been no notes.

I Am Always with You; It Will Become More Obvious

Changing the subject from finding my notes, I observe, "Metude, I am starting to understand how important listening is. I thought it was such a little thing to do at first—it felt insignificant and unexciting. Now, I am beginning to understand that listening means more than merely hearing words with my ears. Listening, imagination, instincts each are the language that can connect me to the invisible reality, the place from which you come. Listening is not only a skill, but a gift."

The corners of her mouth curl, slowly. "Indeed, listening is much more. You are learning your instruction. That is what is being given to you—a gift, indeed. Listening will increase as you are prepared to learn over the next period." Then my discarnate friend leans forward in the rocker stating, "You and the Entity must establish a regular pattern of getting together, and it must be adhered to. You are entering a time of intense learning, given the opportunity for exposure and opening." *Maybe to the other side, where she comes from.*

"Again, thank you for being here with me."

"I am always with you; it will become more obvious." *This is my hope.*

It's like God smiled on me and gave me this wondrous gift that I was initially almost too scared to accept. Thank God, I did accept it. She is changing my whole world.

Bending her head, her voice is softer, and she repeats, "I am always with you. It will become more obvious." *Oh, I hope so!*

Our visits are always so short. Trying to be open to her when she is invisible is hard. And if I sense her, then I second guess myself.

Grandmother on the Other Side ~ A Period of Energizing

Several weeks have gone by since Roger's grandmother died. Once again, I am grateful to be able to ask Metude what happens after someone passes away.

Nodding, she quietly explains, "One is in a period of energizing before she decides what next she wishes to accomplish."

"But I am actually more concerned about May, her daughter, as she is suffering from her loss. Is Gram worried about her?"

"There is a greater awareness, but she is not concerned. Concern is merely a physical, human attribute." *Hmm, why wouldn't Gram be concerned? It's her daughter who is hurting.*

"Oh yes, I get it. You both see a larger picture, don't you, Metude?"

"Yah, indeed." That enigmatic smile hints at the corner of her lips.

Listening to this cottage woman, a new idea pops in my head, "You choose to do this work with us, don't you?"

"Yah, much as you do with me. It is you who grant access. Only with your permission can we share your life."

However, Pam and I didn't know there was permission to give when this ancient disembodied friend started visiting us because we had no idea that she and her "we" existed.

Yet, we did ask Spirit for guidance in our lives many times without knowing there were actually guides. So, Pam must have given permission somehow for our old friend to visit, not at the surface level, but at a deeper level of consciousness.

One Is Not More Advanced Than the Other ~ One Merely Has a Different Lesson

"Will you have a physical life again, Metude?" I inch to the edge of my chair.

"Yah, I have some learning to work out in this method. You have chosen this way too; you and the Entity (Pam) are a brotherhood." *Hmm, I wonder if that is why she initially told us we were like brothers in a previous life experience.*

She continues. "You are as one, have one lesson. It is not that one is more advanced than the other." *Oh honestly, I do see myself the odd time as more advanced in some ways. I have an education, a happy marriage, and I see myself making wiser choices.*

Yet, Pam is certainly more advanced than I in the invisible gifts and sometimes in her larger wisdom. However, Metude, you are right, when we meet, those differences don't mean anything to either of us, we just are the best of friends simply caring for each other.

Again, her words interrupt my thoughts.

"Your lesson in this life experience is what you perceive as advancement. We are all as one. One is not more advanced; one is merely to learn a different lesson. If one judges another as unenlightened, then that is the lesson. There is to be no judgment."

"Oh Metude, can one ever learn all the human lessons?" *I ask, rather awed at the weight and responsibility of such an idea.*

She is quiet. I wait. Then, she starts rocking and saying almost with an air of discovery, "Yah, Tibet, true enlightenment." Then she draws out the words, "Enlightenment is good. Your knowing will be heightened. Trust your own abilities. That is coming. One needs to be reassured on occasion. It is coming. I, through your willingness, am learning, too. . We will proceed." *Hmm, that's surprising, I have never thought of her as needing to learn, too.*

I look at her sitting there by the fire, her wonderful words are again filling my spirit with love and gratitude. Her hands rest serenely in her lap. I want to lean over and almost touch them, but know I am not supposed to. So full of gratitude, I ask, "May I help you, Metude, in any way?"

Reading my mind, she observes, "All things that pass are of mutual benefit, mutual service. *Imagine! I can add fullness to her life. Imagine!*

"Metude, I know it is time to go, but I want to thank you."

She nods. "Our time is at an end. It was a pleasant visit. We would bid you a good day. We have you in our hearts." Then she is gone, at least, physically.

The "we" that bids me a "good day" must refer to others like her in this cottage woman's reality. My old friend has definitely come to me as a real person. *So, there must be other invisible beings like her that I can depend on, trust, and draw from—those who have wisdom, understanding, and love. Those that are much like her. My logic says she can't be the only one out there.*

253

STUMBLING INTO A NINETEENTH-CENTURY GARDEN PARTY

Jan. 4/87 We are in a snowstorm tonight. It has been so wonderful a winter. Roger and I skied around the lake and through the woods this afternoon. Ten above zero Fahrenheit. Everything was clear, distinct, and a strikingly creamy colour of white as the shadows were long and lengthening into the bluest hue over the snow. That lake has become holy ground for me this winter. I took my usual walk down the lane to it last night. The path was beautiful, with the snow-laden spruce and fir trees framing it. No lights, only the moon. I could see the squares of ice that the kids have cleared for skating and hockey.
This past week, Pam attended one of the programs at The Center. Some of the sessions were held in an old farmhouse. After the morning session, we were sitting in the living room talking by ourselves. Suddenly,

*Pam stopped and looked puzzled. I knew
that look. The hair rose on my arms. She
asked if I heard footsteps in the hall. I didn't.
Gingerly, we peeked around the corner,
the hall was empty. I whispered, "Hello?"
hoping, no one would answer. I still had a
weird feeling.
As I leaned back in the chair, Pam frowned,
saying, "I see a young woman swishing
through the hall." I had a full view of the
hall. No one had passed—at least no one
that my little human eyes could see. She
must be seeing with her inner eyes.
Now, having had a few training sessions, I
attempted to shift my stream of consciousness. Either my training sessions were going
well, or the power of her suggestion was
working because now I saw several people
swishing by us. Their dresses were long with
hoops out at the bottom. Sunshine flooded
the room. Others were moving around. Most
people seemed to be out on the veranda, but
we noticed a man with a trimmed beard
and a high-collared coat standing near the
fireplace. Pam and I looked at each other
slightly wide-eyed. She confirmed that
she was seeing the same thing as me. This
would have been extremely unnerving if I
hadn't had the last two years with Metude.
The whole thing felt like an old-timey*

The Cottage Woman

garden party.
The experience faded soon after, but I knew
I would not forget it. Or course, I couldn't
wait to ask the cottage woman about it at
our next visit. Did we really see those people?
Was it a different stream of consciousness?

A TIME OF INTENSE LEARNING ~ MUCH WORK TO FREEING ONESELF

Feedback from "the Garden Party" ~ They Didn't Notice You

Several days later, Pam agrees to a visit, as she is also eager to ask about our experience at the "garden party."

After settling into the rocker, I tell her about the experience. She gives a nod, saying, (almost as if she is explaining the obvious), "There is no time. It happened because of the energy." *Maybe it had something to do with the buildup of energy from the program that was held earlier in the same room.* She continues, "The veil between this side and that side was thinner, making you extra-perceptive. This allowed you to witness the gathering." *Amazing!*

"But Metude, they didn't seem to notice us, and they walked right by us." *Thank goodness!*

"They didn't see you."

"Were we in another time dimension?"

"You might call it that." *She is amused.*

"Well, I am rather shocked I had the experience, as my veil between this side and the other seems a lot thicker than Pam's. How come it happened to me?"

"You have done it before, but you didn't have the basis for it then. You are merely ready to appropriate it again."

Hmm, I wondered if this is part of "the wild ride" she referred to in one of our first visits. Knowing and talking to her feels wild.

Shifting to a Stream of Consciousness ~ You Are Not a Trainee

Wanting to learn as much as I can from the experience, I ask, "How do I learn to be more sensitive? It seems to be out of my control."

Raising that crooked forefinger at me, she instructs, "Trust your information. You are not a trainee. You are already speaking the information. You have the same ability as the Entity, yet you are convinced before you start that you can't do it. Accept that you can do it. Open your mind. Get the feeling. Write it out. Note how many times the Person has confirmed what you have gotten. You will not credit, recognize, or own it. You would gain strength by doing so."

Yes, I feel stronger just listening to her confirm the garden party. Yet, I need to accept that I can do it, open my mind, get the feeling, write it out, and note how many times Pam has confirmed my experiences.

"Now that you have identified and recognized what you have been doing, you are ready for new learnings. If you want proof, go for proof. Ask your question. Sit down, concentrate, and think. Write what happens. Call your friend to see what she gets. You will have your proof. Indeed, we will proceed." *Wow, she hasn't stopped for a breath.*

"Thank you for the exercise. Do I have to stop and pull my energy into the top of my head to reach another stream of consciousness every time, like I did months ago on the railroad tracks and with Joe?"

"No longer do you have to haul it up step by step. It is there momentarily. To think is to bring it to reality. Energy will be up. You are in the process of accepting and owning. You now have a different slant on it." *Maybe I am progressing.*

Metude moves forward, saying, "You have a new information source and you are slow in recognizing it. You must listen to information from the other friend." *Hmm, that's got to be Abby.*

She continues, "You can detect the difference between surface talk and information from the other side. You have been almost rude. Observe her images. You were told to do that, but you did not value them as information." *Oh, but she's right. I do give Pam's images more weight than Abby's since her psychic information has been tried and true over and over. However, I am also not as familiar with Abby's, and neither is she—even with her own images.*

"Oh, thank you, Metude, it excites me to have another resource." *And that you are recommending it.*

In the Process of Freeing Herself ~ Much Is at Work

The next subject I brought up was Pam's continuing difficulties at home. My old friend knows I have to vent.

"Frank and Pam are having a rough time. Frank continues to blame all the supposed wrongs being done to him on her. He says that she is responsible for his and their children's unhappiness. He is a chronic complainer, and she suffers it all. She is like the little Dutch boy in the fairy tale who puts his finger in the dike to hold back the ocean; hers is an ocean of misery, and she is worn out. It is costing her her physical health and emotional well-being. She knows all this, but still can't let go of being responsible and feeling guilty. I think it's because she can't make things right for Frank and the children. It also costs me energy, just helping her to keep balance in the situation. Still, as you know, after considerable persuasion, Frank finally agreed to go to a therapist, which does not seem to be helping. Still, I don't know if things can go on like this for much longer, as Frank may do physical harm to his family or himself."

Metude is nodding as I talk, and her presence is soothing as she responds. "Much is at work. The situation is progressing. Your friend is in the process of freeing herself. Her lack of independence from the other is a result of her having little confidence. Yet, it's being recognized, and it is coming." *Well, it's certainly not obvious.*

"Much venting is necessary," she continues. "Too much uncertainty, not the awareness of where she stands. It is more a matter of her allowing herself to vent. Yet, she adopts a position that she can handle it. Then she is not sure how she really feels, which leads to confusion." *And she can ignore the problems and they don't get resolved.*

"You must call her forth, a very direct confrontation of the confusion. Identify it. Confusion promotes pain, yet through the confusion, one will get direction. She has lost her sense of direction. This is a time of intense learning. There will be many opportunities in the next time frame. Great gains are being made. Many visible signs. Much work is being done; things are approached from many directions. They are as one. It will become clear. Proceed" *Oh, I need to hear this. All our talking and walking must be having some effect.*

Being Overbooked ~ Leave Time for the Unexpected

My old friend then leans toward me, instructing, "Leave time for the impulse of the day." *Oh, boundaries again, but also a spirit caution, I sense.*

"What about my spirituality?"

"New depth to one's spirituality. It is not a change, but has a deepening, calm fullness in it. You don't have to do anything, just allow it to happen. Keep on listening and loving."

"But Metude, my painting is neglected, as I always seem to be dealing with someone else's crisis."

"Yah," she nods, "There is not the time, given what you have booked with other people. One must allow time between bookings. You must avoid committing large blocks of time. Already a lesson. You leave no time for the unexpected. Do not overbook, then no time to maneuver." *Yes, and as you say, no time for the impulse of the day.*

"Learn to leave enough time to be flexible. You do not need a large slot. If the need for free time arose, you would have time to slot in things. There is no flexible time when one is booking things back-to-back."

She continues, "One must schedule, but not rigidly. Establish a pattern, but do not fill at least one time slot every day. Again, leave time for the unexpected. You will be given practice and incidences of being overbooked. Then check out how it feels. Then leave time in order to respond to the need or impulse of that day." *This reminds me of a quote from my Quaker book friend, Thomas Kelly.*

"Never let the demands of the day grow beyond your real needs." I also think of John Woolman, another book friend who wrote, in 1774, "If you want a monk's heart, you must follow the Rule of My Altar. Test the feeling of oneness with things and let that be your yardstick."

Metude shifts in the rocker. I instinctively know that it is time for her parting, and I thank her for coming.

"Yah, indeed. And now we do not have time. Much work is being done. I am with you. Again, we remember you in our hearts. Peace be with each of you and yours. A pleasant visit." Then the muscles in her face begin rearranging themselves, although they are becoming less noticeable as the months go by. And then Pam is back.

• • •

Elizabeth Kubler-Ross ~ Working with Emotional Pain

Working with so much pain reminded me of a week-long workshop I took eight years earlier with Elizabeth Kubler-Ross, who was changing the western face of medicine in regards to the subject of dying. I knew nothing about working with emotional pain in such situations. Until Elizabeth, there was little talk about death. The subject seemed taboo.

When my father died of a brain tumor years previously, the doctor came out of the initial operation telling my mother and me that he only had a short time to live, and that we would shorten his life if we told him the truth. The second doctor I consulted said if I told my father the truth, he would no longer be our doctor. So, when my father asked, I lied, knowing he had counted on me for the truth. Lying to him always sat badly with me. He died several months later at fifty-seven. When I got the opportunity to explore how those who were dying could be treated, the philosophy of Elizabeth Kubler-Ross was something I needed to hear. She supported discussion and truth.

On the first morning of the workshop, which was being held in a city near Seaforth, I entered a large room and found my seat in the back row. People had come from the States and England. At a glance, I noticed the back wall—from ceiling to floor; it was the oddest colour. Then I recognize the colours were a giant pile of tissue boxes stacked against the back wall. So, I assumed a lot of crying would happen. Elizabeth entered the room and introduced herself to seventy participants. Pointing to the back, she said two-thirds of us would work through that colourful wall of tissue boxes before week's end. And they did.

For the first three days, I wanted to go home. I had never observed so much raw pain. The wall of tissues went down fast. One young mother had four young children at home, and she had been given three or four months to live. Her heart pain was unbearable, and her rage was shocking. Every participant had a tragic story. People talked, cried, and raged about their situations and their deepest fears. They were listened to, held, comforted, and allowed to be honest with themselves.

I sat in shocked silence. I was homesick, so I called Roger and asked him to come see me one evening. I snuck down to the backdoor of the building to meet up with him. (We were not allowed to go out or have visitors. I concluded later that she did not want the energy that was building to dissipate.) Roger and I talked it over and, of course, I hugged him goodbye and went back upstairs.

My continued question to myself was, how was Elizabeth going to put these people back together again before they leave? During the day, she sat at the front of the room in a seemingly caring stillness that invited those in pain to open up. She and her team were up most nights, working with the participants. She also talked about her spirit guides. However, prior to the cottage woman, there was no place in my logic for such information.

Then, in the last days of the workshop, an unbelievable occurrence happened. A deep joy began to permeate the participants. People who had spent most of the week being emotionally devastated entered into a nameless, faceless love that touched each of us and felt like a miracle. She had done nothing to the outward eye to create such a shift of the energy in the workshop. Mostly, she just sat quietly in front of the room and listened with a half-smile, which later reminded me of the Buddha—seeming to wait in trust for this ocean of healing, joy, and Presence to sweep through us. It did do that in the last two days.

After the workshop, I walked around in this love-Presence for days. I remember being at the meat counter in our little country store thinking: *I am feeling so much faceless love that I know there is no death. No matter where one is, it is all love.* I asked the Spirit there to never let me forget this feeling and experience, and I have not.

I was no longer afraid of another's tears, and I was no longer afraid when people sobbed and withered from emotional pain. (I had previously thought these things meant a nervous breakdown, or that they were falling apart, never to be put together again.) Instead, I began to understand that these things could be a breakthrough to healing and wholeness. That recognition became an open door in my work with others' pain, as well as my own. Human lessons do not go well if one is too afraid to look.

Another Stream of Consciousness, a Phantom Wall

Several days after the last visit, I dropped in on Pam for tea. We talked about what Metude said about "booking people back-to-back." As Pam was talking, I was looking at her unadorned, living room wall. To my surprise, a scene began to emerge. A phantom sun shone down on a phantom white house surrounded by phantom green grass. My startled eyes darted to Pam. She had not noticed, so I dismissed it, and it began to fade.

A minute later the house reappeared, but this time in vivid detail, with windows and eaves. Disbelieving, again I glanced back at Pam. She had blended into the wall. The weird thing was that she had no solid form. The whole image was like a photographic negative that needed to be developed. After a few seconds, the house began to recede. I was becoming used to seeing images, but this was different. Plus, my eyes felt as big as saucers, as if they had to shrink to get back into their sockets. Telling Pam what I had just seen, I said that I was going to take it as a training session to make it less scary. We laughed, but in hindsight, I think it was a comfort to her, as she was no longer alone in seeing differently.

The Second Spring & Summer

Life changes require a new relatedness.

A DROP-IN VISIT ~ AND AN EFFECTIVE WAY TO PRAY

Spring comes late to the Maritimes. The sun is just beginning to warm the cottage. We can hear water dripping off the eaves. A little excitement always spices the air when we know we are going to meet with this wonderful, wise woman. When she enters, an indescribable sense of settling into her presence is palpable. We exchange greetings. Then, I tell her that I have lost my relationship with my uncle.

Texas Trip Woes ~ Pray for Him and Lend Him Energy

Late in the winter, my Uncle Ned from Texas had called, inviting Roger and me for a visit. He even offered to pay for the tickets. We took a few days to think it over and decided to go. However, unfortunately, I did not think to ask Metude what she thought of the trip. I had some reservations because of Ned's partner, as I knew he wasn't friendly with the family, but I decided to go anyway. I figured we would have enough space from each other, since we would be staying in a motel.

When I asked my old friend just before we went, I could feel the weight in her, and I immediately knew that it was not a good idea. She said that we might as well go, that Roger would be vital support, and that it was important to go outdoors a lot, as it would expand my energy. That was not encouraging. Then, thinking that it might not be bad and that the tickets were already brought, we went.

The visit had been worse than I thought. The first two days the visit seemed okay; however, it was downhill after that. Jim, his partner, didn't want us, and my uncle caved under the pressure. The last two days were spent outside or in our motel. Roger and I are naturally quiet, and we knew enough to try to be invisible. Nothing worked. We could not wait to leave.

I called my uncle once we arrived home. His voice was icy, and the conversation was short. I really needed advice from my ancient friend.

Metude was ready for me. Without a pause and looking intent, she states, "Yah, the trip was a failure in his eyes. He thinks, 'You failed me; you have let me down.'" She looks at me kindly, adding, "He thought you would bring peace and those good things." *Oh, I wanted to! But now I can't even be a friend. I'm sure through those closed eyes she sees disappointment and failure written on my face.*

The rocking chair creaks as she adds, "Giving you the vacation to Texas was a scapegoat. He could vent his anger with it. He thinks, 'What do they want? I gave them a vacation, and they are not even grateful.' " *Oh, that makes me cringe.*

Then she adds, "He must accept his responsibility in the situation. All blame has been put outside of himself. Must own his role. He must be his own person, and he has a right to that. He said and thought what his partner wanted him to." *Oh, I really can't do much about that.* Reading my mind, she adds, "Again, you have not given validity to your own information. You have not recognized it as valid. You must distinguish information from thought." *That's hard. She knew I was trying to understand where I was to blame.*

She is quick to respond: "You need not be troubled. Each person is responsible for their own decisions. Your uncle chooses to hold back."

"Should I call him and try to talk with him again?" *Me wanting to smooth over the situation.*

"You need not do anything at this time. He still is not his own person. He doesn't have the energy with the other and is afraid of all the emotions. Too threatening to face. He thinks his world would come apart. That he can't handle it. You are merely to remain open. Pray for him. Lend energy to his energy level. It is not wasted. Remember his partner in a positive way." *Oh, I need that reminder*! "Negative thought adds to negative energy." *She means mine!* "Hold him in light and caring. Merely a matter of waiting. You must learn to follow your own instincts. Hold fast to what is right. One's instinct is another guidance, when to approach and when to hold back. We will proceed." *Yes, but I hate that he might die thinking badly of me.*

An Effective Way to Pray ~ Set Aside a Certain Time Each Day

"Metude, what is an effective way to pray for his throat cancer?" *At least, I can do that!*

She responds instantly. "Set aside a certain time each day. Sit in the same chair and concentrate on the disease lessening. See and feel the lumps going down. See them receding. Mild warm water, hold it in the mouth. Visualize it positively. Have a proper mental attitude. Stop concentrating on how bad the pain is. Tell him, 'You can have some good times.'" *She must be half talking to Ned. Hmm, and as she says, maybe using the same spot, the same chair, and the same time affects the frequency of the healing energy.*

Being consistent could also make it easier for those on the other side who are working with us. So much is invisible and unanswerable. Often, I pray in blind faith because I cannot see with my human eyes what is physically going on inside the person I am praying for.

She nods her head, then shifting in the rocker, she says, "Now, I must bid you a good day. A short visit, the body is restless." *Oh, that's only two questions! I have others.* However, before I can blink, Pam has opened her eyes and is looking at me, slightly stunned herself. This is the fastest coming out yet; we had planned for at least an hour visit. I tell her Metude just told me that her body was restless. Pam nods and says she thinks her sister from the city is coming.

Six months later, I wrote in my journal,

Ned is in his 9th inning. I followed the cottage woman's step-by-step instructions and prayed that he could feel light and love.

I hope he found some peace. He still remains distant. Maybe he will find what he needs on the other side. Grandmother will be there.

BAKED BEANS, BROWN BREAD, AND PRESENCE

May 6/87 Spring is really here. I hope Roger is having a good weekend. Every spring he goes with four or five other friends from his university days to a cottage back in the woods. They fish and have some hoedowns. I bake the bread for them.

Saturday night, and the smells of baked beans and brown bread waft up from the kitchen. Callie leaves for summer school in another week. We will miss her. These past several weeks we walked, talked about her life, my interest in possibly writing a book or two, and the impact nature has on us both. The song of the loons and wafts of tangy ocean salt filtered through the house in a silence we enjoyed.

Been busy, but I am getting my life back again. A beautiful walk this afternoon, beach, waves, and grasses that sway to the wind and swell in love. Everything moved to a Presence like a current, independent of anything else—so viscerally, with no face, except the breeze against my skin—gift and grace. Thomas Merton, a Trappist monk, describes it well when he says, "(Presence) calls me, I am aware of (it) as Love." And Metude says, "It has been given to you to enjoy, one must enter the joy of that which has been given to you. It is to delight in; enjoy what the moment brings." And thankfully, I can.

Overheard Haley telling her brother yesterday that the love she feels "for Mum" she now recognizes is a God thing and that when I die, she will still have it. I think that's true as any love we hold for anyone is a God thing. How insightful of her and how caring.

A week later . . .

May 14/87 Karate tonight. Sparring is not too bad with the protective gear on. Got a bad bruise on my leg, but I am holding my own. Sometimes I am tempted to quit but if I do, I will never know if I can get a black belt. I pledged myself to another year if I don't get too badly hurt—Blue Belt by December, and then on to Brown and Black. Good talk with Mother about "passing on" and about her not judging herself so harshly. The Spirit gives us much more leeway to make mistakes than we ever do ourselves.

I think people try their best in most situations. Besides, Metude says we are given an opportunity to continue our learning if we don't take it this life experience.

Amazing how we protect ourselves from being wrong. Roger and Callie were telling me I do that at times. It must have been bad for them to mention it. Now to accept this gift and do something about it. I'll ask them to tell me when I do it again, as I surely will.

Pam told me something scary today. Frank apparently told their teenage daughter about someone shooting his wife and two children before he shot himself. We both wondered if it really is someone else, he is talking about. He is so unstable. It keeps me looking out the lane. What more can one do? His doctor and therapist know his situation. It took five mountains of effort just to get him professional help.

She was so upset this afternoon. "Nothing is doing any good. I am stopping our work (which, I am sure, means the cottage woman, too) and will sell the house and move away." I am shocked. I never saw it coming, but it sounds like she means it. Frank would like that. Oh my, she will give the good stuff away for all the bad stuff! What will come of it all?

A CRITICAL TIME, A BREAKDOWN ~ DYSFUNCTION REPEATS ITSELF

Pam is at a breaking point from the stress. Frank's medication doesn't seem to work. The therapist's help is not obvious yet. Pam came down earlier and tells me she doesn't have much time for a visit, but she knows that we both need the cottage woman's wisdom. She is beyond desperate.

My old friend's voice is weak when she enters. I ask if she can speak up as I lament, "Oh Metude, what a dark and harsh time for Pam. A person can only take so much. Now she is talking about selling the house and moving away! She has shocked all of us. Is that from fear?"

She looks thoughtful. I wait, as she settles herself into the rocker. Then begins to speak, "That would be possible, my child, now would it not? One would have to be careful not to use a geographical move to distance oneself from that which they are in fear of exposing."

"Hmm, a fear of being exposed? What are you really saying?"

"That moving away will make a distance from what she fears exposing. Precisely, her uncertainty about working in this area." *Oh, my soul, here I thought it was about Frank and the situation there.*

She continues, "The Entity senses censorship from someone she thinks knows about her special gifts. When you are in the process of working through this it is best to be alerted to what is there. She senses this person has great disbelief in this whole (psychic and invisible) area."

"Oh, thank you. This is so important to know. With all the difficulties in her immediate family, there are also her parents, siblings, or whoever that might be possible suspects." *And this is the very reason we have to keep Metude a secret. I wonder who could possibly guess, but it is very important for me to know.*

"Anything I can do about that?"

"You have been alerted. That would be sufficient. Proceed."

Then, my ancient friend leans forward and points her finger at me, which brings us back to the family situation, "'Tis a crucial time. The body needs food. Much stress and tension. Much needs to be vented, your term for releasing emotions. Opportunity must be taken. Much confusion, much fear. She must be willing to address that, her fears. The body is reaching the breaking point. A need for a lot of emotional talking. She must vent the emotion. Bring up the depths, then one becomes aware of what is within. Again, we see an opportunity for the situation to go whichever way, an opportunity to be held back or set free." *Yes, and doesn't the spirit give us the freedom of choice.*

Metude, my guess is she feels too trapped in the house to vent like that. It's a prison of despair and fear. The only relief for her is to get some space from her home environment, which means her going away somewhere, and I suspect she would only go with me. This presents a big problem in itself. She has never been away from Frank, even for a night since she was married at seventeen. And now she is in her late thirties." *And I don't want to go away with her, I have other things booked.*

If by some miracle she will come away, we will have a ton of miserable work to do. Worse still, Frank is so unstable that he could walk down our driveway any day with his shotgun. I know my old friend knows what I am thinking. I wonder if Pam does. I hope not.

Metude leans toward me stating, "People have different kinds of burdens to carry." *She's right, and Pam's burdens far outweigh my schedule.*

"Create an opportunity to speak to her about going away. There's been enough time for being quiet and holding back. The Person does not have the strength to face the situation on her own." *She really is in trouble.*

"I know, but that's a big responsibility for me."

"The responsibility only lies with the one who hears what one wishes to hear."

"Then it is not mine. Really?"

"Indeed, not." Her old, crooked finger is still pointing at me.

"I suppose I could go to a friend's cottage with her, but I can't imagine Pam will go."

"Confusion. She does not have the ability to make the decision."

"You mean I have to make it for her?" *Now, this does go against my nature.*

Ignoring my resistance, she is resolute. "Again, the Person does not have the strength on their own." *She is telling me I have to strategize my own life for a week and convince Pam, which will be a dicey task in itself. I guess it doesn't matter what I don't like.*

Dysfunction Repeats Itself If It Is Not Interrupted ~ Yet the Fear of Venting

My old friend continues her instruction, "Fear of venting. Must be approached in a casual way. If she expects the discussion, she can back off. Yet there is a trust. An opportunity will be given to you. When one begins to talk, then watch and listen for signs given through the body of the other cutting off the conversation. Do not push one into something when they are not ready. The Person does not have the strength for direct communication. Requires concentration, which she cannot give."

Again, she raises her gaze as if she sees me, then instructs, "Merely to listen. Give her your own signals."

"What would you call my role?"

"Director, if one wishes a term. Much as you usually work." *This means I keep listening, keep monitoring Pam's readiness, and keep asking questions.* Metude continues, "She will not talk willingly, but has a thought that it is the move to make. Heed the warnings. Tread very carefully. Anger will be present. Wise to watch for the beginnings of it, but do not address it prematurely. Keep it channeled where it belongs."

"Yes, but it is hard to remember all this. I'll really need you present."

"Yah, indeed, I will be there. Proceed."

On the surface, Pam might not think she wants this challenge, but this cottage woman is telling me that she is ready for this development at a deeper level, beyond my seeing. Being ready to grow rather than wanting to grow seems to be the motto. It is difficult to discern when a person is pushing out beyond their inner readiness. Obviously, Pam not wanting to do something is not my gauge in this situation.

Metude continues, "Easier for the Person to see from a distance. Needs someone strong enough to help her get some space.

"Ok, I will suggest we go away as it seems the only solution in the moment!"

"One has to do what one has to do. Remind her, one has the freedom to choose to have friends to help. She has to be responsible for herself. Not responsible for anyone else, not even the children. They are old enough. One can influence them. That is different than being responsible for them." *An interesting distinction.*

Then my discarnate friend moves to the edge of her chair again, reiterating, "The Person is responsible for her gifts, to make her body and mind such that her gifts can be used. Try saying it in different ways. Say it over and over. She can hear it when people say it. She has taken total responsibility for the other's life. That is depriving him of his growth. Independence is very healthy for him, too."

I do agree; trying to meet his every wish does not strengthen or encourage him to develop beyond his small and limited culturally conditioned self. Dysfunction repeats itself over and over if it is not interrupted.

Again, I am sure that Pam would be an amazing physical healer if she could free and heal herself. Her gifts—clairaudience, clairvoyance, and being a clear conduit for the other side—are extraordinary. Yet, she has so much fear and denial of them that it is a miracle we can even have these visits. The Spirit needs us to do our human lessons, and one must attend to it if one is to live in an inner freedom and aliveness rather than merely to exist.

However, I am not happy with asking Pam questions she will resist or to invite her to leave her family for a week, which she will certainly balk at. Yet, if we go, she may discover a larger perspective, find a healing strength, and get some rest. Knowing this is just a drop-in visit, I thank this ancient one for coming and her guidance in this crisis. She again assures me she will be with us. *And she will need to be.*

I leave the cottage in a pensive mood, not with my heart singing, as usual, but with my head down and lead in my stomach. How will I ever help this young woman see the value in going away? If she goes, this will be the first time she leaves her family and Frank—ever! Nothing is working right now. Besides, during the last week, I've watched her get sicker and wonder how she will get the strength to do anything. And, aside from the human misery part, continuing to visit Metude depends on Pam surviving.

ATTENDING TO A BREAKDOWN ~ IT'S SCARY

July 10/87 Pam called earlier saying she is having "a nervous breakdown." God, it's scary. She is so fed up with the situation she said, "I've had it. I am going to live in the basement, hidden away and not think." Their basement is half dug out. She will have to leave Frank, but will she?
Later, we took a drive, but she did not want to talk. Keeping in mind Metude's instruction of not holding back, I forged ahead. The conversation became heated at times, but she seemed to listen and finally agreed that she has to get away to survive. It took considerable effort.

Three days later . . .

July 13/87 Human drama when I picked Pam up for her "vacation." The family were all standing in a row on their veranda, Frank not happy, children calling to her and begging her not to go. And Pam crying as she came down her lane. It was all very harsh. When we arrived at our friend's cottage, she went to bed. The next day she was homesick and wanted to go home to her dark, damp basement. Today, she still is in bed and eating very little. When I'd ask Metude what I could do this morning, the answer was, "The Body is resting." Hmm, was it Metude? Getting worried earlier and feeling out of my depth, I called her therapist (who agreed beforehand to the trip), to give her the non-progress report and to check to see if I should take her back home. She felt we should stay. Thank goodness, she began eating supper tonight. And eureka! She began talking without me asking a question or saying a word. It was like she didn't want to stop.

Five days later . . .

July 15/87 Drizzling out, fog hugs the rocks, and isn't that how I feel! In the last few days, everything for Pam seems to come out like an emotional throw-up. We are moving to where she can hear herself and is becoming the observer of the situation. I am watching healing in action.
Unfortunately, I have cabin-fever. Pam is easy to live with and we are starting to

get our humour back, but I am feeling hemmed in, irritated, and frustrated. We work well together, and I have a love for her, but I need a certain distance and this living together doesn't do it. That's just the way it is, and it has not made me happy with myself. "Oh, Metude, it is too bad you do exist on a dicey foundation. I am sorry. And it's not only Pam's shattered-ness, but my reactive-ness that leaves me feeling deficient, small, petty, and down on myself for not being more magnanimous of spirit. As Tiny Tim said so long ago, 'God bless us everyone.'"

Sixth day . . .

July 16/87 Pam and I talked about my cabin-fever this morning. I don't feel so reactive. And she is taking a good look at her situation and is much more herself, thank God.

Roger came down late this morning. It was so good to see him. Now I am sitting out here on the front step listening to the crackle of the fire in the fireplace and hearing them chat.

Frank comes tomorrow. My heart goes out to them. He does not want to be the way he is.

He's like "Jekyll and Hyde," yet he hides it well with Roger and me.

I wonder what she will do her first day back home. What will her insights be in hindsight? Will she be able to hold her gains? She has certainly taken a hard, objective look at the situation.

To sum up . . .

July 20/87 After the first few days, Pam talked from an emotional depth I have not heard before. I listened, questioned, prayed, and watched her shattered self continue to shatter and then begin to mend. (It reminded me of the week with Elizabeth Kubler-Ross. After the emotional storm, the participants started to heal.) Pam slept, vented, felt safe for those seven days, and put some distance between her and her situation, which seemed to give her space and a larger perspective. She is a remarkable person. We even discussed her leaving Frank. By the time we drove home, she was also closer to going to university. I knew it was an immense stretch, but it offers her a future, and I knew she could do it. Earning her high school equivalency last year motivated her, and continues to give her confidence.

As a mature student, she could get a student loan. Plus, maybe these past few days have helped her. I prayed a lot while she was in bed, and I was thinking this morning— prayer is the physical positioning that forms the chalice part of my spiritual life. However, it may also be a while before Metude and I can talk face-to-face again, but at least I am sure we will. Pam does get the life-giving force of the cottage woman. Unfortunately, for all my experience, my old friend and her reality still feels distant when she isn't sitting directly in front of me.

And what of Pam and me? Our relationship is not too understandable. At times, my caring for her is muted. Other times, we just are on a fun wavelength of humour, wisdom, and magic.

This trip also shows me how hectic my life has become at home. Sometimes, I feel like a country doctor on call. Far too often. It seems to go with working with people in crisis. Thankfully, Roger and I go sailing most nights. An excellent and much needed balancer.

TWO WEEKS LATER ~ VACATION TIME FOR ROGER AND ME

August 1/87 Prince Edward Island—warm breeze and vacation time. We needed a break. We had yummy lobster sandwiches for lunch, stopped at an art gallery, took a nap, and I just had a swim over eelgrass and red sand. I love the smell of the ocean water, and now the sun is drying little patches of white salt on my skin. These gorgeous days go lightning fast, and each summer seems to be shorter.

Roger was working on some fiddle tunes, so I had my second swim today. The sunny day turned into rain and wind. The terns swooped and dove. The gulls hunkered down on the rocks and the jellyfish stung my legs, especially when the water was rough. The red ones hurt more than the white, but at least I could see the former coming toward me more easily.

Tonight, we are going out and having one of

those famous lobster suppers we see advertised everywhere.

Two days later . . .

August 3/87 Home again, and it was renewing. While away, I updated Roger on Pam's crisis in more detail than I usually would because of their privacy. I did it so he wouldn't be too shocked if Frank became noticeably violent. It's a good thing I did. Pam just called and said it is worse than it has ever been. Frank's anger is fueled again. That didn't take long. He is depressed and has quit going to his therapist. He hates his job, his life, his house, and it goes on and on. He needs to be in the hospital. And thankfully, Pam's voice told me she has the strength to put him there tonight. He refuses, of course. Where is his doctor and therapist? It's concerning.

What will she do? He is so resistant to going back to the therapist. Yet she is physically trapped since she has no training in anything and could never in this world support herself or three teenage children. This dismal situation does feel insurmountable, and she can't leave without them.

WHAT CONSTITUTES A FAMILY IS HOW ONE PERCEIVES IT?

Pam arrives; she had called earlier, and she is really wanting to visit the cottage woman. To say that I am pleased is an understatement, and I interpret her desire as progress. Brooke is here too. Metude has a bit of a struggle to come in. It's a miracle that she can continue to visit. I haven't dared think we'd get to visit for the next few months, but here she is—her wonderfully, wise, grounded presence; I feel it instantly. It's like none of this chaos touches her. Amazing, really.

I am worried again about Pam surviving. My old friend nods and responds without me asking, "The person will live to an older age." *Oh, thank God.*

Metude Does Not Feel Physical Pain ~ Use Mind Power

"Yes, but Metude, Pam is having an awful time. Plus, now she has shingles! They are so painful. What can she do for them?"

"Inflammation, virus. Rest. Use her mind power to control pain. Progress could be halted. Shingles, a potential for pain and prolonged illness is there, but use her mind."

"Do you feel her pain from the shingles, Metude?"

She pauses as if feeling around her insides, then states, "I do not feel the pain. This is sufficient. Proceed."

"Metude, the good news is since we came back from being away, Pam seems to have more strength to make her own choices."

"Indeed, yet an area of indecision for the Entity. Much change, but there is confusion. She is to help him by presenting options rather than her choosing the options for him. Proceed." *Hmm, she is pressing him to go back for some professional help and change his ways.*

I think Metude is saying that Frank must be allowed to have the freedom to make his own choices, bad or good. And she needs to make hers, whether they are helpful to him or not. You certainly can't always help the other.

Special Needs ~ Not as Difficult as the Mother Thinks

The next question, which was given to me by a friend, is about her son, who has special needs. He is a four-year-old in a forty-year-old body.

Metude nods, "Not as difficult as the mother thinks. Yet, he is wearing his mother down." *So true.*

"How can the situation be helped?"

"The human body that this Spirit uses is damaged. Again, not as challenging as it appears. The mother needs to be helped with acceptance. Love him as he is. Much healing in the mother to see your friend's love and acceptance (of her son). Balm for the mother. And peace be with them both. We will proceed."

What Constitutes a Family ~ Humans Have So Limited Their Relationships

Abby's daughter is getting married in a couple of weeks and she asked if I would sit with the family as her sister at the wedding. I agreed, but I am uncomfortable. Although I can relate to our spiritual bond like a sister, I feel deceptive calling her that when we are not related by blood. *I need to hear how cottage woman sees it.*

A year earlier, Abby had arrived at my house one morning just before her birthday and had asked the guides for a birthday gift. To her surprise, she saw an image of two little girls, twins in a gypsy wagon several centuries ago. The mother was poor and had to give one of the twins away. She felt they were us and the one given away had died shortly after. Was this true or just her imagination? Yet, we do have some soul connection, a similar love of God, and a special interest in art and music.

Thus, I ask, "What constitutes a family, Metude?"

She leans forward in the rocker and replies instantly—of course, knowing the reason I ask. "Love is family. Adopt a child, why not a sister? Relax with it and share her joy. It is how one perceives it is, how one goes after the illusion that comes under the term family. What constitutes family? Family is a term. It is not a reality. Bonds tie one to another. Family is not man-made." *She might mean like marriage: that instantly makes a husband-and-wife family in the eyes of the world, even though they are not blood or gene related.*

She continues, "The one that is perceived as not family may be more family than the one perceived as family. Is not the one that is loved, true family? Indeed, is one speaking of blood or spiritual relationship? There are different bonds. Bonding is of an active nature. How one thinks limits the term."

"Oh Metude, you are so right. We humans have created such limits to our relationships. I think of family as relating through blood and genes, yet Roger and I were considered family by everybody since the moment we said 'I do,' without blood or genes. I hadn't thought of that."

Wouldn't the world be a loving place if we extended our feeling of family to all those we love? And doesn't that make it look different?

"Yah, indeed. One excludes much. We will proceed."

Do Not Fear the Future ~ a New Relationship

I nod to Brooke, as she has been patiently waiting for her questions. She has begun dating a young man she met at university a year ago. Now, she is considering going to another university a thousand miles away. She is concerned about leaving this relatively new relationship and wants to know if the distance will damage it.

"Ah, the young one need not fear for her relationship. Do not worry what might happen. It's not to talk of an ending when it's just the beginning. One must enter the joy of that which has been given to you. It is to delight in. Do not fear for the future. One does not live only for the moment, but enjoys what the moment brings."

"Oh, thank you Metude." *Brooke is delighted.*

Our old friend continues, "The relationship provides more opportunity to grow into the whole you are to become. You have been given the gift of discernment, of listening, too. It is one of your most valuable tools, a tool to enable you to live life to the fullest extent, as you move directly into intuitive awareness." *Oh, you are so right. My relationships certainly offer me a human schoolroom.*

My wise old friend, turning her head toward Brooke, continues, "Go within yourself. It is not necessarily rational or reasonable what you recognize as truth, but it is receiving information. In a very deliberate way, exercise it. Take a subject, settle, allow one to perceive what one sees as the answer." She pauses, then adds, "A different manner than of (intuitive listening), a flavour of your own. Yet, could work in much the same manner (*I think she means as I do*) in building confidence. Have confidence. So be it. The human side requires confidence. Use human wisdom at this time. Proceed."

Hmm, use human wisdom for this situation because it is on the human side. What an interesting distinction. Are there different wisdoms? Maybe there are, according to the frequency of our vibration.

Brooke, changing the subject, asks about Pam's cold. The cottage woman pauses, then says, "Let me search the body." She nods and states simply, "I see germs moving around." Brooke and I look at each other and break out laughing. *I assume cold germs.*

Then, without pause, Metude shifts in the rocker, observing, "This body is impatient. A short visit." I expect this is because Pam does have shingles and a cold. Brooke and I thank her for her wisdom.

Then Metude adds, "We will be with each of you. There is not a barrier that exists between us. And now I must bid you good day." Again, after a little muscle change, Pam is back and stretching.

In her wake, as usual, this ancient, remarkable woman leaves an overwhelming feeling of gratitude and largeness. Maybe it was a short visit, but the information is important to understanding situations, and saves a lot of wasted energy. I now see that with the special needs child only the body he uses is damaged and it is not as bad as the mother thinks or we think. In other words, the boy is not his body. Also, in regard to Abby seeing us as sisters, she said that family is not defined or limited by genes and is defined by relationship, love, and bondedness. Thus, she always leaves me thinking outside my little box, which continually changes my perception of reality and opens me to a grander world.

LOVING THE RAW LIFE OF IT ALL

August 10/87 My, it was good to talk to Metude in person. We haven't done so since before Pam's breakdown. I told my old friend that I feel distant from her when I don't meet her in person. She said I think of her as being separate, so I experience her presence as separate. I do experience it as separate, as she is always sitting across from me in the rocker. It's hard to do otherwise. Apparently, I make it separate when she is with me in the invisible. How often does she feed my actions or feelings, in a certain situation, back to me in our next visit when I have a question? Amazing really, when I think of how "with me" she is! She knows the details of conversations and actions when Pam is totally absent. In fact, most of the time, the latter is at her house buried in a family crisis. Didn't I fall off the bike going to karate tonight? The country roads are so narrow that one has to get off on the shoulder when a car passes. I slid down the gravel into the ditch, face down! It hurt, but I continued on to karate. However, I am writing this with a skinned palm embedded with gravel and a chin that is road-burned, which is still stinging. The saltwater swim afterward helps to keep the infection out. But in spite of the slide, how blessed am I to be able to workout at karate, ride the bike to the dojo, fly home on it in the dark, and especially jump in the ocean when I get here. I love the vigor and raw life of it all. In fact, I thrive on it. The other day, my dear neighbour, Mila, was saying that when she goes back to Prague in the winter, the image that always comes to her is of me swimming down past her beach in any kind of weather—be it rain, fog, or whatever. Quite frankly, I don't know what would keep me out.

A few days later . . .

August 13/87 We had our wedding anniversary feast today. We had supper at the Yacht Club. Showed our wedding film and another of when we were first going together. I was 19 and Roger 23.
Then, with Mila and her husband, we took two canoes down the river. Mist covered the hills on both sides. The water was still. The sky from the setting sun was a

panorama of colour, muted pinks, yellows, magenta and cobalt-blues. "Red sky at night, sailors' delight…"

The highlight of the day was Roger's anniversary present. He built us a bed out of pine with a back board and shelves on the headboard to hold books, even though he doesn't read.

Also, thank goodness, Pam and I are back laughing and feeling together again. Those days away at Sally's cottage were valuable, and I think it was worth doing. Time will tell.

• • •

Identifying Another Stream of Consciousness, It Is in Everything

Following the cottage woman's hints, I started listening to Abby's guide information more closely. I had begun to note subtle changes, at odd times, to her tone and inflection. She was not aware of the shift, as it was so natural. Working with the cottage woman was different. She was sitting right in front of me, whereas Abby's guides were invisible and seemingly more happenstance.

One afternoon, a week after the last visit with Metude, I caught that subtle shift in Abby's voice so asked if they were the guides that had talked to us last fall which were on her left side. They were and she seemed to be taking it all normally, so I asked if they had anything to say. The first suggestion was not to set up a regular time for meeting. "Allow it to be more spontaneous as fluidity and flexibility will be part of it. Yours is a questioning position. You question, then you transport the information to where it is needed, that makes the information one piece. You are like a factory. You are to get what you hear out to people." *Oh, my land, I have never thought of myself that way, but what a neat way of putting it! Well, I do pass the information on.*

She continues, "However, at the same time, when you are with others, the information comes through in other unusual ways. Watch for it. You are not limited to your friends. Information is in everything: trees, rocks, birds, everything. Just keep awake. When you don't, it is to your detriment. It is in everything that happens around you. Some ways are just weaker than others." *I am sure this must be from another stream of consciousness.*

"You have been given great faith. It is because you can hear and believe that the others can be clear conduits to other streams of consciousness. She needs to use her imagery."

Interestingly, Abby often speaks using metaphors and images, which at times, cleverly brings mental clarity to complex situations. Yet, she seems to be unaware of how important the information can be.

Taking the opportunity while the stream of consciousness was still running, I asked again about writing a book. Abby turns and looks through the window at the trees observing, "Fall will be a beginning of compiling and preparation for a book. It is essential that you conserve energy. Do not take on new people. Set aside a couple times a week, a couple of afternoons for gathering your information. If you don't, it won't get done. Not to be the burden one thinks." *Oh, it does feel like a mountain of work.* "You'll get in the rhythm and there will be a space in between. Simple, you will be a writer. Much joy in it for you."

Then I asked about Abby and I being sisters and what it would be like. Again, there was a change of tone and feeling as she responded, "Sisters, do not deny, it will serve no purpose. The work is done. Like a filling station, a long and lasting friendship. You were brought together for love, by love, and not for information. It is uncomplicated. The information access will help strengthen the relationship. Again, do not deny being sisters. It would serve no purpose."

Then, just as suddenly as the guides started talking, the energies changed. Later, Abby added that the guides had been standing by an old mill like last time. I also asked if they knew Metude, but they did not know her *personally*, which is a rather interesting qualifier.

As I write this thirty some years later, Abby and I still visit these two monks of the left side which she sees in her inner vision. And they still offer us invaluable wisdom and, at times, still meet us by that old mill.

A WORLD RAPIDLY CHANGING ~ I STAYED TOO LONG

August 20/87 Pam looks terrible, and they are living in hell. Thank God, Frank consented to go into hospital after the doctor ordered it this afternoon. She took him in earlier. Oh, that they work with him! The kids were against it. Of course, they don't want their father going into the "psych ward." But God, what choice did she have? Their world is rapidly changing. Pam can hardly work with people now. The visits with Metude are short. Her life is in such turmoil. Oh, that they can help him. Had the best talk with her this morning. She has gone through the fire, but I feel her strength, her detachment, and her wish for freedom. And that is a good piece of work done by both of us. We have such a sweet spirit with a real twinkle between us. Too bad it gets squashed at times.

Just bought some fish from Pam's youngest. They have nice boys, and it is sad that they have to live in. Amazing that people continue to smile.

The Pam I knew years ago is gone. A new person is emerging. Her innocence is gone. Their home of the past is no more. They will move, separately or together. This has been a wonderful, meaningful era of friendship for us—fifteen years. Well, and will it be the end of a long, hard-rock road for her and Frank? We'll see.

Three days later . . .

August 23/87 Out here on the lawn, I need this silence, this aloneness. Metude tells me, "You must provide for your own isolation, your own aloneness, your own time for silence." She is right.
Oh, yes, I ordered a new karate gi made of a heavier canvas this morning to go with my new, hard-earned green belt. Driving to the grading, my karate friend Rod and I wondered why we put ourselves through it. However, my body has never been so well worked out. I sweat buckets, come home, and have a night swim with the terns. Maybe they are bats.
Pam called. The hospital won't keep Frank! My oh my, all it takes is a pair of eyes and ears. Why does it have to get so dragged out? Talk about human endurance—years of it. What does he have to do, shoot them

all and himself? It is so bad. Pam said tonight, "I've stayed too long." Talk about an understatement.

Letting go of making it better . . .

August 25/87 Back to this silence, which is wrapping and enfolding me at this moment. Mila gave me a birthday gift—a poem. It read, "A blazing fire in your heart and may the wind of the spirit blow it into the darkness of others. May you reach out your hand daily." Thank you, dear friend. I will try.

She is also helping me clarify this situation with Pam and Frank. I keep trying to make it better; maybe I can't and need to accept it as a fact. It may never be better or something worse will happen. Yet, I want Pam to be free, be safe, in light, and live life rather than this miserable struggle to exist.

Visiting with my ancient friend is threatened. However, I must also remember my people work does not rest on the whim of Frank and Pam's future. That was well established before Metude blessed us with her presence, her great other side experience, and her wisdom. But oh, how I would feel orphaned without her!

ALLOW PAIN TO BE WITH WHOM IT BELONGS ~ MUCH FREEDOM

As bleak as it is for Pam, she called yesterday suggesting we have a visit today. Brooke is here, but she has to leave early. Abby is now joining us at times, thanks to Metude giving a few more people permission to visit. Initially, it is always an adjustment for new people to watch the transition from Pam to the cottage woman. In my years of visiting with her, I do not think I ever thought it ordinary even though the changing of muscles became less obvious as time passed. New visitors generally take their own notes as I, of course, continue to do.

After greetings, we settle in and I ask the most pressing concern: how is Pam holding up under all her family stress? *Her stiff upper lip can betray what really is going on and it's hard to work with what I can't see.*

Surprisingly, my ancient friend seems quite perky. "Much freedom. It is as told; this body will attain age. It is good. Much was said, much was heard, and much was addressed (our week away). It's coming. It is good to give

what is due. When one decides to let go, back on the path. It is coming. There is a realization by the Person, how one creates one's own barriers by fear. Now back on the path."
Oh, this surprises me, but I am so thankful. These weeks of her venting must be working. And wouldn't you know, just when I am thinking of letting go of trying to make it better.

My old friend pauses, and I hear a note of caution, "Yet, she will be more disbelieving about medium (psychic) talk. Much lies ahead for her. Very difficult time. So be it. Proceed." *Then, so be it.*

"Metude, another person we have worked with for the last couple of years is gaining much freedom, too. Fran told me yesterday, 'I know who I am. I now have more confidence in myself.' That is the statement of her coming home to herself and now she, too, is looking forward to a more caring future. And it is all payment for the hard, human-lesson work she has accomplished and the help from you."

Nodding again with a hint of a smile, this discarnate friend says, "Indeed, we are pleased much work has been done."

The "stake" was gradually removed from Fran's chest during months of pain work using the breathing process. In time, she separated from her mother and claimed her own identity as she witnessed above. Years later, when Fran had healed significantly and her mother had passed away, her mother appeared to her in much love. I happened to be with her at the time and the love was so strong it made us both tearful. In the image or visitation, her mother showed her a padlock. It had been open, which reminded me of what Fran was always saying, "If I can heal, my mother will be healed, too." Experiencing her mother's caring presence seemed to suggest that on some level, she had.

Past Moments Need Not Be Past ~ One Cannot Be of Service to All

I look over to Brooke, knowing she needs to ask a question for her younger brother. He wants to know how he "can meditate and get to a spiritual place."

Metude replies instantly, saying brightly, "Ah yah, the young man with the love of the sea. It would be helpful in his mind if he would recreate sailing episodes when he felt so at peace with himself and at one with the universe. Would also be helpful if he would struggle less. To be gentler with himself. Then gently dismiss struggling thoughts rather than becoming impatient with himself. When that happens, it would be helpful to check his breathing. The most beneficial exercise is the move back in the extra peace within himself that he finds when sailing."

She pauses, I wait, and she then adds, "In a sense, his experience has to be re-lived and thus, it will become real again. A reality to him. It should not be thought of in terms of the past. We will proceed." *How interesting, she is really saying there is no past. He can recall and re-experience the meditative power of sailing's beauty, harmony, and power in the present. Those meaningful moments can nurture us right now.*

Brooke continues, "Thank you, Metude. He also always wants to know if you have any wisdom to give him for doing his human lessons."

Slightly amused she responds, "There is not much I can do about the natural process of maturing." *Brooke is laughing and so am I. She is so right; I'd love to hurry my maturity along.*

She continues, "He is a thinker, not a talker. Thinks and mulls. Sometimes he goes past mulling to struggling. Time is for him to be growing and maturing, which he is doing." She pauses, as if checking it out, then nods, "Good, indeed, good."

Several of Brooke's friends come from more difficult family situations. Metude, intuiting her next question, looks at Brooke, kindly saying. "My child, you cannot be of service to all. Do you understand that?"

Brooke does try to pass on what she learns from these visits to them, but their problems can be overwhelming. Our old friend continues, "Yet, wise to access your sense of responsibility with your friends. 'Tis merely to offer choices, not to make them for them. Lessons are not always apparent by what appears on the surface. Search your heart for what you really want for them, but don't accept responsibility for what they do or do not do. 'Tis good that, you are positive. One of the friends in particular is aware, much as a vibration one gives off. One need not always be happy, but is to remain positive. Do you understand this? Do you need more understanding?"

"I will think about it. Thank you."

I interrupt, as Brooke has to leave. "Is there a word of wisdom for her personally, Metude?"

Nodding, she observes, "A busy life." Then adds gently as an aside, "Would be nice if she would enjoy this day.

To note the sunshine and the crispness of the air and to lay aside the problems for the moment. They will still be there." *I laugh, knowing how true that statement is for each of us.* Brooke laughs too, then she thanks both of us on her way out.

I now ask how Abby is doing with her growth work as this is a chance for her to hear about it in person and not second-hand from me.

Rocking, she nods, "Struggles, yet her progress is good. The breathing and questioning process you use with her is good." *Yes, the same one I use with others is effective.*

Also, there are questions that lead to identifying emotions that often drive our actions like fear and guilt, which we are good at hiding from. Also, the simple breathing out and in at different speeds works to release pain. Plus, of course, the logical "how to" directions she gives me for different problems in almost every visit.

Abby has been gaining more self-esteem and awareness. However, now she is questioning her relationship with her husband, Stan. Television and football are his focus, and he has seemingly no interest in meaningful conversation. She is lonely and wonders if he loves her at all. It rather reminds me of others I have worked with. These husbands are threatened when their wives start feeling their own personal value and want more meaningful relating.

Abby's husband is generally a gentle, soft-spoken man, but he occasionally makes damaging comments, like calling her a demeaning name. I cringe hearing him sometimes. Initially, she did not seem to notice, but now she is becoming acutely aware of how harmful such remarks are.

However, she excuses him by saying he was deprived of relationships as a child, then she feels so badly for him it seems to stop her from making progress herself. *It is almost like a misplaced compassion, if there is such a thing, as it keeps her from challenging him in several areas that could be healthier for both of them. So, I want her to hear this wise old woman's words directly.*

Metude nodding, adjusts her position in the rocker, "Have her focus on needs in herself, not other things. She must allow pain to be with whom it belongs. Recognize that she carries what in this case is not her own (pain, but his pain). This causes confusion." Turning her head toward Abby she continues, "Carrying another's pain does not make you a good person. Must be addressed." *Hmm, we humans do go around carrying others' pain too often.*

Abby, seeming relaxed, asks, "But how can I encourage him to talk to me and really see me as a person and not just a wife?" *Good question!*

"Much is buried in the person; he looks on the surface. The relationship is not in reality where he thinks it is. Follow the information given you."

The day before, I had asked Pam for an image of their situation. She saw Abby standing before Stan, but she was significantly smaller. The image called to mind the tomb portraits of the ancient Egyptian pharaohs being disproportionately large compared to the much smaller figures of their surrounding family members and retinue. The image's information had disturbed me. Women have been considered less than equal to men for a long, long time.

My old friend reading my mind continues, "She must find a way to up her stature. Her mate is looking straight ahead, masked, and blindfolded. Make time for his exposure to truth, as the light will hurt his eyes. Love him and pray for him. He is blinded somewhat." *What an astute caution. The light will initially hurt his eyes. Hmmm, we pray for light, but apparently can only stand it to the degree our human work has enlarged our capacity to receive.*

"'Tis good and now we will proceed."

Bonding with Those on the Other Side ~ Give It Attention

Abby's father passed away when she was seventeen. He was a great love for her. As her spiritual sensitivities develop, she notices she is becoming increasingly aware of his presence so asks if she is really sensing her father after all these years?

There is that small enigmatic smile, "Yah, indeed, the bond is increasing. Awareness may promote it by turning one's thoughts to him. Must realign thoughts. Death does not remove him from you. Also, others who have passed are not removed."

My old friend pauses a moment, then continues, "Such as a grandmother who has a deep love for you." *The grandmother Metude must be referring to is Abby's father's mother, who lived in Italy during World War II. Abby had never met her.*

Metude pauses, then adds, "There are others. 'Tis good, we will proceed." *Now that is a teaser. I wonder who the others are and how many times this ancient woman has witnessed the fact that we live on—not as flesh, but as being or a human form without skin and bone!*

Speaking about people who have made that transition to the other side, my next question is about Roger's aunt May. I seem to be helping May and Roger since Grandmother passed when I talk to them about it, but I want to check it out with my deep-seeing friend.

Again, she pauses then observes, "There is a father with a child sitting on his lap. She is listening to him." *The child must be May.* "The way they look at each other: a mind-thought bond. Fulfilling for the father in particular. Do not fear tears or emotion." *And I know May has them. And she has told me about that bond so often and it has always been there for her. Maybe it is more fulfilling for her father now, as he may feel it more not having a human body of skin and bone to interfere.*

Metude lifts her head as she slightly turns closed eyes toward me, saying, "Tears are not negative. You will be there for them. Wings and shadow that is you." *What a curious description.*

Feeling the energy begin to shift, knowing it is time for my old friend to leave, she turns to Abby, nodding, "I will be with you. When you have moments of despair, you have but to turn. We will speak again soon. (Many) barriers are down. May you each walk in light." And she is gone.

LATE SUMMER TRANSITION ~ AND TOO MUCH COMPANY

August 25/87 Ah, one of those crazy back-to-back company times which so often happens in August. The children are all home, so we have to put the company in the cottage tonight. And without exaggerating, most nights we sit ten at the table in the summer. I like the people that come and love some of them, but the work of it is laborious. This is one place Roger and I are not lined up. He loves having company, and for me an afternoon visit does fine. I need space—not more people, baking, changing beds, and sitting, talking for hours as he goes out to work around in the yard. Four different sets of company in two weeks is too much. And it is most annoying when Roger turns and asks, "Why are you tired?"
Yet, even he is telling me he is tired tonight. I said nothing. And thank God I am going camping—a necessary getaway. "Create your own isolation," as Metude suggests. And here I come.

A few days later, an ocean retreat . . .

August 29/87 Abby and I are camping here at Risser's Beach. It's a great break. As usual, I am the first one up. I've just meditated for half an hour to the early morning smells of pine, spruce, fir, and salt water. I am truly in heaven. Plus, I will get to paint all day in the sun with the sound of seagulls and the ocean.

Yesterday, I did a seascape of Little Harbor. It was wonderful sitting alongside the road painting that small fish shack in the warmth, people wandering by, and I had lunch on the hill overlooking the sea. Did a couple of okay paintings. Back to camp for a swim in the breakers. Diving into one wave after another, I couldn't get enough of it. My, it is like holding heaven in my eyes being in these places.

Abby's up and cooking breakfast—here's the aromatic smell of Lunenburg sausage, eggs, fried potatoes, and onions. She is seriously considering university in the fall. Will she, do it? I keep encouraging her. After all the personal work she has done, she deserves to get out and engage a larger arena than being a housewife. Her children are mostly grown as well.

The Third Fall & Winter

'Tis harder to screen through a human body that is not mine.

LIFE CHANGES REQUIRE OF ME A NEW RELATEDNESS ~ A NEW WINE

Sept. 3/87 These fall changes certainly require a new relatedness. The kids will be back to university shortly. My friends are considering launching forth in their own educational directions. Wow. It does require letting go of what I have loved, but now new wine needs to fill new wine skins. Some sadness for me, like when the kids were younger, and I'd watch them walk across the field for that first day of school. Every fall was different, even though everything looked the same on the surface. It wasn't.

The little hitch for me is that what has been for twenty years plus is no longer. The children growing up makes me think of what used to be. Thus, it's vital for me to accept this new reality and let go of the old one. An era of raising children successfully, to date at least, is finished. God that's wonderful. Now they will walk with others and, of course,

*that is what has been happening anyway.
And oh yes, last night, after Callie was
watching me struggle with the weeds in
the garden, she said, "You are whole, you
have influenced each of our lives." Later she
thanked me for the choices and the discipline
that I followed along the way. Then said,
"You took care of yourself." Well, I tried. It
is so important for mothers and mentors to
do so.*

A week later, working on university . . .

*Sept. 10/87 Pam's lost her spark, but gained
her strength, value, and much more of her
own separateness as a person. However, her
old world has come crashing down since
spring. The shingles on her back are still
ugly. A dark winter for her unless something
happens. She said, "It would have been
easier if Frank had died." It does feel
like that.
I first dared to mention the possibility of her
going to university during our week away in
the summer. Now, I really can't see any other
future for her unless she does. Yet, it feels
like such a gigantic leap. I know she has the
smarts for it. We have been and are working
on her resistance to it—not only her fears,
but her excuses. How vital and life giving*

a move that could be. It would balance the desperate weight of her home life, introduce her to new people, new ideas, a new way of living, and give her more self-value. Right now, it just looks like that half dug-out basement waits. I will check out with Metude when we visit Friday.

A FEW DAYS LATER ~ POSSIBLY A GIANT STEP

Sept. 15/87 Eureka! I think Pam is going to university, but she still gets iffy on it. I am excited. Roger has investigated the entrance requirements for mature students the last few weeks and student loans are available. At nights, he and Pam have worked on filling out the applications, just in case she might go. She keeps telling me she is not ready, which I know is partially true. I keep telling her I believe in her, that she is smart enough to do it. I am also trying to leave her enough space for her choices as the cottage woman suggests. We keep peeling away the excuses, fears, and have walked miles in the last few days—from defeat to hopefully a new spirit and strength. I wonder if the university will mean a lot less time for Metude's visits. I have worked alone before and will again, if need be.

I can feel that Pam is a bit excited. Thank You, God. The door is open. A good week's work. And Frank is softening up a bit, or maybe Pam is just getting stronger. He even agreed to go back to his therapist which seems to be helping him somewhat.

• • •

A Fledgling Attempt for a Cottage Woman-Like Wisdom ~ A Purple Pillow

Brooke dropped in to see if she could ask the other stream of consciousness (guides) for some information without going through Metude. So, I stretched out on the bed without a lot of confidence and tried to relax. Then, I paused until my entire body felt weightless, maybe like what an astronaut feels floating in a space module.

An answer came, but it seemed ordinary so I didn't tell her. She repeated the question. This time, I decided not to judge whether the information was true or not, so told her, "Take a pen, then ask your question at a time when you are alone and utterly relaxed. Listen into the silence. Listen. You will know when you get the answer. Early morning, after supper, and late evening are beneficial times. Yet, as you already know, it can happen in a moment. Find the time of day that is good for you and practise it. Make it a habit. Turn your mind to the expectation of it. Trust it. You will gain confidence." This all came out in a burst, but I felt I was probably copying the cottage woman. So, as I told Brooke to proceed, we both laughed.

Then, she asked if she would find a place to live near the university. Again, waiting a little, an image appeared with information. "A place to live is not hard to find. I see a family around a table having an evening meal. It's an older house. The family will be okay for you. Yet I sense an atmosphere, not negative, yet not a lot of fun." I was shocked as I actually could hear the chatter which reminded me of the experience Pam and I had of the garden party in the 1800s that happened several months ago at The Center.

"How will I recognize it?" she asked. *Hmm, how would she recognize it?*

I told her the question is too hard for me. She suggested I try. Then, instantly, I heard, "When you are looking for a room, notice a purple pillow." And with that, I was eager to end the session. I could not imagine she'd ever see a purple pillow. No wonder Pam struggles with giving out information." *I'll have to ask Metude about what happens if one gives out the "wrong information."*

This reminded me of her telling me, "You are getting more information than you realize." And yes, I am beginning to recognize that. Maybe, I did get a purple pillow. As, at times, the stream of information really seems right there on the tip of my tongue. Yet, it's to listen and then when you hear or see something the question is, how to interpret it?

Now, during a crisis or when I have serious questions and Pam and I cannot meet with the cottage woman for a visit, Abby and I are learning what we call "doing guide information." Later, when checking it out with Metude, she tells me that information is "of the same essence" as hers. However, again we have to be careful we don't get in the way and misinterpret it in our enthusiasm.

AN OPPORTUNITY TO GROW, EXPLORING A NEW FRONTIER

Another eureka: the big news is that Pam is taking four courses. Amazing. Metude said the other day, "Your friend will see this as a year of great learning. There is a significant gain in freedom from the past, as well as the present. It will become easier to maintain the balance. One needs reassurance that the bonds that have been set will remain. Merely know that and trust that."

Pam called this morning. She has a bad cold, but she wants to visit with the cottage woman. She is eager to hear about her new possibilities at university. I also need her wisdom because next weekend we are going down to Mother's. After Pam is comfortable, the rocking chair begins to move, and it feels like the room is filling up with a liquid calm. Greeting Metude, I ask about the information of the purple pillow— is it really a sign of where Brooke might live? *Metude hints at a smile. Of course, she knows the question is coming.*

"Ah, indeed, the purple pillow is like a minor clue. Significance will come at a later time. Will be revealed. A heightened perception." *Hmm, so Brooke may actually see a purple pillow!*

"Oh, thank you Metude! That is so helpful." *Imagine: It might be real information I'm receiving. Now, I need the proof.* (Several weeks later, I wrote in my journal, "Brooke called, and she found a place to stay. In her room was a purple pillow. Now that's proof.")

Asking Questions ~ Like Exploring a New Frontier

My question now is, "Why do we have to be so specific when asking you questions?" She made this specification when we first met, and she has mentioned it several times since.

My ancient friend leans forward. "It becomes harder to screen work through a human body that is not mine. Continue to question; do not be as doubting. Phrasing your questions positively is most helpful, do not phrase them in the negative. When asking your questions, think of it as exploring a new frontier. 'Tis a learning experience for you. Welcome the question, the new thought. The door will open. Do not fear. Future is never to be feared. You must tread boldly, my child. Much awaits you, many challenges. Indeed, 'tis good. We will proceed."

"And, oh Metude, isn't it wonderful that Pam is going to university? It feels like a victory for both of us."

My old friend begins to rock, nodding, "Again it will be seen as a year of great learning and freedom. Relationships will hold. A mountain climbed, much like a beginning step. Yah, 'tis very good. It is much like a beginning step. The Person has not fully realized it yet."

Neither have I, really, but it does feel like the end of a long road. And she has certainly climbed more than one emotional mountain to get here. Then she leans toward me again, frowning, "Yet, not the need for a cold in the body, a chronic cold. The person had been told what to do. She is not sure if it is true." *Sounds like me second guessing my information. Obviously, whatever Pam was told, she has not yet done. I'll remind her when she comes back in.*

Accused of Being Selfish ~ An Opportunity to Grow

"Pam wants me to ask how you feel about her first few days of university?"

Metude seems pleased. "Much progress, much learning will follow, a path freshly started. New opportunities presented in a way she does not expect. Areas to test new-found strength." *Oh, thank goodness, it's working.*

I reflect, "Now she can make new friends and find her independence from us all—husband, family, and me. Yet, her family continues to accuse her of being selfish and of putting herself first, which causes both guilt and stress. We wives and mothers have all been taught that we serve others before ourselves and not to do so is being selfish." *And who wants to be seen as a selfish person? Again, the airlines have it right, put on your own oxygen mask first before helping someone else.*

Metude moves forward in the rocker and instantly responds. "Putting oneself first is not what is expected. What she is doing is not selfish, but rather an opportunity for growth. Serves no purpose to follow another's directive. If she follows her mate, then neither is fulfilled. What the Person really wants to do is not selfish. Serves no purpose to preach one thing while the heart does another. When one follows a true course, the rest falls in place. To put husband and family before oneself is conditioning and what is expected."

She continues, "Ask oneself the question, what does one really want to do? Then list what stands in the way—for example, social perception, conditioning, or what is brutally laid upon one. The reasons become more factual when put on paper. This is not meant to make light of responsibility, but to clarify responsibility." Again, she repeats, "What she is doing is not selfish, but is an opportunity for growth. Serves no purpose to follow another's directive, (her husband's), then neither is fulfilled. Serves no purpose to preach one thing while the heart does another. When one follows a true course, the rest falls in place."

Again, Metude asks the question, "What does one really want to do?"

"I feel uneasy as she still may quit university because of the family's resistance." To be forewarned is to be forearmed.

Nodding to my thoughts, my old friend responds, "A great gain of strength for her. The potential is there, but watch motivation." *Oh, she is warning me.* "Much growth. Many opportunities. A decision has yet to be made."

My old friend continues, "We see the value of choices."

She's right; now I have to step back. The choices are Pam's. "There will be a block, not of your making but presented. Move through it when it comes. That is good. We will proceed."

"What about her family? The pressure is on her."

"Much pain and tears, but healing. Wholeness will follow. Tears, do not fear them."

We know tears are healing, but we never seem to shed them—a good dose of the "stiff upper lip" mentality growing up here in the Maritimes, probably, due in part to our Canadian-British history.

My ancient friend continues, "The person is ridding herself of guilt that is not hers to carry. She will be provided with more people she needs to walk with."

Then Metude's face has the slightest change of expression as she says caringly, "Do not trouble your heart over her down periods. 'Tis good."

"I know. Thank you." *But my heart is still troubled.* I need to ask, "How is my growth-work coming?

An Intimacy Shared ~ When One Works with the Depths of Another

"Metude, I have another slight concern because of the work, painting, and music that brings Abby and me together a lot. I hope there is enough balance in our relationship."

Appearing thoughtful she replies, "Becomes easier to maintain the balance. One needs reassurance that the bond has set and will remain. Merely to know that is to trust it. The image of the past life is for you to work with. We work with them too—another working tool. It means she is more receptive to you than others." *It seems we are kindred. She must be referring to our being sisters at one time.*

"Well, Metude, I do like our togetherness, but I want the relationship to be separate and independent. So does she."

"There is an emotional intimacy shared when one works with the depths of another's soul work that can lead to dependency. More learning to be given. More opportunity to be exercised. In one's individual, unique journey, there is glory in this honouring of separateness. It is in existence already. Move into owning it. It will grow. Freedom alone will bring closeness."

"Oh, thank you, Metude. Is that freedom coming along, okay?" *I sensed early in the relationship that Abby is independent by nature.*

"'Tis good your friend sees this. Great year of learning for her. A significant gain in freedom from the past, too, as well as the present. College is merely a piece of the whole picture. Other doors will be open. Exposure to people that she has not yet met. Not relaxed yet. As one progresses outward, new things will surface, given the need. Once missed the first time, given later."

We are always reassured by this consistent assertion that "they" give us mortals many chances to learn what we need to learn in this dimension.

Positive Thought Transfers Information ~ Your Heart Is Loving

My discarnate friend's words to Abby about separation and independence reminds me of my issues with my mother.

Our hearts seem to have been hurting about our relationship all my life. There was a chasm between us that I could never quite bridge even though now I understand it much better. I know she needs me to call her more than once a week, but it is safer for me to love her by keeping a little distance. Yet, our imperfect dynamic can make me feel guilty.

Metude interrupts my reverie: "Your positive thoughts are transferring communication. Need not get in touch. One is doing her own work. She sees problems in her own way. Trust your instincts, child." *This beyond wise, ancient friend looks at me with such compassion that I almost come to tears.*

"Oh, Metude, these words are so comforting. I have felt bad forever about not being more attentive to her.

She moves forward in the rocker and thrusts out her forefinger, saying, "Your heart is loving. Trust your instincts." *Oh, I don't think I know that. I have a loving heart.*

Interesting. I had written in my journal a couple of days before that I dreamed of Mother. She came and told me that I had not called. In other words, she was telling me I was neglecting her—or at least, that is how I interpreted it. I hate that. Anyway, I called her. Then on the phone, she began telling me she had a dream, saying, "I saw your name Augusta written in capital letters on a sign in my dream. The letters were raised in gold and silver." Her thought was to buy it for me. We had a good chat, but I felt worse when I hung up. She would pay whatever it cost for that sign, out of devotion to me, in spite of the challenges in our relationship.

Fear of the Unknown –
What She Calls Dying

Having another question, I ask, "How is Mother, really? She has a lot of physical pain." Her backbone is beginning to collapse from osteoporosis.

"Physical illness is present. The body panics, a severe emotional correlation between fear and illness. She fights against the unseen, as if it's the enemy, when fear itself is the greatest enemy. Fear of pain, fear of the unknown. What she calls dying." Metude is thoughtful as she observes, "She has refused to let go and allow you to become who you are. Your distancing is interpreted as not caring. Causes her grief, as well as anger. She expresses anger, not to you but to others." *Oh. She talks to others about me. I hate that.*

"She has not identified the sources of her panic. Physical stress is caused by panic and fear. Much damage is done to the physical body by self-creating stress."

"Should I try to go after those feelings this weekend?"

"It would not be helpful. Better if one expressed concern and caring as in being supportive. Not a time for challenging." *Oh, what a relief.*

"What are my options?" I ask, desperate for a strategy.

"Visit her. She will interpret that as caring. What one says will not fall on deaf ears. Her body would benefit from rest, sunlight, and music. She responds to gentle caresses. Much soothing comes to this one by gentle touches. Time for touching rather than talking." *Now that will be hard as I am keen on keeping my distance, not touching.*

My old friend continues. "Key is in the gentleness of the approach. Harshness is to be avoided. What one (she) perceives as harshness is not harsh but perceived as harsh. Much tenderness is vital here. Pain throws perspective out of focus. Hang onto your truth. That alone must guide your words and actions. One can't compromise a truth and have it still exist as truth. What you could hear will be disturbing to you, but it need not be. You will possibly be confronted with questions. Answers do not need to be forthcoming on the spot. One needs time to feel what the answer must be." *Too often I want a question to be answered instantly, but, of course, I need time to feel it deeper.*

"Thank you, Metude; you do ground me in a larger and richer place." *You surely do.*

One Cannot Judge ~ We Do Not Have the Whole Picture

I have another question from a friend; she is concerned about her son, who is a fundamentalist. I tell Metude that my friend finds it a narrow way of thinking. Does she have any comments?

Nodding her head, she responds, "There are pathways. Some choose a narrow pathway to follow. If one chooses an open pathway, one questions. Learning only happens when one remains open. The one that becomes closed, they have all the answers." *Does this not apply to fundamentalist anything, be it religion, politics, or how one "should" live their life?*

My wise friend continues, "There is a continued opportunity for this young one to hear. Yet the closed path does not negate the lessons one learns. Do not judge. Lessons are not valid or invalid. One learns in one's own time. Again, do not judge. One doesn't have the complete picture." She pauses a moment and then states, "Neither do I." *How interesting. Even she doesn't.*

Maybe it is part of her learning, too. This also applies when we closed our mind to Metude. And think of all the wisdom we would have missed, and all the people not helped!

The rocker stops as I hear, "And now the body is restless. Again, we are not far from you. There is hope. Many blessings and much light to each."

"Oh, thank you Metude. A million times over and peace be with you and yours."

JAN REVISITS ~ A LOVING HEART

Oct. 17/87 Had a wonderful talk with Metude yesterday. There was so much energy in the cottage. And she is always changing my small-boxed perspectives. It was so helpful to hear that she thinks I have a loving heart and, most importantly, to hear it from someone like the cottage woman. It feels freeing and healing.
Mother and I had a beneficial talk, I think. Later, she also told me about her will. She is leaving her savings to me and a thousand dollars for each of the grandchildren. Maybe I am better understanding our relationship. It allows me to stand outside it, to an extent. I don't seem to get caught so much in old stuff.

A week later . . .

Oct. 24/87 Sunday evening, and my cousin Jan has arrived from the west. Her first visit since she helped bring in Metude two and a half years ago. It is also Pam's birthday. There is only six years difference in our ages, but I always think of her as being much younger.

We went to the Sheraton Hotel for lunch—it was fun, and we did some reminiscing about our ancient friend. We talked about her traumatic entrance, and then the terrifying sound of Beat in the living room after that first visit. I reminded them how they all said we shouldn't meet with her again. Yet, if I hadn't made the deal with God on the cement veranda, I never would have had another visit either. And my old friend has been true to her word: "Love, I teach love." That statement has permeated every visit and much of our lives since. We have also arranged a visit for this week, and Jan has some interesting questions.

A REUNION, THE COTTAGE WOMAN MUST BE INVITED

It is late fall, and the snow is already building up under the cottage. The wood stove is stacked, and everyone is wrapped. Brooke has dropped in as well. Our discarnate friend comes in with relative ease. Jan has heard a lot about her in the last couple of years, and she is eager for a visit. The warmth from her presence in the room is palpable. *What a difference from those first scary encounters. This cottage woman is now a very special friend.*

Once we settle in and have a bit of a reunion, I tell Metude that Jan has several questions. She had been working with a friend out west who began to communicate through a guide called "Spokesperson." Apparently, the person doesn't physically come in like she does through someone's body. It's more like a sense-feeling, similar to Abby's guides on the left side.

Jan's question is, "Do you know about Spokesperson?"

She pauses. We wait. Then after a little she nods. "Indeed, more than one. Main one is a person which others rely on to speak for them. They are informed of (her friend's) disbelief. She wavers yes, maybe no." *So true.*

I interrupt, "Can Jan open up to someone one like you, Metude? She was saying last night that she wants the full experience of a spirit-person actually coming in and changing her body." *I wonder how we would respond this time? Scared again, probably."*

"I do not have that information. Tis not a gift. The body's energy vibration needs to be at a certain frequency. All have it in unique ways." *I think the key is in different ways.*

Interjecting, I observe, "I lie on my bed trying to practise 'out of body' (leaving my body while conscious), but nothing happens. Can I do it or am I wasting my time?"

"No, timing is not there. Each has the work that they are meant to do. Great progress is being made." *In other words, I also have my work designated and it is not "out of body" for the present, at least.*

Needing Proof ~ Then Go for Proof

Jan then tells Metude that her friend needs some proof that Spokesperson is real. *This should be interesting. Isn't that the hardest thing for each of us to get a hold of?*

"Yah, 'tis good that is the prime concern."

"What would you consider proof, Metude?" *Oh, excellent question, cousin. I can't wait for this answer.*

"One must always be very careful. The proof is found in one's heart. Often people are well meant in intention, but they deceive themselves. 'Tis not deliberate, but a misguided sense of wanting to help. At some point, you are given information from another source where you know one couldn't get it any other way." *So, that's one way of identifying it.*

Jan continues, "Well, my friend does sense-hear helpful information, but does not want to share it fearing she might be wrong and how it will affect the other person receiving it."

"Sense-hearing is valid information. One does not take responsibility for another's hearing. One does not own the information. That person has merely to search her heart to discover what is truth for her. It is important to watch how she phrases her information. Helpful that she does not take responsibility for it to herself. She could say 'I sense' instead of, 'I know.' She accepts responsibility when she should just merely allow it."

How often have Pam and I both struggled with whether the information is true or not? We wouldn't want to misguide anyone.

Jan is smiling. "Oh, thank you, Metude; she will be glad to hear Spokesperson was not just her imagination."

"Indeed not. We will proceed."

Pam wants me to ask about Frank, as he is more difficult again. My wise old friend responds instantly, "Seek medical attention. He is a hazard to his own health. Her body sense is correct. His emotional condition is not good. It has intensified." *It will never end.* She continues, "He is demanding and difficult. The Entity is to be aware of feeling guilt. All is being done. Much is held back. Opportunities for him if one wants doors to open. We will proceed."

Brooke has been taking notes for Jan, but she looks up hoping it is her turn. I tell Metude happily that Brooke was twenty-one last week. Not being sure whether my old friend knows how special this is, I add, "Twenty-one is like a magical age for us on earth as it marks one becoming an adult."

My old friend hesitates, "Yah, indeed a special age, yet it is important to value the child part of oneself." Nodding she adds, "A possibility of a good twenty-first year. The young one has many choices. Next few months, a time of choices, exploring what is wanted and other facets. Beware of making hasty decisions now and later. Wise to have second choices. Many other decisions have to be made. Not only yours." *Of course, our choices also are affected by others' choices.*

Brooke then asked if Metude was present the other night at the supper she had with her friends.

"My presence was not there. Proceed." *Oh really, I assume it is everywhere. Apparently not. Maybe that is why we have to ask for them to be present.*

I Must Be Invited First ~ The Body Has a Tendency to Ignore

Pam was telling me yesterday, which delightfully surprised me, that she and her neighbour might visit the latter's mother, who lives in a nearby province, sometime in the coming year. She wants to ask about it.

My old friend, looking slightly amused, responds, "Growth is emerging." *Yes, it seems to be. Thank goodness.*

"Will you be with her?" *She is quiet. I can't imagine she won't be.*

"I must be invited first." After a slight pause, she responds, "Ah, yah, but a great possibility." *Wow, she really does have to be invited. Let it be known wise woman, you have an open invitation from me. Yet, how important it is to ask.*

"But will Pam feel the joy of you like I do?"

"The opportunity exists, whether used, I cannot say. The body has a tendency to ignore and not pick up." *Interesting, and Pam is a hundred times more sensitive than myself. I'd think it'd take a considerable effort to ignore you!*

A Hug ~ But How Is the Question

Watching my old friend, wrapped in a blanket to keep out the cold (apparently only for Pam's sake), I am moved by how much love she constantly gives us just by sitting there by the fire, without saying a word. I want to hug her, but I am never sure if it is appropriate. Plus, originally, she said I could not touch "the Body." So, daring a bit, I tell her I'd like to hug her, and I ask her if that is possible.

The corners of her mouth turn up slightly as she rocks gently. *What will she say?*

"Yah, indeed, 'hug' is a term of joy and happiness. But let me know first, then hug. In a sense, both occupy one body." Hesitating, I then move slowly toward her, bending down, putting my hands on her shoulders and am very careful not to squeeze, as she feels a bit brittle. She does not hug me back. *Yet, I think I feel her pleasure and amusement.*

I sense that she is ready to leave. She pauses, as if there is difficulty. I ask, "What is it Metude?"

"Much distance with the Person this eve." *Oh, she means between Pam and her.* "Yet, much will be accomplished in the next work. 'Tis good. It has been a pleasure to visit. Ah, it has done my heart much good. Enjoy your community and we bid you good eve." *Jan's heart is in good shape too, she is all smiles.*

Later that evening, I wrote in my journal, "Metude, thank you for meeting with us. All my smallness needs to be thrown out the window and I need to give everyone an extra mile." *If I can only remember to do it.*

A MINI VISIT AND A LITTLE PARTY - TWO GLASSES OF WINE

Pam came down for supper. Mila and Abby have dropped in too. Jan leaves tomorrow for home. Thus, it ends up being a little going away party. We have had lobster, wine, and now have a little glow. Since it is their last night, I ask Pam if we can have a mini visit with Metude. I am wondering how the wine will affect our old friend when she comes in. *I feel a slight concern.*

After greetings, I tell Metude about the party and the wine, and I ask how she feels. She waits a minute, then nods, "A strange effect on one's body. It is interesting to observe." *Oh, she feels the wine. Jan and Mila are looking on with mischievous little grins.*

"Well, Pam has had two glasses, which is rare for her," I explain.

"Two glasses, nice for me, yah." *That's funny. We giggle. She likes it.*

However, after a long pause, she begins to frown and states, "Yah, yah, wine and blood pressure." After a little silence, she observes, "We will fix it." *Hmm, oh, wine must raise Pam's blood pressure, maybe it is not so funny.*

"How?"

"We are merely slowing the blood rates." *We wait.* Then she nods saying, "Proceed." *I must tell Pam that she needs to be more careful with wine.*

God Is Not Contained ~ Boundaries Are Put in by Humankind

Leaning forward, Jan signals me with her eyebrows that she has a question, "Metude, my friend told me that Spokesperson said God is not finished. You don't hear that in church. What do you think?"

My old friend is silent, then responds thoughtfully, "Much is in this statement. God is ongoing. It relates to infinity. God is present in each—never finished. God is not contained—'tis boundless. Boundaries are only put in by humankind. One's spirituality can be called forth. Sweet as the air you breathe. The vibrational level increases with reading material that will stimulate other human contact in this area." *Oh, she is right, I can feel when a certain spiritual book does change my energy.*

Thanking Metude, Jan now asks about the loneliness she experiences in her marriage. *Oh, this is news to me. Yet, how many women ask that question? It feels like an epidemic.*

My ancient friend "observes" my cousin kindly and responds, "Isolate your problem. Loneliness causes sadness within. Not having a home or root within oneself requires work, acknowledgement, and refinement. Follow it to its root. Follow it further. It is an inner element not recognized yet. It is not to be feared. It is a process. All questions are for a reason. Stop, say to yourself, 'This is for a reason. What am I to do with it?' We will proceed."

Jan nods, "Thank you for taking time with my questions."

"Need not worry about questioning, I do not mind. But now we will proceed."

How Past Lives Affect Us ~ They Are Recessed

And with that invitation, Jan asks how past lives affect us. *Another good question, cousin.*

This cottage woman begins to rock and looking with closed eyes in Jan's direction, begins to speak, "Remains with choice. What one learns from other life experiences is the sum total of who you are. This life experience is what one chooses to put into play and does not use all past life experiences. They are not visible, not lived, not upfront. They are recessed, not active but latent." *How interesting. So maybe we can choose to live certain life experiences which we call lifetimes in the one larger life that is our soul self.*

The rocker stops as our old friend says, "And now it is time to go. We bid you a good evening. Peace with each. Enjoy your community. It is a gift. Yah, indeed, it is a blessing. And remember, spirituality is as sweet as the air you breath." She then leans in Jan's direction adding, "We will not be far from you. Ask your questions." *I think she means when she goes back west tomorrow.*

Augusta

We thank her for dropping in on our party. Jan is smiling. Pam is back, stretching, yet she hasn't been out long. We tell her what the cottage woman said about the wine and her blood pressure. She laughs, but I sense a little concern.

COURT - ACTING AS A SATELLITE WHEN PRAYING

Oct. 20/87 Went for a walk on Salty Beach earlier. Sunny, cold, and heavy seas. Such wildness with the wind blowing. It rattles our upstairs windows. The maples have lost their reds, yellows, and oranges. I am now so much more at one in feeling the earth, the colour of the trees, and the melancholy awareness on the wharf at Northwest Cove a year ago. This season is over, the leaves are in their last throes of curly crispness and indeed are melancholy. It also reminds me of going to court this week.

About six months ago, Philip, the young father who has a brain tumour, told me about his cousin, Don. He was a teacher accused of sexual harassment by a student. Philip felt his cousin was innocent and from what he told me, I suspected he was. I asked Metude, and she confirmed it. She also felt I could be supportive. Thus, I began walking a painful journey with him. It also was a high-profile case in the newspapers, on the radio, and on television. Finally, it went to trial. Before going to court, I asked my old friend how I could be most helpful in court. She responded that I could act as a satellite by praying for light, as all in the courtroom needed prayer. And she stressed 'all.'

Several days later ~ the trial continues

Oct. 23/87 Court again tomorrow. The trial has taken most of the week. The truth of his innocence was literally felt in the courtroom. I just kept beaming prayer. He was excellent on the stand, but he was death-white. Yet, his co-workers revealed that he was a great guy when they each took the stand. Roger and Philip sat in on some of it. We had several fish-chowder lunches together.

Next day . . .

Oct. 24/87 I am so relieved it is over! It is also the end of the crisis phone calls. Ultimately, it came to light that the little girl accusing him had been influenced by an issue in her own home. And the big news is that Philip's cousin was acquitted. Now, it is for him to pick up his shattered life and his ruined reputation. He says he will never go back to teaching. He also told me, "You will never know how you kept me going when I was thinking of killing myself." I didn't really know that, but thank you, God.

GUIDES ARE PRESENTED TO DIFFERENT PEOPLE IN DIFFERENT WAYS

Pam and Abby are challenged, but both are liking university, and both want to visit with the cottage woman this afternoon. We can still see our breath, but the warmth of the stove is beginning to make it cozy. I always love the smell of applewood burning. After Pam is wrapped in the blanket, the rocker begins to move. Our discarnate friend settles in nicely. My friend whose son is the fundamentalist, wants me to ask about him again, as he is coming home for Christmas. Apparently, he is now considering a master's degree at a liberal university next fall. His mother is wondering how that will work out.

Her Prayers Are the Road He Travels On ~ It's Actually Moving Him

So, I ask the cottage woman what she thinks, and she replies, "Same uncompromised truth will set this one free. His idol is a book. The Spirit of the book has yet to be met." *Ah, the*

Bible. Hmm, it's helpful for me to consider it as two separate things: Spirit and book.

"Will he meet the Spirit of it soon?" *My friend says she can't stand "being saved" another Christmas.*

"He is choosing life which will change for him soon, for the Spirit world watches over him carefully." *Oh, his mother will find this comforting.*

She continues, "Nothing to fear in this on his mother's part. He is tenderly held."

"But when they can't communicate, she feels he walks away from her."

"It is a walk that carries no anxiety. He is only searching for more. This will help him understand his mother's stand and will eventually unite their spirits. Her prayers are the road he travels on, guiding him. Prayer is actually moving him. Holding him tenderly. We will proceed." *Oh, she is going to love to hear that her prayers are having an effect.*

Several years later, his mother told me that after three years at university he announced that "big walls had fallen down." He was referring to the rigidity of his fundamentalism and now was much more open and easier to talk with.

Compassion ~ Go Down Deep Enough, the Roots Are the Same

I also want to know how Roger is doing. When I ask him, he always says fine, and that is it. What would be helpful for him? He certainly seems not to be doing personal work.

"What is it you wish to know?" She asks almost curiously as she tilts her head towards me.

"Well, I don't know." I sigh. "Getting him to pursue different things that are really interesting for him. He sails in the summer, but I'd like him to have more interesting things to do in the winter, like I do."

"What is it he wishes to do?" *What an astute question.*

She nods, "Right, that is the question. He is pursuing what he wishes to pursue."

"Really?" *Oh, I am thankful. It's actually a relief.*

She looks at me kindly, "All you have to do is support him in who he is in the moment. To allow that it is you who thinks he needs to be motivated, or you who feels he is in some place he is not. And that, my child, is not a reprimand." *It kind of feels like one.*

"No Metude, it's okay. That's fine and most helpful to hear. I just want him to be happy." *I don't want to be happy without him.*

"Yah, indeed, a loving heart." *Hmm, wonder if she means mine or his; I'll bet both.*

"Well, I'm asking because life is engaging and meaningful for me, and I want that for him. He says it is when I ask him, but I still am not sure."

She continues thoughtfully, "One does not experience life the same way. It is to value the person where they are. It would be wise if you followed the path down far enough you would find it rooted in the same thing." *I don't get it.*

"Now you have lost me a bit."

"Follow the path down far enough, look inward—compassion. Yah." She explains with delight.

I laugh saying instantly, "That's him. We do share that compassion for people."

"The surface may be presented in a slightly different way, but the roots are the same, my child. They merely take a different expression."

Becoming More Sensitive ~ Feelings of Love Are in Essence Your Guide

I then ask about my guides. I still struggle for a clearer awareness of their presence. My old friend raises the index finger, "Your guide is with you. Listen. You learn to listen." *She must get tired of telling me this.*

"Well, how do I hear?" *Sometimes, I think it is coming and other times I don't think I am hearing anything but the clock.*

Now she looks at me kindly through closed eyes and with great patience instructs, "Take your pen. Put down what you think are random thoughts—in reality, they are true for you. Helpful to feel, sense what it is you feel, that which one cannot attribute to oneself. As I have said, feelings of peace that steal over one are your guide, feelings of love are in essence your guide."

"What about feelings of longing?"

"Longing is the distance from your guide." *Really?*

"But I feel cut off from them."

"You are cut off," she adds gently. "For you, quietly close your eyes and concentrate on the feeling of love you know so well. You will call (the help) forth. You have the ability to have images." *I feel a long way from doing that.*

Metude begins to rock slowly, saying, "We have been together before, and will be together again. Sometimes, I am there in what you perceive as the peaceful silence, much as a buffer when it's difficult for you." Repeating what she said earlier, she continues. "When troubled, take pen in hand and write your questions down. When you feel deeply hemmed in, put on your coat, go out the door. Let the sun warm and the breeze wash over you. Watch the amount of physical tension in the hands, arms, and jaw. One has the habit of holding the body tense, especially the jaw. Each day, deliberately allow your body to loosen. 'Tis good, 'tis beneficial. We will proceed."

Much as a Final Struggle ~ Wear Good Shoes

My next question is about how Pam is doing. Her home situation is intensifying and with so much negativity, I don't know how she studies. "Do you have any words of encouragement for her?"

Metude draws a noticeable breath. "Much as a final struggle. Has to regulate her time better—lacks routine. Body requires a steady diet, nourishment. Her tooth must be filled. Much delay, seen as unimportant. Will affect her health if left unattended. Regular rest and nourishment. Tends to drive the body further than it is nurtured. Problems of circulation in legs coming up. Careful to wear good shoes. 'Tis good. We would proceed." *Oh, this reminds me of a story in the New Testament.*

When the angel was helping Paul escape from prison, it looked after him down to the smallest detail, reminding him to tie up his sandals so he would not trip on the way out—now here is the cottage woman telling Pam to get her teeth filled and wear good shoes.

Handling Stress ~ Ask One's Guides Right on the Hot Griddle

Then I ask, "How can she feel her guide's presence in moments of stress?"

Metude is thoughtful for a minute, then nods. "Severe emotional stress. First things first, calm one's inner being. Merely proceed to open one's self. The guides may be identified as feeling calm and becoming peaceful. When in an emotional intensity, that is what provides a block to her thinking. In this situation, one panics. Only when one moves into panic and fear, the block arises. One moves to these emotions rather than standing back. It is to say that in the situation, one panics only when one moves into fear. She must take the first step and say again, no to panic and fear. That is when you ask the guides for help. Ask right on the hot griddle.

"Would also be helpful to watch one's breathing as it provides distance from panic and fear, then merely the need to listen. Guides are presented to different people in different ways, some in calmness, some in peace, and some hear what to do. Merely one's translation. Breathing creates inner space and distance for clarity. We will proceed."

"Oh, thank you Metude, that is so helpful."

And decades later, the spiritual teacher, Eckhart Tolle wrote that to be in a moment of Presence is stepping out of the voice in one's head, and it is the rising of inner consciousness which, he suggests, can take one out of emotional turmoil.

Being Discouraged ~ Doubt Must Be Watched as It Creeps In Unnoticed

"Metude, I have another question for Abby that I am curious about as well. Is Abby's husband open to his guides even though he doesn't believe in them?"

"Only to the extent that he allows, by time. Yet, it's not beneficial to mention it to him."

This is why we cannot tell anyone beyond our small group about the cottage woman. Sometimes, I think of what she could offer our bruised world directly, but I know it would not be beneficial to out her now in the 1980s. It is not only our country road that is not ready for this person who occupies someone else's, but it's everyone else I know!

I continue, "But Abby is so discouraged about his non-relating and his indifference to her."

Nodding and rocking, she begins to speak, "She must not lose faith, must hold to her truth. Must not be doubting the wisdom of the choice she makes. Doubt must be watched as it creeps in unnoticed. Must recognize what is doubt, what appearance it has. She will recognize it. Most often comes in moments when tired and then is closely followed by discouragement. To re-evaluate is helpful to her. Keeps her goals uppermost. Clarifies. She needs to be told it is progress, the whole situation."

"What is my role with her in the situation at this time?"

"Truth. Much as a sounding board. Helpful for her to hear she is making progress. 'Tis good, even though it is very difficult. It is her truth she struggles for. Their paths have been deliberately intertwined: mutual learning. She must be positive in her thoughts; that it is progress."

I continue to be surprised that the very act of thinking a positive thought rather than a negative thought is viewed as progress. It seems such a small thing, yet it apparently achieves such a big reward—the soul's progress, I suppose.

Always aware when our visit is soon ending, I again ask about Pam's feeling of loneliness even though she is surrounded by people at home.

"The Person is good. More will unfold for her, what is it she wishes to do about her relationship with her mate? Misconceptions around her choice. One might as well be lonely outside as in a relationship." *Thank God I don't feel that way with Roger. He is always right there.* She continues, "Elements for her not yet introduced. They are forthcoming. New elements that will enter, but are not there now. This is sufficient."

Pam dreamed yesterday that she survived and made a successful new life for herself. I hope it is prophetic, but will she? She is stronger, but still has those pockets of despair, hopelessness, and still lives with Frank. However, financially, there seems to be no other option.

The rocker stops. I know instantly, in the silence, that Metude has to leave. She says, "It has been a pleasant visit. Ah, yah, it has been a blessing. Take good joy in it. Peace to troubled hearts. I will be with each of you." And she is gone, leaving us with a wonderful peace and light-heartedness in spite of it all. Pam told me later that she had been more stressed than usual before the visit, but she sensed a quiet joy that evening as she walked down the road back to her home. *I'll bet that's Metude, taking care of things.*

BLESSED ARE THOSE WHO KNOW THEY HAVE HELPERS

Nov. 16/87 Dusk and just came back from a cold, snowy, windy but invigorating walk on the beach. As Metude says, "Your time of day." Blue, grey-green water mutes the sky—hues of blues with streaks of pink as clouds swoop across it. On the shore, a dark drama of rocks and seaweed are silhouetted against water. These are the energies that shift, allowing us humans to exist in such exquisiteness.

I also thought today in the wilderness of the snow, wind, and beach that a day has a thousand colours and then thought: every person does, too.

I have grown to feel teamwork with the other realm, the larger consciousness. There is another side, and there are more like the cottage woman who have this great universal love, compassion, and understanding. These helpers desire to not only share it with us humans, but as the cottage woman states, she is here to learn and her life is much like ours.

*Maybe every human form is learning. Yet
she is not sure she will come back here again
for another life experience. It sounds like she
hasn't decided.*

*The odd time she cautions me, "Humans need
to be careful how they move—you may not be
alone or occupy the space by yourselves." Yes,
wise-friend and blessed are those who know
they have these invisible, to us at least, helpers.
My consciousness is shifting more into a
oneness that I have not known before. It's
rather surprising and rather awesome.*

Two days later . . .

*Nov. 19/87 Sunday and surprise! The sun.
Sitting here outdoors with my fur hat tied
tightly around my chin, I am wrapped in a
wool blanket. Gus, our bird-killer cat and
Ginny, our love-cat, lift their legs delicately, as
if that will cause them to avoid the powdery
snow which is already halfway up their legs.
They are framed by a brilliant blue sea behind
them. Quite striking as, one is orange and one,
white and black.*

*I hear Metude's words, "Note the sunshine, feel
the crispness of the air, set your troubles aside
for the moment as you journey through this
day." I am setting everyone else's troubles aside,
even the cats.*

The Cottage Woman

Wrote the Christmas letter this a.m. before anyone was up, and it came together in a stroke. Yet, too bad I cannot talk about one of the most significant influences in my life—the cottage woman. It would be unbelievable, unacceptable, and considered nuts.

Also walked to the end of the point tonight with Mila's mother and granddaughter. Stars were bright, snow falling. We walked arm and arm. It came to me to step back and catch the enchantment and charm of where I was, who I was with in the moment, and to be present. When we turned at the bluff to come back to the house, the snowflakes were falling on the child's face. Then I looked up to see the old, loving eyes of her grandmother, watching, too. It doesn't take much, only a glance to feel it all.

• • •

Seaforth Christmas Letter ~ Making Gentle a Bruised World

We are simply asked to make gentle a bruised world, to tame its savageness, to be compassionate to all, including ourselves.

~ *Peter Byrne, S.J.*

This is the wondrous season of Advent, with its sprinkling of snow, lights, planning of gifts, and the practising of carols. I am wondering again what the meaning of this ordinary event that occurred in a barn two thousand years ago could possibly have in our lives today. And yet, each year, I am discovering how alive the event truly is in its ordinariness. A person is born, attempts to live the seed of truth with family, friends, strangers and in doing so becomes light, compassion, and hope in a bruised world.

Now, for some of those ordinary pieces of family news. This past summer, we sailed almost every night in the Spitfire. Our two youngest were often at the tiller. Roger has a major cupboard project going here in the kitchen, which has kept him busy this fall. His newly formed company, *The Seaforth Boat Works,* has also produced a bed for our twenty-fifth wedding anniversary this past June. However, he lives in hope of producing boats in the future.

I also painted along the shore: mostly gulls, fish shacks, boats, and wharfs. I got another belt in karate, also continue to do human development programs at The Center and do hospice work. The children are home from university for the holidays. Mother and her husband will arrive like Santa's impersonators in a few days. And tonight, we are doing a jazz version of three Christmas carols with eighteen children.

As I look up from writing, I hear the sound of a lobster boat just off our beach, and I see another across the water checking their traps, the season has begun. More snow flurries, and I am off for a walk to the bluff before the family wakes.

We wish each of you a season of joy and wonder as we indeed attempt "to make gentle a bruised world" and as Dickens had Tiny Tim exclaim, "May God Bless us one and all . . ."

CHRISTMAS ~ RECOLLECTIONS

Dec. 15/87 Shock, shock, shock! Pam dropped in after supper. We were all in the kitchen with the kids. I felt her happiness and could see it on her face even before I knew why she had come. Gleefully, she announced she is giving Roger and I a ticket for a trip to Germany and France. The plans were made, and we will travel with Mila who lives over there in the winter. Talk about being stunned! We were speechless. She added that it is a gift of love for us and that her father, who recently passed, left her some money. Even though I knew we couldn't take it, love seemed to fill the kitchen.

We didn't want to hurt her, as she was so happy making the announcement. We all thanked her, hugged her, and said as gently as we could that definitely we could not take her money! She would not hear any arguments. Then, she asked us to do it as a gift for her. We ended up laughing, as we were both resolute in our decisions.

> Then I asked if Frank had agreed, and
> he had! Oh God, you just can't tell by the
> surface of things.

Four days later . . .

> Dec. 19/87 Christmas . . . What a storm last
> night. The snow laden soft woods are silent
> and beautiful. Again, the big pine tree in
> the backyard looks like an ill-shaped snow
> woman with a long, bulky dress.
> Mother and Lee arrived a few days ago,
> again with the car filled to the roof with
> gifts and baked goods as they do each year.
> They add so much to Christmas. We went to
> church this morning.
> I watched Mother. Life has been harsh for
> her. She looked at me one Christmas Eve
> a year or two ago and said, almost with a
> sense of achievement, "Well, we survived."
> All the hardness of her life and the victory
> seemed to be distilled in those three words.
> I agreed that indeed we did, yet it was
> her love, strength, and integrity that was
> the beacon.
> Mother and I went to town shopping
> this afternoon. Haley called me to say the
> fruitcake had burned. They are a lot of
> work. Apparently, it went up in smoke,
> literally. Mother had mistakenly jacked the

oven up to 500 degrees, and that did it. Then my wonderfully resourceful daughter took the hammer to the almonds and threw, I am sure, literally, another one together. The place was as clean as a whistle when I got back, and everyone was smiling—this daughter of mine is amazing, and not just for the fruitcake rescue. She always goes the extra mile.

Mila sent us a beautiful, wood-carved Christmas candle holder from Italy. I miss her spirit, its joy, and warmth.

Two days before Christmas . . .

Dec 23/87 Woke up feeling for Presence and it was not there! My meditation the last few days has fallen prey to the busyness of the season. However, this afternoon I have had enough space to move into Presence. So, I sit here in love, appreciating that there is such a season, no matter what religion. Jesus was an enlightened being, as was Buddha and Lao Tzu.

Later . . .

The boys are sitting here on the kitchen floor playing Santa Claus. Lots of presents to wrap.

We seem to do our one-on-one talking visits by walking to the end of the point with each other. I love standing there with the fierceness of the North Atlantic at its best, with someone I love, looking out into the cold, grey-snowy, white-crested water, as if it was being churned into buttermilk. Be it mate, child, or friend.

Haley informed me last night, "It's important you visit people as they feel something beyond the social with you." Hmm, I am not really a visitor, unfortunately.

Caught Roger's eyes twinkling at me tonight with love and friendship. It is one of the most beautiful gifts of my life. We still haven't told Pam anything definite about the trip. It is hard to accept it, but in spite of our initial reaction, I'm starting to think that we should.

A CHRISTMAS VISIT ~ MUCH ILLUMINATION, MUST LET THE HEART SING

Pam, Abby, and Brooke dropped in for tea and fruitcake earlier. We were wondering what Metude's experience of Christmas is, even though I am sure her light, love, and wisdom don't belong to any one religion. Pam spontaneously suggested we meet with her. Brooke, Abby, and I always have questions and readily agree.

Metude's Christmas ~ Much the Same as When One Is on Earth

The fire in the wood stove has been crackling since morning because I was painting earlier. Pam tucks into the rocker and tries to relax. I add more wood. My old friend has a bit of a struggle but again, nothing like the first year. After greetings, she welcomes "the young one" back for the holiday.

This season has to be one of my favourite times of the year because it is such a joyous family celebration. On Christmas Eve, we always have lobster. We then sing carols and Mother reads the Christmas story from Grandmother's bible. Friends and neighbours drop in. We also have cake and sing happy birthday to this babe born in a manger.

Thus, I ask Metude, in my usual holiday enthusiasm, "Isn't the Christmas season wonderful?" *Oh, a slight frown. She is not sharing my enthusiasm. In fact, she is looking rather somber.*

"Yah, special for you, indeed. As each perceives it to be, so it is. Yet, stress for others in their relationships, also sadness. We will proceed." *Ouch, that's me being insensitive. How many homes are unhappy and Pam's being one? I need to stop talking about being blessed. Will I ever, ever get it?*

Hearing her word "proceed," I change the subject telling her that the four grandchildren quite enjoy their grandmother.

Haley and Callie had been visiting Mother every summer since they were seven. It seemed to be a magical time for them. Callie was telling me the other day that they always had "a wonderful time and there was a wonderful lightness to them." We all would visit on a half dozen weekends during the year.

My ancient friend nods, "Ah, they relate as friends, precisely. This is so pleasant. Yah, indeed, Grams are such nice people." *That's funny but you are right, Grams are.*

Still wanting to ask Metude about Christmas in her dimension, I persist, "What is Christmas like for you?"

"It is as one perceives, as you perceive it. Much the same as when one is on earth. When one thinks positively, then it will be positive, when one thinks negatively, then it will be negative. Much illumination in positive thought. Eased greatly by what one thinks. Your thought creates what your future will be. One shapes one's own environment, same as with you. There are no limits."

Hmm, is she saying thoughts shape their life on the other side, too? Maybe, there are limits with her as with us. My land, the power that thought has.

She nods, again answering my thoughts. "Each is as one. Proceed."

"Hmm, interesting, thank you."

Still puzzled, I nod to Brooke to ask her questions. She had called me up after she got home and told me she felt threatened by the possibility of being harassed by a certain individual while she was away. The stress caused her to feel like "broken stones." She had wanted to ask me about it. Feeling a little more confident since the purple pillow, I agreed. After she asked several questions, I saw an image of a lynch pin. Neither of us knew what it meant, other than it releases something if one pulls the pin out. Good or bad, we were not sure. Could it mean something would explode, grenade like? Again, from experience, I was learning there can be more meanings to an image than first thought. Plus, I still didn't know when my information was right.

Now, Metude can correct or confirm what the lynch pin means, and she is quick to respond. "The young one is to pull it and release the fear. It is deep-seated. Two different fears, one is vulnerability, yet when identified, it will be her greatest asset. The second fear has been there for a long, long time. Find out its roots, where it comes from. Also discover what is hers to be upset about. Set aside what is not. One reacts to situations when one doesn't have to." *Yes, and I am learning to react less myself.*

Advice for a Down Feeling ~ Do Not Give In and Do Not Just Drift

Reading Brooke's mind, our ancient friend continues, "One must not give in to the down feeling. Say to one's self, 'I will not give in to it.' Go outside. Feel the sunshine. Do not just drift through it. Watch the blue sky, see the blue sky, and the sparkling snow. Breathe light and life into yourself. Put music on, be happy. One will literally have to shake oneself physically. Move your body, don't just slump." *Brooke is smiling and taking notes. This is great for her to hear and for the rest of us too, as who doesn't feel down at times?*

"Is there anything more that can help her, Metude?"

"Ah, the young one's thoughts are very confused. Suffers from what one could call a very light form of depression. Not the need for medication. Much to be accomplished as we are working to go through it. Decide what she wishes to know. Key is in the process. One needs to take out and explore the emotions. Deep and slow breathing. 'Tis good. Most valuable, if one keeps to the instructions given." *This applies to everyone I should think.*

Turning toward Brooke, this wise woman continues, "You do have control. The emotion is not to be feared. It is merely that: emotion. Will become much clearer (and less fearful) as one identifies the emotion and where it stems from. The main lesson is that you need not react. You are in control—if you choose. Decide if you wish to give in to this emotion or, using your word, bracket it. Bracket is a good word."

My old friend looks slightly amused as she knows I know she is borrowing one of our colloquialisms, again. Like she says, she too has to learn to communicate with language that is meaningful to us.

We often used the term bracket when we wanted to work on a certain aspect of a situation, but did not want to lose sight of its other aspects. We then could put the other parts of the problem on hold to deal with later. For example, Brooke needed to address one emotion at a time so as not to be overwhelmed.

She leans forward and asks, "What led to my feeling down, Metude?"

"Being homesick. It was not identified and dealt with. To identify, get in touch with the emotion. Take pen in hand and write what you are feeling."

"I don't think there will be enough paper." My young friend sighs.

"As one talks, write; it becomes less."

"I did not deal well with the strangeness of being away from home?"

Metude nods, "Initially, the feeling was not threatening, but you had a feeling of being foreign and misplaced, yet not being identified compounded it into feeling threatened. These factors will be revealed as you work. Wise decision not to dwell there. Christmas is a time for peace and joy. Move into the feeling of being loved and celebrated. That is what you are intended to do. Lay your burden aside. Much lightness will come, if you allow it. Call your friend tonight and let him hear the joy in you. This is what has been missing." She adds, serenely.

Let Out the Heart and Let It Sing ~ The Young One Need Not Fear

As Metude rocks before the fire, the cottage actually seems cozy, as it has warmed up. We can't see our breath now. I stock the stove again, and it's doing its best to warm the room, in spite of the skiff of snow that has blown through a crack in the window. We sit here in this lovely, really indescribable silence. I look at our ancient cottage woman wrapped in a wool blanket. Suddenly, as she rocks, she begins to talk unbidden, again, taking an initiative that happens rarely.

"Ah, Christmas is much the same as when one is on earth. I love to rock. I have sat many hours in front of the fire and knitted. It is the essence of who I am. I had many grandchildren, and they so enjoyed peppermint sticks."

Oh, she must be referring to a past Christmas. I wonder if this is her past-life experience in Sweden. She moves her head toward Brooke and with a caring expression, encourages, "Enjoy. Be kind to yourself. Let out the heart and let it sing. Young one, you need not fear. It's to that which people react. Fear is the greatest enemy. Makes you vulnerable. Set it aside. Must let the heart sing. You are very much loved. It is a time for joy, and you shall have that, my child. We will proceed."

Speaking of joy, Brooke and her family sometimes drop in after supper for a little sing-along which reminds me to ask, "Metude, as you know the family jazzed up some carols for several of the concerts around the Bay. It was so fun. Were you there and if so, did you enjoy it?"

With a lilt and a tilt of her head, she responds, "Yah, indeed, 'tis good. Enjoyed the music, but prefer the impromptu get-togethers." *Oh, that's funny. She likes the home music better.*

So, she must be present when we play in the living room after supper. Ah, let me remember an invisible guest who knows what we lack in musicianship we make up for with enthusiasm. Everyone that drops in is also given sticks, bones, or shakers to bang on if they wish.

My ancient friend nods, "'Tis good. Celebrate with the children. Christmas is a time for that."

I reply excitedly, thinking of our kids, "Yes, aren't the children great?"

"Ah, you see them as they are becoming and who they will become. 'Tis good."

Then she bends toward me and in a deeper tone whispers so kindly, "Such a blessed visit."

Metude now turns to Brooke and quips, "Your older friend here has earned her vacation." Then she turns my way with the slightest smile. *Oh, she means Pam's gift-trip.* She continues with a lilt, "A good trip. You will absorb much time of rekindling for you and your man. Much need for one another to share, much walking, listen, and hearing one another. The trip has been given to you both. You will be touched by much that you will see."

"Yes, as you know it is a struggle for us to accept. Yet, ultimately, it just seems like it needs to be accepted as a love gift."

"Yah, indeed, 'tis that." *I knew it and we have been through so much together.*

"I need to ask though, while we are away, are there any alerts for us to watch out for, Metude?"

"Stick to your daily routine; your daily way of life, times of silence, set times to be outdoors, and be present in the moment. Proceed."

Roger and I accepted the gift a week later. Pam brought down the money with a lovely card saying, "My family." And I knew in certain ways that was true. Now, everyone is contributing money for our trip, the kids, family, and friends. Mila will meet us in Frankfurt, and we will travel through several countries with her. It is all truly amazing.

Energy Forms ~ Life Energy That Has Outgrown the Human Shell

I know our ancient friend is nearing her leaving time, but I have one other question. Sometimes, when seemingly unusual things happen, Metude takes the opportunity to expand our knowledge beyond our physical world. Today, I want to ask about Mother losing her potato masher. She was sure it was on the counter when she left the kitchen. Yet, when she came back later, it was gone. Apparently, she gave a good look for it, but no potato masher. However, later she came back in the kitchen and there it was lying on the counter.

Plus, the other day, Jerry, our neighbour across the road, had a different thing happen to him that he was asking me about. He thought he lost the plug to his sink. After looking all over his bathroom, he came back later and there it was. He was so scared he ran outdoors and threw the plug in the woods. *It really doesn't take much to spook us humans and just think if I told him about Metude.* "Do you have any knowledge of what might be going on in each of the missing incidents, if anything?"

My old friend is quiet. *I think she is checking out the situations.* Then nods and states, "Does have two causes. Energy movement is one and the human error in the other."

Brooke interjects, "Why would Jerry's plug be back in the sink though?"

Metude shook her head saying, "Human error, given his state of mind!" *Interesting; so, mother's must be the energy movement.*

"Really, well, what about mother's missing potato masher? As a limited human I don't understand this."

She explains, "All is energy, but one does not necessarily see this life form." *The potato masher is energy but surely not a life form?*

"Okay, that potato masher would not put itself back on the counter. Right?"

My ancient friend moves forward, thrusting her hand toward me, "Oh no. 'Tis energy forms." *I think she is telling me energy forms moved the potato masher. Wait till I tell Mother this.*

She nods her head vigorously, "Ah, yah. Indeed. We now will proceed."

Abby, who has been on the edge of her seat, speaks up, "Do we call these energy forms ghosts, Metude?" *Oh, what an interesting question!*

"Ah, yah, not to be feared." She assures us quickly as she continues to rock.

Abby and I both chime in unconvincingly, "No, no, we aren't fearful." *Oh, but I am.*

Seeing a ghost would be scary and I have hoped they haven't existed. Yet, thinking of it as an energy form instead of a ghost is better and kind of exciting. Oh, I need to ask about Pam's spoons. She feels they are being moved around at her house.

"Is it the same with Pam's spoons?" *She will be most interested in this as often her spoons go missing and then resurface, which has bothered her for a while.*

My old friend almost laughs, which is extremely unusual. "Oh indeed, energy forms are very active there." She retorts. *Oh, a bit of humour! But she is serious.*

"So, the energy forms are very active!" I parrot, not knowing what else to say.

Abby is quite excited. Here is someone we totally trust telling us about ghosts. We have all heard of them, but with significate skepticism. She asks, "Are these, hmm . . . were these (energy forms) once human or are they spirits? What are they? What is a ghost?" *It's hard to know what to ask, but she's doing well.*

This ancient friend calmly continues, "Energy, life energy as occupies your human self. As one out grows the need for the human shell. All life exists eternally."

I interject, "Metude, that is fascinating; fascinating." *Hmm, could it be as we move toward making our transition (her word for death), our spirit outgrows the body, skin, and bone-part which is merely a shell? Maybe that is what we mean when in high spirits we feel bigger than life? That's something to think about!*

"And is there a reason for the 'energy forms' to be active or are they just playing with us?"

"They are active for many reasons."

"And with the potato masher, they knew Mother needed it so they helped her out." I add.

"Yah, indeed. Quite often, that is the case."

Then Abby softly adds, "That is a very loving thing to do for someone."

All Energy Forms Are Light and Love ~ Move Quietly and Gently in Their World

The rocker picks up speed as our old friend spreads out her hand. "Ahhhh, there lies our key. All energy forms are light and love. Indeed, indeed." *The three of us looked at each other in amazement. This is the cottage woman telling us there are energy forms that help us, and **s**he is like a witness from that same invisible, caring world, too. I am out of my depth.*

"Hmm, well that's incredible. Energy forms? Really all this feels too big for me to process. Is there anything else you want to say, Metude?"

"There is much you have yet to understand. It would be wise if people would learn to move gently in their world. They do not occupy this space unto themselves." *Ohhh, is she saying there are life forms around us here in this cottage?*

Reading my thoughts, she replies, "Yah, indeed, 'tis good."

"Ah, we don't occupy our space by ourselves; really, Metude, really?"

"Yah." Abby and Brooke are laughing at my incredulity. *They don't often see me stunned.*

Our discarnate friend continues, "Yah, quite often humans unconsciously and subconsciously are sensitive to the energy light forms around them. They have a sense of someone being there, but they dismiss it because their human eyes do not see. A sense of knowing someone is there when they don't believe it is possible because they do not see with physical eyes. All life is eternal. Let us proceed."

We Will Have Many Talks in the Future ~ A Great Unity Not Yet Understood

I know it is past time for her to leave, but Abby has another question before we go. She continues to be beside herself with her husband's lack of response to the lethargy in their relationship.

Metude pauses as if checking, then states, moving her head slightly toward Abby, "Progress is good. A need to relax, enjoy family, and holiday. Stop working with it (the issues.)

Enjoy. Take the emphasis off expectations and attempting to understand your mate. Christmas, a time of joy given if one chooses. The struggle can be picked up again. Why do it now?" *How wise and indeed why do it now?*

I interject, "Oh, I know you have to go, but I have one more question about my friend in the city who is concerned about her fundamentalist son that I've asked about. He is now home for the holidays. Again, she is still worried about the distance that might get created between them.

"Encourage the mother; she has but to love, listen, and trust herself. She can do it. She needs to relax; they merely have to be with each other. A great unity that she does not yet understand, one with the other. Hardly fathomable to her. They have come back this time and the gift is given." *Oh, and I think she means from a past life experience. Hmm, what a mysterious woman you are my old friend.*

"Thank you, that will be so comforting for her to hear. She talks about him a lot and I suspect she will understand about the unity. Seeing them together, it is there when they look at each other like some silent knowledge."

"Yah, indeed." She, looking at me and seemingly out of the blue, states, "We are with your youngest a lot. He has a dawning awareness. He has access to another realm of which I am merely a part." *Really, I wonder what that means, and I am guessing she is not going to tell me.*

She stops rocking, saying, "We will have many talks like this in the future. Again, enjoy the community, 'tis a gift. Remember me in the music and laughter. And now we are out of time."

"Oh Metude, it's been a good visit. And we got it on tape, on this contraption that you are hooked up to." *We had a new mic pinned to Pam's sweater. We laugh, knowing how much trouble this recorder gives us. It feels like a victory just getting it to work.*

"I thank you so much for coming to us." *My land, it is such a privilege every time she comes. I am sitting here, and the love is palpable.*

Then my ancient friend leans forward saying, "I do enjoy our visits."

"Oh Metude, we do too." *Abby and Brooke are nodding vigorously as well.*

She responds, "Creates community, indeed. There is much joy in that, much Presence. Even in the moments of solitude there is Presence. Yah, a blessed visit and now 'tis time to go."

"Yes, and peace be with you and your 'we.'"

"We will meet again soon."

We thank her in unison and wish her blessings.

I add, "What a Christmas gift you are!" Then she is gone to our visible eye, and Pam is stirring in the rocker.

YOUR WORK ~ COMPASSION FOR OTHERS, THE FOUNDATION OF LIFE AND LIGHT

This is the third New Year with the cottage woman, and a nor'easter wind is fierce off the Atlantic. The drifts of snow are so high we waded up to our knees to get to the cottage. The house is full as the children are getting ready to go back to university this week. Pam was free for a visit so we put up with the storm to take advantage of the opportunity.

Brooke and I huddle around the pot belly stove which is doing its best to warm us. A skiff of snow has drifted across the floor again. We wrap Pam in a blanket by the fire and keep our jackets and scarves on. The wind is howling.

The Cottage Woman Enjoys the Wind ~ Are We the Only People You Visit

Metude comes in comfortably and we wish her a Happy New Year. "Indeed, it is." She responds brightly. I am concerned she will be as cold as we are. As if reading my mind, she responds, "Cool, but very good. I am not cold." Then she raises her head slightly, "Wind, I am very familiar with the sound of it. Much wind in Sweden, a last life experience."

I love it when she talks about her other-side life. She must mean the one she mentioned as a clockmaker when she first started visiting with us or maybe it was when she was a grandmother or both.

"When was that, Metude?"

"Early 1800s." Then she sighs, keeps rocking and seemingly quite contentedly adds, "I so enjoy the wind." *Hmm, it's a bit like she is missing it.* (In later years, she would look kindly, saying, "And you think of it only as wind." *And I still tend to.*)

"Do you work with other people aside from us?"

She nods with a slight smile. "Many. Those that call. There are others, but more like as your guides work, through your imagination, instincts, and listening."

"I mean, do you work with people like you do with us, being physically present in Pam's body and talking to us directly like this?"

She pauses, then shakes her head emphatically, "I do not." *Hmm, I thought there would be others.*

She then pauses, frowns somewhat, saying, "The body is weary. We will fix that."

Your Work Is in Compassion for Others ~ For All Energy, All Life Forms

We wait in silence, then she nods, and I ask about our continuing work with people this year.

Looking thoughtful, my old friend reflects, "Ah, your work is in compassion for others."

"Yes, I can feel that is true for both Pam and me."

She tilts her head toward me, "Yah, all is made possible when one has compassion. It is the foundation on which life and light are based. One cannot have light in their life if they do not have compassion." *She is so right.*

Her voice is lilted, "All is possible when one lives their life in compassion. Yah, that is to the universe as well as with others. One must not neglect the importance, one for the other. Compassion for all energy, all life forms." *I never, never thought of having compassion for the universe. I suppose she means everything on earth and in the sky. I have a lot to think about.*

Feeling Down ~ Advice Much Heeded & Joy in All Elements

"Brooke wants to know how she has been doing with the advice you gave her about feeling down in our recent visit. She has been busy with friends and her family in the next village, so I will be interested to hear. Yet, knowing her family, a lot of love has been coming her way."

Nodding, my old friend responds, "The information given to her in our visit before was much heeded. A real gift. Indeed, joy in the moment. Trust in the future. Difficult for most humans. Key is joy in the moment—joy in all elements. Even when sad, one can feel the caring of others. 'Tis a matter of owning what one hears. We will proceed."

One is Always Guided ~ A Matter of Energies and Frequencies

Brooke, pulling the flaps of her wool cap tighter under her chin, then asks, "Can you help me again with some suggestions on how to contact guides when I am away?"

"My child, much is available to you. Search your mind. You can find out many of the answers for yourself. When alone you have but to call. Then through mind and heart connection reach out and call. You will get us." Then she pauses and adds as reinforcement, "Yah, indeed. Remember, watch fear, your greatest enemy. You must watch, knowing in your heart you are protected. Identify it. You are never alone. Say no to fear. Much practice is needed in this area, you have been given much instruction. Saying no is difficult in other things too."

"Thank you, Metude, but what about a really upfront guide for me?" *Ha, she must mean more physical.*

"One is always guided. Has to do with energy, frequencies, and levels. We will proceed."

Talking about levels of energies, Pam would never want to relive the last year so I need to ask, "What will the New Year be like for Pam?"

Metude shifts in the rocker, observing, "Can be a year of good learning for the person." *Yet, good often means challenges and struggles in this human school.* "The Person needs to pay more attention to the work and needs to ask, 'Is my physical body healthy?'" *A tricky question as physical healing is problematic for her, possibly because of fears from that past life experience of being killed.*

A Past-Life Fear ~ Affecting This Lifetime

One day, I asked Pam about her resistance to physically healing people. My instincts told me she has the ability. The question ignited a traumatic experience which panicked her and scared me. I was glad the cat was outdoors, as it had had a fit when she got the images of my last life with Marcus. This time, she found herself in New England at the time of the witch burnings. This young woman was considered a healer in her village, but it was thought by some as the devil's work. Describing the scene, she became agitated. Then as if reliving the event, she found herself running in fear from men chasing her on horseback across a field. This seeming terror ended in mid-sentence. Silence. Then, struggling to speak, she croaked almost in a whisper, "I think they killed me."

So, this could account for her avoidance of the subject and why that tape recorder got turned off every time the subject of physical healing came up. Now it makes sense.

Much Is Given, Much Is Earned ~ Learning Is Brought into This Life Experience

Now, wondering about my immediate past-life experience, I ask, "Can you tell me what my last life experience was, Metude?" *She is thoughtful, but frowns slightly.*

"Hmm, not a long life. Eight years old when you left. You knew you were going to leave, but you could not communicate with your mother. I don't see any other family. That experience provided a feeling of loneliness in this life for you. An experience that you recognized as a child, but could not name. You also made a decision when you passed from that life experience to choose a very quick return. A decision to try again. You have a wonderful life here. Much is given and much is earned." *Oh, so true. What a gift this life is to me and hopefully to those around me.*

My ancient friend continues, "You chose to learn. This life experience is for refinement, in other words, using what you know. Much was already known when you came into this lifetime. That is why your wisdom feels so familiar to you. You are following the path you have chosen. Now one is able to recognize and understand one's path better." *She is actually smiling slightly, and so am I.*

God, it makes sense, I can so relate to what she is saying. Since I can remember, my wisdom was always a comfort and strength to me. When I was a child, at times, I used to look at grown-ups and think, I feel older than them. I had also hoped we didn't come back but now I think we might have a choice. If that is right, I'd want to come back with wisdom.

Then I thought to ask, "Metude, are you really, really in our house when I am not visiting with you like this?" *I just need to keep hearing her say it as the invisible just seems so . . . invisible.*

She half-smiles, "Yah, often in this house. Enjoy the wit and banter."

"Oh, I like knowing that. One of the children called our home 'the love house' the other day." *I liked that too, keeping in mind that love doesn't mean it's perfect. I'd say it is beautifully human.*

This old woman muses with the slightest smile. "Much has been given, as well, to us." *Oh my, she means herself and her "we."*

Imagine, our home might give joy to them on the other side, as well. Now that is exciting. And who'd have ever thought that when we were petrified of that Beat the first time, we met this cottage woman? And how many people would not have been helped if we had gone with our reason and logic? She is true to who she said she is—universal love and wisdom.

There Is No Death as It Is Perceived ~ No Ending of Life

Pam and I had been talking about death before the visit, and we both thought it was funny I hadn't asked before about Metude's death. So, my last question this visit is, "Was it a shock when you died in that last life experience, the Swedish one?"

My ancient friend takes her time responding, "Merely crystallized what I had thought. Sharpened one's vision of what one believed." *Oh, that is something like how she responded after Mrs. Jordan passed over. She found that deep faith she was looking for.*

"Yah, indeed. There is an instinctive yearning, a hunger in all humans to know about death. There is no death as it is perceived, no ending to life. As I have said, that is not the word we use." *And how many endless times has she told me that. Thank you again.*

She shifts in the rocker. The wind is still howling. The stove is red hot as I have been jumping up feeding it wood throughout the visit. Yet, before leaving, she pauses, then repeats, "I so enjoy the wind, much like home. Love to tap my toes to the fiddle, do enjoy music." *Pam's feet just might be moving slightly, maybe she is listening to the fiddle? It's quite funny. I love knowing Metude is there when we play.*

We thank her as she is leaving. The joy is palpable. And in her wake, as usual, this ancient, remarkable woman leaves an overwhelming feeling of gratitude and wellness with love in our hearts in spite of all the human struggles. Even Pam got some good news, a coming year of greater learning and probably the same is ahead for each of us. If we choose.

MUCH LIKE OLD FRIENDS
~ A CLEAR CONDUIT

Jan. 14/88 A winter wonder world out there now, but there was quite a wind-driven storm yesterday. The trees are laden and heavy with snow. Our neighbour's big pine tree crashed to the ground as well. Haley said it was a weird feeling as she stood in the kitchen and watched it fall in slow motion, just missing the cottage. I have walked beaches so many times, saw so many moons, always knew I was touched by Presence, but also knew I had fallen short. Yet tonight—this thumbnail moon, not even a full one, with the snow on the trees, the waves lapping the iced sand, and blue-grey mist over the water—shifts me in an aliveness and fulfillment I have not experienced before. Pam came down for tea this afternoon. We sat in the kitchen and talked for a while. At one point, we looked at each other and started laughing. She said, "There are more than us in the kitchen—can you feel the peace, gentleness, and compassion?" I did. It was indeed tangible. She then held out her hands. "I know it by my hands. As the feelings increase, so does the tingling in my hands. I am never without awe when this happens. For these things that come through me, I feel great gratitude." This is one of the first times I have heard her articulate being thankful for her great gifts and one of them most certainly is being a clear conduit for our ancient friend. Plus, every time we visit the cottage woman, it seems our compassion for others and understanding of ourselves increases because we can see below the surface and into the pain that rests in our own hearts and thus, others. The visits now seem to be more conversational, less stilted and formal, possibly because our relationship has grown with this seemingly ancient, wise woman and her "we." As she put it a year or so ago, "Much like old friends—an ocean current moving back and forth." And in her visits I feel her joy as she rocks—the vibration of love that slowly fills the cottage like the initial Beat did the first time we met, but without the sound this time. Remembering back to the Beat, she had stated, "Ah, that Beat takes great energy. It is the love of the universe. You needed it." Then she informed us, "Love, I teach love."

And in each visit, true to her word she does in every human situation we bring to her. "And yes Metude, I have always loved the wind, too. Now, it will remind me of you. I know that someday, we will bid each other adieu for the last time, on this side, at least." And as my book friend the great Quaker John Woolman echoes, "A love clothes my mind as I write." And so, it does. Thank you, my ancient friend, and will this not be an end with a new beginning?

EPILOGUE - AN END WITH A NEW BEGINNING

In the years since the cottage woman's visits, universities like Princeton, Stanford, Cornell, and the University of Arizona in Tucson, among others, have researched different aspects of altered states of consciousness (some have focused on mediums, shamans, spiritual guides, and after-death experiences.) Three and a half decades ago, this knowledge would have helped us understand our old friend better if we had had exposure to such literature and the new science before she came into our life.

Because we did not know anything, we felt alone and somewhat threatened. We were talking to someone who was different than the person she came through, and yet this ancient woman was a real person who was enlarging our lives in such a beautiful way. Our culture's comprehension, then, was not of a multidimensional universe. Family, friends, neighbours, and everyone we knew could easily have dismissed and demeaned the experience. Thus, our motto to each other was, "Tell no one." And we didn't. In fact, we would not have believed it ourselves if she had not been sitting in front of us. Thus, we continued to meet secretly for five years and learned that there is more to reality than what the eye can see. There is another side intimately interwoven with our human one.

Update on a Few Who Took the Adventure

Pam was a clear conduit not only for the cottage woman, but also for other streams of consciousness. In some sense, her greatest fears were her extraordinary gifts. However, through the years, she did her human lesson work and discovered a newfound freedom. During this period, she upgraded her education, and two years into the cottage woman's visits was ready to begin university. She lived with Frank for several more years and then left him.

A couple of years later, he took the dog out into the woods and shot it; then he shot himself. Pam told me later that if she had been there, she knows he would have shot her, too.

Pam earned her undergraduate and master's degrees. After she graduated, she worked in her profession for several decades, eventually meeting a life partner, and although continuing to use her wisdom in service to others, she kept her gifts a secret. I am writing this book now because she has crossed over to the other side, and society is more ready to learn these lessons.

Fran did achieve independence from her mother, claimed her self-identity, and is now living her hard-earned freedom.

Abby earned her Bachelor's degree in Fine Arts, has taught art for these past decades, has given workshops in southern France, and is a well-known Maritime artist. We also still consult with the guides of the left side.

Donna did not kill herself. Knowing she had made progress and had other support, I terminated her work-sessions. She was not happy, and I never heard from her again. Shortly after, I heard she had met a man whom she had known for a few weeks and was now married.

Brooke, "the young one," as our ancient friend called her, is senior in her profession and living the spirited and fruitful life of her choice. She now receives and recognizes her own "information" from the other side, as do others in our enlarging circle.

Since that time, I have become a writer and in 2016, I self-published my first book, *Moments That Blink Back*. I also stuck it out with karate and did earn my black belt.

This book has covered the first two and a half years of our visits. My hope is that in the next few years, I will write the second half of our time together.

Walk in silence and love, all is holy ground

The Cottage Woman herself was certainly wiser and more human than anyone I have met. I told her, "You don't have a solid body, yet you feel solid. I know now you are definitely real and are a part of our reality, but you belong to this other reality that isn't a reality by our human, normal definitions."

Thus, nodding to me, she kindly suggested, "You have a limited scope of understanding and have enough to assimilate." Her definition of herself when I asked was, "I merely exist at a different frequency. I am a part of a stream of consciousness and each stream has its own vibrations. Not as you understand, but my life is much the same as yours. I am here to learn too. I have not decided if I will come back. It is quite dense for humans." (I felt she was referring to our frequencies but had to laugh, as dense is what our humanity feels to be at times.)

When the cottage woman left us after five years, it was time.

"To everything, there is a season . . . There is a time to plant and a time to harvest…" (Ecclesiastes 3:1).

We had all changed, our physical lives were changing. The bulb has to split for there to be new bulbs for new gardens. And hopefully this book will sow some of those new seeds.

Again, I will let my ancient friend have the final say, "Every moment has meaning, every step, every breath. Be very sensitive to air, light—it engulfs and enfolds you. Every raindrop has meaning. Walk in the silence, in love. Carry it about your person. Breathe it. All is holy ground."

ACKNOWLEDGEMENTS AND GRATITUDE

> *"What makes our dreams become a reality . . . (they) are the people we surround ourselves with who share in our vision, who subscribe to a similar purpose, who support us in (numerous) ways."*
>
> *~ Joe Dispenza*

Books are not written without help, encouragement, and confirmation, nor are they written without the people who sustain the life from which the experiences emerge. I am deeply grateful to those who have supported me in countless ways, and not necessarily directly with the project. Many people help hold up one's sky. Some assisted directly with the project, some saw the vision, and some did not. And others who sustained me were already on the other side and yet, I had a feeling at different times they might have dropped in. The following are those I am deeply grateful for:

For the original community of good friends who dared to embark on the adventure that took them beyond their beliefs, their fears, and what was considered normal for the time.

For Pam, who took her courage against the odds and obstacles in her life and allowed her friendship with the cottage woman to develop. She was a seer, and I am thankful for the gifts she offered our community.

For Joan who helped initiate the introduction to the cottage woman. Her support of the community throughout the years never wavered and she flew across the country on more than one occasion to meet with our ancient friend.

For j'anna whose thought and conversation take one to the place that the mystic Rumi refers to as "the field"—a place of larger awareness. I am also thankful that she has not only walked the path of this book and offered insight, but had the confidence in my ability to write it. She also visited with the cottage woman those five years she was in our life.

For Lorna who has also walked the path of the creation of this book. She has listened, offered creative thought, disagreed with me, given honest comment, helped edit the book more than once, and often twigged my grammar. I also thank her, too, for her confidence in my ability to write the way I knew the book needed to be written.

For Laura, who in the early days, years ago, when beginning this project, generously gave her time and her editing skills.

For my mother, father, my grandmother, and former husband (now all on the other side): They had the integrity, the strength, and courage to hear their own song (even if sometimes I didn't agree), and they encouraged me to sing mine.

For my four children, for their wisdom, and devoted support in a myriad of personal ways too countless to name.

I am also thankful for my book friends, the ancient sages, and seers throughout history. They have often been a lodestar.

ABOUT THE AUTHOR

Augusta is an established author. Her first book is titled *Moments That Blink Back* (2016). She is a contributing writer in *Contemporary Literary Horizon*, an international magazine of culture and spirituality that is published in several languages. Some of her writings are also found in the *Goose River Anthology* (2017), published in New England. She belongs to the Writer's Federation of Nova Scotia and has maintained a bi-monthly blog for the last nine years (augustaspen.blogspot.com). Her website is augustaswritings.com.

She has several decades experience in adult education, national conference planning, workshop leadership, and personal counselling. Augusta's formal education includes a Bachelor's degree in Psychology and Education, and a Master's degree in Theological Studies. She also has a black belt in Okinawan Karate and is a portrait and landscape artist.

Augusta chaired the National Celebration Worship Committee of the United Church of Canada, which required her to develop policy manuals for conferences and numerous educational programs at the national level.

She also participated in the first hospice pilot project developed by the Victoria General Hospital for the Maritime provinces and was one of its early developers.

Eight months of the year she lives on a lake in Nova Scotia embraced by family, friends, loons, and ducklings. In the winter, she lives on her own in Tucson, Arizona, with visitors, yellow finches, mesquite trees, and cactus.

When not writing, Augusta enjoys nature, piano, hiking, art, and accompanying people on their spiritual journeys. In addition, four children, two grandchildren, and close friends grace her life.

augustaswritings.com
augustaspen.blogspot.com
quillmark@yahoo.com

CPSIA information can be obtained
at www.ICGtesting.com
Printed in the USA
LVHW112041080622
720817LV00001B/22